SIMONIS DE KÉZA

GESTA HUNGARORUM

SIMON OF KÉZA

THE DEEDS OF THE HUNGARIANS

CENTRAL EUROPEAN MEDIEVAL TEXTS

General Editors

JÁNOS M. BAK
URSZULA BORKOWSKA
GILES CONSTABLE
GÁBOR KLANICZAY

SIMONIS DE KÉZA
GESTA HUNGARORUM

SIMON OF KÉZA
THE DEEDS OF THE HUNGARIANS

Edited and translated by
LÁSZLÓ VESZPRÉMY and FRANK SCHAER

With a study by
JENŐ SZŰCS

CEU PRESS
Central European University Press

English edition published by
Central European University Press

Október 6. utca 12
H-1051 Budapest
Hungary

400 West 59th Street
New York, NY 10019
USA

Translated by Frank Schaer

Distributed in the UK and Western Europe by
Plymbridge Distributors Ltd., Estover Road, Plymouth PL6 7PZ,
United Kingdom

ISBN 963-9116-31-9

Library of Congress Cataloging in Publication Data
A CIP catalog record for this book is available upon request

Printed in Hungary by Akadémiai Nyomda Kft., Budapest

CONTENTS

J. SZŰCS
THEORETICAL ELEMENTS IN MASTER SIMON OF KÉZA'S
GESTA HUNGARORUM (1282–1285)

GENERAL EDITORS' PREFACE

While interest in the medieval and early modern history of the central European region is definitely growing, knowledge of the medieval languages (mainly Latin) in which the story is usually told has been declining for some time. Just as historians in the rest of Europe realised that modern language translations are of great value in presenting the picture of their country's history, central Europeans also did their best to translate their past chroniclers into the local vernaculars. However, very little has been done to make these highly important narrative sources available to readers not familiar with the relevant central European languages.

The General Editors' plan is, therefore, to follow the example of such highly acclaimed enterprises as the *Oxford* (previously *Nelson*) *Medieval Texts* by launching a series of narrative sources on medieval Bohemia, Croatia, Hungary, Poland, and their neighbouring countries. Each volume will contain the Latin (or medieval vernacular) text, its English translation, an introductory essay, annotations, indexes, and the usual scholarly apparatus, edited by the best experts in the region and beyond. Since these sources are mostly available in good, relatively recent critical editions, *Central European Medieval Texts* will print the original language texts with only select textual variants. However, extensive notes will be added on features, persons, and institutions of the region perhaps less known to readers outside it.

It is envisaged that at least one volume will be published yearly, so we hope that the series will have made the most important narrative and hagiographical sources of the region available within a decade or so.

The General Editors would like to take the opportunity to invite colleagues working on such texts to join the team of scholars editing *Central European Medieval Texts*, so that the series can proceed in good speed to deliver editions and translations of first class quality. Readers, in turn, are encouraged to communicate to the General Editors their comments on the volumes and their suggestions for further texts to be included in the series.

J. M. B. – U. B. – G. C. – G. K.

ABBREVIATIONS

ABBREVIATED REFERENCES
TO FREQUENTLY QUOTED TITLES
(For other short titles, consult the Bibliography on pp. 187–216)

AASS   *Acta Sanctorum*. Edited by J. Bollandus, G. Henschenius, et al. Antwerp, etc., 1643–.

ÁMTF   Györffy, György. *Az Árpád-kori Magyarország történeti földrajza* (Historical geography of medieval Hungary under the Árpád dynasty). 3 vols. (A-P). Budapest: Akadémiai, 1963–98.

Anonymus   *Die Gesta Hungarorum des anonymen Notars*. Edited by Gabriel Silagi with László Veszprémy. Sigmaringen: Thorbecke, 1991; also *SRH* 1: 33–117.

ÁUO   *Árpádkori Új Okmánytár / Codex diplomaticus Arpadianus continuatus*. Edited by Gusztáv Wenczel. Pest, Budapest: MTA, 1860–74.

CCCM   *Corpus Christianorum: Continuatio Mediaevalis*. Turnholt: Brepols, 1966–.

CCSL   *Corpus Christianorum: Series Latina*. Turnholt: Brepols, 1953–.

CSEL   *Corpus Scriptorum Ecclesiasticorum Latinorum*. Vienna: Akademie der Wissenschaften, 1866–.

DRMH   *Decreta Regni Mediaevalis Hungariae / The
            Laws of the Medieval Kingdom of Hungary.*
            Edited by János M. Bak, Leslie S. Domokos,
            and James Ross Sweeney. Bakersfield etc.:
            Schlacks, 1989–.

ELTE   Eötvös Loránd Tudományegyetem (Eötvös
            Loránd University, Budapest)

FvS   *Freiherr von Stein-Gedächtnisausgabe. Aus-
            gewählte Quellen zur Deutschen Geschichte
            des Mittelalters.* Darmstadt: Wissenschaft-
            liche Buchgesellschaft.

KMTL   *Korai magyar történeti lexikon, 9–14. század*
            (Early Hungarian historical lexicon, 9th–
            14th centuries). Edited by Gyula Kristó, Pál
            Engel, and Ferenc Makk. Budapest: Akadé-
            miai, 1994.

LexMA   *Lexicon Latinitatis Medii Aevi Hungariae.*
            Edited by János Harmatta, Iván Boronkai,
            and Kornél Szovák. Budapest: Akadémiai,
            later Argumentum, 1987–.

LMas   *Lexikon des Mittelalters.* Munich and Zurich:
            Artemis, 1977–.

MGH   *Monumenta Germaniae Historica*

  Dt. Chr. *Deutsche Chroniken*

  SS   *Scriptores*

  SS AA   *Scriptores Antiquissimi*

  SSrerLang *Scriptores rerum Langobardicarum et Italicarum*

SSrerMer	*Scriptores rerum Merovingicarum*
SSrG	*Scriptores rerum Germanicarum in usum scholarum separatim editi*
SSrG NS	*Scriptores rerum Germanicarum. Series Nova*
MTA	Magyar Tudományos Akadémia (Hungarian Academy of Sciences, Budapest)
OSzK	Országos Széchényi Könyvtár (Széchényi National Library, Budapest)
PL	*Patrologiae cursus completus: Series Latina.* Edited by J.-P. Migne. Paris: Migne, 1844–55, 1862–65.
PSRL	*Polnoe sobranie russkich letopisej.* Moscow and St. Petersburg, 1926-.
PVL	*Povest' vremennych let. Vol. 1. Teksti perevod.* Edited by D. S. Lihačova. Moscow, St. Petersburg, 1950.
RA	*Az Árpádházi királyok okleveleinek kritikai jegyzéke. / Regesta regum stirpis Arpadiane critico-diplomatica.* Edited by Imre Szentpétery and Iván Borsa. Budapest: MTA, later Akadémiai, 1923–87.
Sinica	*Sinica Franciscana: Itinera et relationes Fratrum Minorum saeculi XIII et XIV.* Edited by Anastasius van den Wyngaert. Vol. 1, Quaracchi, 1929.
SRH	*Scriptores rerum Hungaricarum.* 2 vols. Edited by Imre Szentpétery. Budapest: Academia Litteraria Hungarica, 1937–38.

Witnesses

K   Library of the Academy of Sciences, Buda-
             pest, Ms. Tört. in 4° 139. (18th century;
             followed by the *SRH* and this edition).

H   University Library, Budapest, Collectio
             Hevenesiana, Ms. vol. LXX. (18th century).

E   *Simonis de Keza Chronicon Hungaricum*. Ed-
             ited by A. Horányi. 2nd ed., rev. Buda: Lan-
             derer, 1782.

S   Széchényi National Library, Budapest, Ms.
             Cod. Lat. 406 (the Codex Sambucus; 15th
             century).

OTHER ABBREVIATIONS AND CONVENTIONS

ad ann.   under the year
add.   *addit*
Germ.   German
Hung.   Hungarian
om.   *omittit*

1205/9   of uncertain date, between 1205-09
Sophie/   alternate names for the same person
Judith

LIST OF MAPS, FIGURES AND TABLES

Codex Sambucus
(OSzK, Ms. Cod. Lat. 406. f. 1 recto)

INTRODUCTION

The present work is the first bilingual annotated edition of the *Gesta Hungarorum* (ca. 1280) of Simon of Kéza (in Hungarian, Kézai Simon). Simon was court cleric to King Ladislas IV, and his chronicle is a highly important record of traditions, or fictions, relating to the origins of the Hungarian nation, the Huns and the Hungarians, and the immigrant noble families in Hungary. Based on his readings in Roman and canon law, French and German epic traditions, oral sources, and diverse other information gathered by sight or hearing in the course of his European travels, his account of Hungarian history not only exercised a long-lasting influence on his countrymen's view of their past but was read by Italian historians as well. The standard edition of the Latin text is in the *Scriptores rerum Hungaricarum* series (henceforth, SRH).[1]

THE MANUSCRIPTS

To the best of present knowledge, no medieval manuscript has survived of Simon's *Gesta*. We know, however, about one of them, which was used for the first editions and

---

[1] *Scriptores rerum Hungaricarum tempore ducum regumque stirpis Arpadianae gestarum*, ed. Emericus Szentpétery, 2 vols. (Budapest: Magyar Tudományos Akadémia, 1937).

served as the basis of all the surviving eighteenth-century copies. This manuscript was described by Daniel Cornides (1732–87), professor of diplomatics at Budapest University, in a letter of 22 January 1782: "This is an almost square parchment manuscript of 35 folios, each of them having 22 lines." The size was given by Cornides as 131 by 100 mm, but as he states that there were wide margins, these measurements must refer to the written space, which, as he noted, was marked by scratched-in lining. The space for initials had been left empty but the chapter titles were written in red. "The writing is of the late thirteenth-century, thick and rounded, and can be dated by the consistently used dot above the letter *y* and the occasionally accented letter *i*. The wooden boards of the codex were covered by pigskin, and fastened with clasps of which only the remnants survive. The mode of the binding also speaks for the age of the book."[2]

This codex was first mentioned in the early eighteenth century. It was then in the library of the Esterházy family

[2] Quoted by Alexander (Sándor) Domanovszky: *Codex membranaceus fere quadratus, absolvitur foliis 35, quorum quodlibet 22 lineae continet. Foliorum magnitudinem subiectae duae lineae patefacient, quarum prior AB folii longitudinem, posterior ab folii latitudinem aequat:— AB: 13,1 cm, — ab: 10 cm. Litterae Capitum initiales omissae sunt, sed pro iis spatium vacuum relictum est, eo fine, ut olim expinguantur. Lemmata Capitum minio sunt exarata, margines undiquaque sic satis largi. Scriptura est saeculi XIII. exeuntis, id quod e litterarum characteribus crassis et pinguinsculis, et littera (ẏ) puncto semper notata et ex accentu acuto litterae (í) interdum imposito licet colligere. Theca codicis lignea, suilla obtecta, fibulisque, quarum non nisi vestigia supersunt, munita et modus Compactionis, venerandam pro se ferunt vetustatem* ("Kézai kódexéről," 85).

in Kismarton (Eisenstadt), where the Jesuit Gábor Hevenesi (1656–1717), one of the founders of historical scholarship in Hungary, made a copy of it on 16 May 1701. This
copy, referred to by the sigil **H**, is now in the University
Library, Budapest (ELTE, Collectio Hevenesiana, vol.
LXX). This copy was the basis of a further copy, referred
to as **P**, made by another Jesuit historian, George Pray
(1723–1801), and presently also in the University Library
(Collectio Prayana, vol. XXIX). Finally, Pray's copy was
copied by Daniel Cornides, many years before he had the
medieval codex in hand. This copy was purchased by Count
Joseph Teleki, and is now in the Teleki Library in Tîrgu
Mureş (Marosvásárhely), with the old shelfmark fol. 1030.[3]
Being a copy of copies, this manuscript was not cited in the
SRH edition, nor is it in ours.

The original manuscript in the Esterházy collection—in
1713 bequeathed together with the entire family library to
the Franciscan convent in Eisenstadt—was used by the
editor of the first printed edition, the Piarist Elek Horányi
(1736–1809). It can be assumed that Jenő Kósa, provincial
of the Friars Minor, had noticed the codex in the Esterházy collection and took it with him to Bratislava (Po-
zsony, Pressburg) in 1768 in order to prepare an edition.
He there showed it to Horányi and lent it to him for a day.
Horányi printed an edition in Vienna in 1781, but having
acknowledged its mistakes he prepared a second edition
for publication in Buda a year later (to which Cornides
offered his assistance); this *editio princeps* is referred to

---

[3] We are grateful to Prof. György Györffy for affording us the opportunity to inspect a copy of this manuscript, even if it proved to be of
marginal use for the present edition.

as **E.**[4] Horányi did not have a good press among his contemporaries. Cornides, for example, wrote that "it is to be feared that Horányi will dreadfully distort Simon, not necessarily by ill will, but because of his usual haste and carelessness."[5] Indeed, his fears seem to be confirmed by the fact that Horányi attempted to "improve" upon the text he had in front of him in order to produce, with the help of the fourteenth-century chronicles, an "authentic" version. Horányi described his exemplar as a "parchment manuscript in Gothic script duodecimo size with 69 columns."[6] Judging by the already cited description of Domanovszky, this refers to the same codex which Cornides described as containing 35 óne-column folios, in which the last page may have been left empty, leaving sixty-nine written pages. In short, Horányi clearly used the former Esterházy-library manuscript.

Finally, another eighteenth-century copy of unknown origin reached the library of the Hungarian Academy of Sciences (present shelfmark Tört. in 4o 139) in 1838 from the collection of the Counts of Batthyány at Rohonc (Rechnitz). It seems to derive from the same medieval codex, but is more accurate than Hevenesi's, and was hence followed both by the SRH editors and in the present edition, except where badly corrupted. It will be cited as **K** (for Kézai).

---

[4] For a detailed description of the editions see the Bibliography.

[5] Quoted by Domanovszky, "Kézai kódexéről," 85.

[6] 2nd edition (Buda, 1782), 5: *charactere gotico in membrana . . . Codex hic in forma duodecima, novem et sexaginta columnis absolvitur.*

The history of the medieval copy can thus be followed till 1782, when it was still with Horányi in Buda. It was at that time that Cornides saw it. A year later the Franciscan provincial Kósa died, and apparently the Pressburg Franciscans forgot about the "one-day loan" and no one asked for the manuscript back from Horányi. At any rate by 1833 Joseph Podhraczky (1795–1870), historian and editor of a number of chronicles, could no longer find it and was forced to use **H**. Earlier this century, historians tried assiduously to locate the codex in one of the Franciscan or Piarist houses, but to no avail. Because of its small format this slim volume, or its medieval sisters, may have easily ended up in *colligata* and could be hiding undetected in Hungary or abroad. Beyond the borders of historical Hungary and Austria, Italy, perhaps, suggests itself, as Simon's work was certainly known there. Paolino da Venezia, father confessor of Pope John XXII, later bishop of Pozzuoli, quotes from him extensively; but so far no copy of the *Gesta* has been located in an Italian library.

However "ancient" (Cornides' word) the codex from the Esterházy library may have been, it was hardly an autograph, as can be clearly seen from the many misspelled toponyms in all the copies made from it, most of which must go back to earlier miscopyings (for an example see ch. 41, note 1). The many misreadings in the dedication and initial chapters also point to the same conclusion.

DATE AND INFLUENCE

Evidence for the date of the *Gesta* is provided by the fact that it notes the campaign against the Cumans in the autumn of 1282, but does not mention the victory over the Mongols who raided Hungary in the spring of 1285. It has been convincingly argued,[7] based on the relationships of Hungary and the papacy around that time, that the work was originally commissioned for propagandistic purposes, specifically with a view to an Italian audience, and copies may have reached the peninsula soon after it was written. If this were the motive, Simon, a royal notary versed in the Italian language and familiar with that land, would no doubt have seemed a fitting choice as author, and Italian readers would presumably have appreciated the many Italicisms of the text. Simon is eager to present his king, Ladislas IV, as a Christian ruler of Hungary of a stature only comparable to Attila among the pagans. It is only Simon among Hungarian chroniclers who does not explicitly link the genealogy of the Árpádians (including his royal patron) to Attila.[8] The whole structure of the work is influenced by the intention to demonstrate that Hungary was always a lawful polity, in which even its Hunnish predecessors lived and were ruled *Romano more*, and where the workings of government as well as the relations between free and servile elements were based on customary and statute law. The special chapter on the "immigrants" is

---

[7] Cf. Szűcs, below, pp. LII–LIII.

[8] The Hungarian Anonymus (c. 1200) as well as the fourteenth-century chronicles (*SRH* 1: 284–85) constructed a complicated and muddled genealogy for the native dynasty from Noah and Japheth through Bendegúz, Attila, and Csaba to Álmos, father of Árpád.

also aimed at pointing out that the foreigners who came to
the kingdom enjoyed freedom and chances for advance-
ment guaranteed by the laws of the realm. Simon implies,
though never says so, that the Cumans, too, will one day
find their place in the Christian Hungarian society. The
commemoration of the victory over the rebellious Cumans
at Lake Hód seems specifically included to reinforce the
latter message; indeed, this may have been another of the
motives behind the commissioning of the *Gesta*.

However, even if the work was originally aimed at an
"international" audience, it was copied and survived in
Hungary as well. This is obvious from the fact that the
Hungarian chronicles compiled and/or copied in the fourteenth century regularly include passages from Simon's
narrative. It seems that this was done not in one but in
several stages, as the *Chronicon Budense* (in the Sambucus
codex, Hungarian National Library OSzK Cod. Lat. 406,
referred to as **S**) and the version in the so-called *Chronicon
Pictum Vindobonense* (now OSzK Cod. Lat. 404, here **V**)
include different fragments of the *Gesta Hungarorum*.
Some passages are cited only in the one or the other
redaction. Simon's prologue was copied into the fifteenth-
century Sambucus codex[9] at the beginning of the Buda
Chronicle. Because of this, the chronicle was for long time

---

[9] This codex, written in a fifteenth-century Humanist hand, was acquired by the bibliophile John Sambucus (Zsámboki) from the Abbot
of Pistoia in 1563, whence it came into the Vienna Hofbibliothek and
in 1920 to the Hungarian National Library. It contains a very good text
of the *Gesta*'s introductory passages, most of which (with the exception of the dedication to King Ladislas IV) was taken by Simon from
older chronicle redactions.

ascribed to Simon: Wadding, who chanced upon S, described him as the author of this text,[10] and Simon became known as such both in Hungary and abroad.[11] Since the best copy of the introductory parts of the *Gesta* is in S, the present editors have followed the editors of SRH in utilising this version to amend the text of the first three chapters.

SOURCES

It has been long debated whether Master Simon was the author of all or only parts of the historical work that came down to us in the late copies. His authorship of the entire *"opusculum"* was convincingly argued by, among others, Imre Madzsar, János Horváth Jr., and Jenő Szűcs,[12] though they acknowledged that Simon utilised and re-worked the texts of older (and in their original form no longer extant) Hungarian chronicles and gesta. However, it is still unclear which passages originate in these older texts and what was Simon's own contribution. The passages which appear in the so-called fourteenth-century compilation of chronicles (as in the *Chronicon Pictum* and other versions) will be identified in the notes by reference to the critical edition in the first volume of the SRH series (up to now the standard, and indeed only edition of Hungarian medieval narrative sources). Simon certainly "made notes" (as Szűcs

[10] Wadding, Lucas, *Annales Minorum seu Trium ordinum a S. Francisco institutorum* (Rome: R. Bernabo, 1732), 2: 166; (1733), 7: 259.

[11] Cf. Domanovszky, *Kézai Simon*, 17.

[12] Madzsar, "Hun krónika," 77–79; Horváth, *Stílusproblémák*, 370; Szűcs, below.

aptly put it) from the thirteenth-century Hungarian Anonymus,[13] of which a near-contemporary copy has come
down to us, and most likely also followed his predecessors, among them Master Ákos, chancellor of King Stephen V (1270–72)—the original version of whose chronicle
is lost—for Hungarian pre-history and the post-1000
events.[14] There is, however, a reasonable consensus that
certain parts of the work are Simon's own contribution:
the introduction, the "Deeds of the Huns," the passages
on the reign of Ladislas IV, the chapter on the *udvarnok*,
and good parts of the list of the immigrant kindreds.
The SRH edition attempted to identify the passages most
probably "original" in Simon (those not found in any other manuscript than the copies of Simon's work), and marked
these in italics.[15] This is, however, somewhat misleading, because there are passages in the later chronicles that
utilised Simon's text. Simon's own contributions are often recognisable by his Italicisms and by his extensive use

---

[13] Szűcs, below, p. LX.

[14] Mályusz, *Az V. István-kori gesta*, passim.

[15] These were, according to Simon's chapters: 1–2, 74–75, 83, 89, 93,
95–99 in their entirety, and chapters 6, 26–7, 33, 39–41, 57, 61, 64, 73,
76–8, 91–2 in significant parts. This list would exclude in particular the
Hun story (chs. 7–22), because this was fully taken over by the later
chronicles, while they are clearly original to Simon, as proven by their
appearance in Paolino da Venezia. In chs. 25–73 the situation is the
opposite: Simon abbreviated, summarised, but also augmented with
colourful details the older chronicles (which went then into the fourteenth-century texts), and re-worked chapters 3–6 according to his
own experiences. In some cases Simon was the source for the later
chronicles in chapters 25–73 as well, as for example when in ch. 48 he
comments that the Austrians do not have dukes but margraves.

of Jordanes, Paul the Deacon, Godfrey of Viterbo, the Alexander-material, and the Hungarian Anonymus, as well as his own travel experiences.[16]

There are, however, scholars who wish to see the origin of the "Deeds of the Huns" in an earlier and no longer extant Hun history.[17] We agree with Györffy[18] that the Hungarian Anonymus and the *Chronicon Hungaro-Polonicum* (ca. 1220) contain certain elements of the history of the Huns which Simon also utilised, but Simon's version, complete with references to Roman ruins, different local legends, and literary references to the Attila tradition and German poetry, is his own creation. It was, indeed, the most individual and original redaction of the Hungarian Attila and Hun tradition of his age and may claim, precisely because of its extensive use of local lore and etymologies, a unique place in medieval European literature. Modern readers—but medieval ones before them as well—have read Simon mainly for his Hunnish story and, of course, for the political theory expressed in the work.[19]

EDITORIAL PRINCIPLES

We have followed the SRH in using *Gesta Hungarorum* as the title of the work, even though the eighteenth-century editions occasionally referred to it as the *Chronicon Hun-*

[16] See Szűcs, below, p. XLVIII.

[17] E. G. Macartney, *Historians*, 89–108; Csóka, *Történeti irodalom*, 565–601.

[18] Györffy, *Krónikáink*, 188–191.

[19] See Szűcs, above, pp. XLI–LXXII.

garicum. However, as Horányi himself admitted, the latter title may be a later addition,[20] and we feel that the accepted title better reflects the genre of this work. Our Latin text does not claim to be a critical edition, but follows, with minor corrections, the text as printed in SRH (where full textual variants are cited). For easier reference to that edition, we note its page numbers in brackets; the chapter divisions and numeration introduced by Domanovszky in the SRH have also been retained. Since we have no medieval manuscript, we have usually followed the punctuation and capitalisation of the SRH edition, as well as their normalisation of *U* and *V*. However, we were able to add in the notes a number of references to Simon's sources not available in the 1938 edition.

It is not always easy to make sense of Simon's narrative, whether due to conscious or unconscious ambiguity on the author's part or to the derivative textual tradition. His language shows a varied register, from classical and biblical vocabulary to borrowings from the contemporary vernaculars. The translation has not attempted to reproduce the original word for word, but rather to present a narrative which reads smoothly and intelligibly, while still retaining something of the rhetorical ornament of the original.

As the present edition is the first that contains a translation into a modern foreign language, we have also added explanatory notes for readers less familiar with central European history and literature. Our notes aim to identify toponyms and less well known persons, as well as to in-

[20] See *E* witness p. 17.

clude as many references as possible to the author's probable or possible sources. Moreover, in order to indicate the context of Simon's work in the development of historical and political thought in Hungary, we have included a study by the late Jenő Szűcs on Simon's work and its "theoretical elements."[21] Finally, among the extensive Hungarian scholarly literature on Simon we particularly wish to draw attention to the important work of such scholars as Sándor Domanovszky, Sándor Eckhardt, Jakab Bleyer, Imre Madzsar, János Horváth Jr., and József Gerics, which we have consulted extensively, even if we do not refer to them at every instance. For the Hungarian chronicles (a great part of which overlap Simon's work, as discussed above), readers can now consult the up-to-date Latin commentaries (with ample bibliography) by Elemér Mályusz and Gyula Kristó in their critical edition of the Chronicle of Johannes de Thurócz.[22]

The translation of the Latin text was primarily Frank Schaer's contribution; however, both he and the editor

[21] We are grateful to Ms Elisabeth Szűcs for having permitted us to re-print—in a linguistically improved version, thanks to Frank Schaer's careful copy editing, for which he also utilised the German translation of the article—the study, originally published in *Etudes historiques* 1975. Readers familiar with Szűcs's oeuvre will recognise that in this study (the Hungarian version of which, published in *Századok*, is much more detailed) the author has adumbrated the ideas elaborated both in his later famous *Three Historical Regions of Europe* and his studies on medieval Hungarian national consciousness (cf. the studies in *Nation und Geschichte Studien,* Budapest: Corvina, 1981) and now also his "Zwei Fragmente," in *East Central Europe/l'Europe du Centre-Est: Eine wissenschaftliche Zeitschrift*, 20–23 (1993–96): pt. 2, 55–90.

[22] Mályusz-Kristó, *Johannes de Thurocz.*

profited much of the discussions with graduate students in "translation seminars" at the Central European University in the academic years 1996–97 and 1997–98. Among the general editors of the series, János M. Bak assisted the translator and editor in establishing a "norm" that should serve as a guide for future volumes of the series. Finally, we all wish to thank the editor and staff of the Central European University Press for their help in producing a pleasing volume out of the manuscript we submitted.

Budapest, 1 January, 1999

L. V. – F. S.

J. SZŰCS: THEORETICAL ELEMENTS IN MASTER SIMON OF KÉZA'S *GESTA HUNGARORUM* (1282–1285) *

THE BACKGROUND: THE EMERGENCE OF A EUROPEAN STRUCTURAL UNITY

One can only begin to speak properly of European history once the term Europe ceased to be merely a geographic concept and came to refer to something new: a structural unity. But at what point can one begin to speak of "European" structures? This is not an easy question to answer, as it is a matter of viewpoint where and in which combination of criteria one chooses to identify the essential, determining circumstance within the thousand-year process that began with the dissolution of the ancient world and led to modern Europe.

Certain primary conditions undoubtedly already lay concealed in that process which shifted the focus of history from the ancient centre of civilisation, the Mediterranean, further north toward the periphery of the late ancient

---

*Revised version of the translated article, first published under the same title in *Etudes historiques 1975*, I (Budapest: Akadémiai, 1975) (for the Hungarian original, see below, n. 8, "Társadalomelmélet"). The subtitles were borrowed from the German version ("Theoretische Elemente . . . " in J. Szűcs, *Nation und Geschichte: Studien* (Budapest: Corvina, 1981), 263–328), which has occasionally been used to clarify infelicitous translations. Some notes were abbreviated in order to reduce duplication with the notes to the main texts, and at some points references to more recent publications were inserted, without attempting a thorough up-date of the article. The kind assistance of Mr Gábor Tóth in editing the notes is gratefully acknowledged.

world, toward the interior of a Europe which, though not unknown to ancient geography, was of rather uncertain definition. There is, therefore, some justification for the commonly held view which ties the "making of Europe" to the centuries of the early Middle Ages. It is significant that by the time of Charlemagne, around 800, Europe first appears as the expression of a totality of specific social and cultural ideas, a synonym for *Christianitas (societas fidelium Christianorum)*—in other words, as the conceptual framework of a specific "structure" we term Christian feudal society.[1] The Carolingian unity, conceived of as an *imperium Christi*, can be considered as the first experiment in the creation of a new synthesis, containing within its borders virtually the whole of the new historical area which had been coalescing since the fall of the western half of the *imperium Romanum* (the Islamic conquest having finally completed the dissolution of the ancient Mediterranean by detaching the southern half of the former *orbis Latinus* in the middle of the eighth century). This synthesis represented the result of three centuries of internal transformation, as the antagonism between the late antique Romano-Christian and the Germanic-barbarian worlds was finally overcome and a symbiosis gradually emerged. Indeed, much of the Europe-to-be is adumbrated in this process; the two elements, in part cancelling each other, in part permeating one another, became the first medium of an emerging structure which was by then neither "Roman" nor "barbarian", but of a new quality: medieval.

---

[1] W. Ullmann, *A History of Political Thought: The Middle Ages* (Harmondsworth: Penguin, 1965), 70.

However, this transitional phase (the sixth to the eighth centuries) created merely the crystallising nucleus of Europe. On the one side, this Europe lacked Hispania, then in Islamic hands; Britannia, too, was only loosely connected with it. On the other, its eastern limits terminated in the area stretching from the Elbe to the western edge of the former Pannonia where the *orbis Christianus* ended. The northern part of Europe and its eastern half were at this time and throughout the next two or three centuries still referred to by the same collective name applied in the fifth century to the world beyond the Rhine: "barbarians." Even in the tenth century, the Saxon Widukind spoke of the defeat of the Magyars at Augsburg (955) as a victory over the enemies of "Europe." At the same time, at the other end of the future Europe of the Middle Ages stood Byzantium, in retreat from the waves of "barbarians" and largely isolated from the emerging western Christiandom, still guarding with defensive rigidity whatever it could of the Roman tradition.

In truth, it was only when the gap between the geographical and socio-cultural senses of the term was bridged and the framework filled in with more or less identical content that Europe was, so-to-speak, "born." It took a new historical phase, the ninth to the eleventh centuries, for even the preconditions for this to emerge. However, there exist some analogies between this phase and the earlier one. For even as in the fourth and fifth centuries the beginning was announced by the "barbarian" invasions, so it was again "barbarian" invasions which threatened the Christian world. The Slavic and other mass-migrations originating in the steppes had already filled the space between the West

and Byzantium, but in the course of the eighth to the tenth
centuries, Viking raids from the North and the Magyar
invasions from the East were threats which could still
inspire apocalyptic dread in contemporaries. Consolidation finally came around the turn of the first millennium
with the transformation of these peoples into new Christian nations. Europe now stretched from Scandinavia all
the way down to Byzantium, embracing the areas periph-
eral to the former Carolingian Europe and the nomadic
remnants now confined to the eastern boundaries of geographical Europe. In this new synthesis *Europa* around
1100 embraces the totality of the expanded *orbis Christianus*, and thus in practice coincides with its geographical
limits from now on. The preconditions were now in place
for a unified "European history."[2]

To be sure, from the outset there was always something
relative in this unity. Even the early nucleus of Europe
was marked by regional differences. The larger units—the
Mediterranean, Britannia, the areas west and east of the
former Roman *limes*, and the Rhine—preserved many of
the distinguishing characteristics of their historical genesis,

[2] For the details, see H. Gollwitzer, "Zur Wortgeschichte und Sinndeu-
tung von 'Europa,'" *Saeculum* 2 (1951): 161–72; G. Barraclough, "Die
Einheit Europas im Mittelalter," *Die Welt als Geschichte* 11 (1951):
97–122; H. Aubin, "Der Aufbau des Abendlandes im Mittelalter,"
Historische Zeitschrift 187 (1957): 497–520; O. Halecki, *The Limits and
Divisions of European History* (Notre Dame, Ind.: University of Notre
Dame Press, 1950). For the discussion of problems relating to the "old"
and "new" barbarians, see L. Musset, *Les Invasions: Les vagues ger-
maniques* (Paris: Presses Universitaires de France, 1965), and *Les
Invasions: Le second assaut contre l'Europe chrétienne (VIIe-XIe siècles)*
(Paris: Presses Universitaires de France, 1965).

to say nothing of Byzantium at the other pole. However, in the economic and social spheres the sharpest line of demarcation occurred between the new regions on the one hand and all of old Europe on the other—and this in spite of the paradoxical fact that the great Schism of 1054 had already split the *neophitae gentes* into two camps. The Schism produced cultural and intellectual spheres of influence for *Europa occidens* and Byzantium which did not coincide with the line of demarcation mentioned above but which nevertheless were later to have powerful repercussions in the social and economic spheres as well.[3]

At the turn of the first millennium European structures are still fundamentally "asynchronous." In northern or eastern Europe the concept of High Middle Ages (*"Hochmittelalter"*) makes no sense. These societies continued to live in their own "early Middle Ages" until the beginning of the thirteenth century, displaying many features more analogous to the Western European structures of the sixth to ninth centuries than to the feudal society of the contemporary West (to say nothing of the peculiar world of

[3] The reason for making an exception, among disputed and disputable modern terms for regional demarcations, of the term "East Central Europe" is that this area shares certain common characteristics evident in the early modern age whose roots stretched back to earlier times. The kingdoms of Bohemia, Poland, and Hungary (with Croatia), and in some sense even the German territories east of the Elbe and Austria, display more or less "eastern" characteristics in the economic and social sense, but peculiarly "central" European ones in a cultural sense. [On this complex issue see more recently J. Szűcs, *Vázlat Európa három történeti régiójáról*, Budapest: Magvető, 1983, the best translation of which is by V. Charaire, G. Klaniczay, and Ph. Thureau-Dangin, *Les trois Europes* (Paris: Harmattan, 1985).]

Byzantium). The Normans, Poles, and Magyars of the eleventh century, even as the subjects of Christian states, were still generally regarded and referred to as "barbarians"; in the middle of the twelfth century Bishop Otto of Freising spoke of the thoroughly barbarian characteristics he had encountered in Pannonia. In the course of the thirteenth century, however, one can observe a fundamental and surprisingly rapid transformation. A shift in attitude is discernible around 1200 when the new peoples receive their due place in the biblically derived genealogies of peoples and languages. By around 1300 no traveller from "old" Europe visiting the middle and lower stretches of the Danube or Vistula had any more the feeling that he was in an alien culture or in a "Europe" different from his native land, even if his eye might have been struck here and there by some things that seemed strange. When a Dominican at the Synod of Lyons (1274) reviewed the former and present enemies of Christendom and assessed Europe's situation, he concluded that the "barbarians" (Poles, Magyars, etc.) had mostly disappeared and been assimilated into the larger family of Christendom—so much so, indeed, that he declares that "except for the Tartars, there are no barbarians." Indeed, the new papal legate to Hungary about the same time (1279) singled out the *more Christiano* lifestyle and culture of the Magyars as an example to be imitated by the Cumans, a new "barbarian" people now belatedly expected to be incorporated.[4] This anecdotal

---

[4] On the terminology, see R. Buchner, "Die politische Vorstellungswelt Adams von Bremen," *Archiv für Kulturgeschichte* 45 (1963): 15–59. — Otto of Freising (*MGH SS* 20: 368). The *Chanson de Roland* (of around 1100) counts among the 13 "pagan" peoples the Bulgarians, the Magyars, and in general the "Slavs." For the lists of peoples see

evidence by and large reflects the reality. In this new historical phase (from about the year 1000 to the middle of the thirteenth century) the geographical and political consolidation of Europe opened the way to something new in European history, a genuine structural unity, even if this unity manifested itself in regional heterogeneity and a characteristic Latin-Western vs. Orthodox-Eastern dualism.

Of course, the relevance of this dimension is not even admitted in the one-sidedly "western" or "eastern" historical viewpoints which still persist as a heritage of the nineteenth century. If, following Ranke, one narrows down the content of "Europe" to its "original" entities (his *Einheit der romanischen und germanischen Völker*"), everything else, naturally, becomes some appendage, some *Randgebiet*, and so, effectively, some *quantité négligeable*. On the other hand, if one chooses to see historical development during the Middle Ages as the gradually evening out of the initial "phase-differences"—with whatever is left over be-

---

A. Borst, *Der Turmbau von Babel: Geschichte der Meinungen über Ursprung und Vielfalt der Sprachen und Völker* (Stuttgart: Hiersemann, 1957–63), 2: 580ff., 734ff. For Humbertus de Romanis' remarks at Lyons, see J. D. Mansi, *Sacrorum conciliorum nova et amplissima collectio* (Venice and Florence, 1780; reprint Graz: Akademische Druck- und Verlagsanstalt, 1960–1), 24: 110 (cited below note 22). — For the deeper socio-cultural content of the phrase *more Christiano* in the so-called "Cuman law" of 1279 [now in J. M. Bak, Gy. Bónis, and J. R. Sweeney, eds., *The Laws of the Medieval Kingdom of Hungary/Decreta Regni Mediaevalis Hungariae*, Vol. 1 (1000–1301), 2nd ed. (Idyllwild: Schlacks, 1998), 71], see M. Kring (Komjáthy), "Kun és jász társadalomelemek a középkorban" (Cuman and Jazygian Social Elements in the Middle Ages), *Századok* 66 (1932): 42.

ing some "qualité négligeable"—this considerably over-
simplifies the problem, and leaves open the question
whether or not there were infrastructural preconditions to
the separate development of eastern and western Europe
after the sixteenth century. As if this were not enough, a
variety of inherited myths cloud the discussion. In practice
it is unimportant whether these are modern versions of
the Romantics' ethnic myths with their misleading dualism
between "Romano–Germanic" and "Slavic" worlds, or
whether they are newer civilisation myths (the theory, for
instance, that "feudalism" is peculiar to the West and did
not develop elsewhere, or only imperfectly).

Without question there are analogies between the separate
historical phases outlined above. Both the fifth and the
tenth centuries led to a symbiosis between a higher unity
and a heterogeneity of "barbarians," even if the half-mil-
lennium that separated these two processes inevitably
made them very different from each other. But in neither
case were the "barbarians" some primitive tribe or tribal
conglomerate (which would had been swept away in the
historical conflict), but organised societies possessing a
developed leadership and a system of rule based on military
retinues. The Germanic *Gefolgschaft*, the Slavic *družina*, or
the early Magyar stratum of *jobbágy* (corresponding to the
Old-Turkish *buyruq*, originally meaning "member of the
retinue") are essentially equivalent. They are all the basis
of a rudimentary *"Personenverbandstaat"* (Th. Mayer). The
subsequent development, peculiar to the proto-feudal
structure, of free (*maiores, milites, vulgares*) and nonfree
(*servi*) social elements relates the old and new barbarians
much more closely than historians, still excessively en-

thralled by ethnic and civilisation myths, generally like to admit.[5] (The use of "Germanic", "Slavic", and such terms as categories of social history is simply another myth.) The ultimate persistence of these original characteristics is debatable, however. Certain "original characteristics" in the economic, social, and political structures of eleventh and twelfth century Eastern Europe are comparable to proto-feudal conditions in the West. But it took five hundred years for the *par excellence* "European"—that is, Christian-feudal—structural characteristics to evolve, and only the "old" Europe worked to produce them—thus in turn providing finished models and schemes to hand over to the new barbarians around the turn of the millennium. So in this sense the two historical situations are not analogous, and to a degree Europe's younger regions must be judged of secondary significance.

Indeed, the two phases are not comparable in other respects either. For in the final analysis the old barbarians vanquished Rome, even if the early Middle Ages absorbed the victors as ethnic and political units. The new barbarians, on the other hand, were "vanquished" by Christian Europe, at least in the sense that the situation convinced their rulers of the expediency of at least a degree of assimilation. The Europe of the millennium may have been less imposing

---

[5] For details and further literature see L. Makkai, "Les caractères originaux de l'histoire économique et sociale de l'Europe orientale pendant le moyen âge," *Acta Historica Acad. Sc. Hungaricae* 16 (1970): 261–86; Fr. Graus, "Deutsche und slawische Verfassungsgeschichte?" *Historische Zeitschrift* 31 (1959): 191–229; J. Szűcs, "König Stephan in der Sicht der modernen ungarischen Geschichtsforschung," *Südost-Forschungen* 31 (1972): 17–40.

than Rome had been even in her fall; but within it, forces of expansion and internal transformation were already straining to find expression. The political and institutional medium for this was once again a "renewed" and "Roman" *Imperium*, or at the other pole the true heir of Rome, Byzantium. The period which saw the beginnings of the fusion of the old Europe with the newer regions (about 1050–1100) was marked by the emergence of a complex of new phenomena. These included demographic expansion and improvements in agrarian technology, the beginning of economic and social mobility, and an intellectual revival. This combination of factors was to transform the face of Europe within the next two hundred years. The dynamism of this "second feudal age" (M. Bloch) was peculiar to the Western part of Europe, in contrast to the more rigid eastern (Byzantine) sphere,[6] and its integrative force accelerated the new European symbiosis. However, this time, unlike in the early Middle Ages, there was little reciprocity in the process, and the relationship between the "old" and "new" regions was mostly unidirectional.

The result was a peculiar dichotomy.[7] On the one hand, processes analogous to those which had taken place in Europe's older regions appeared again about 1200 in a more

[6] M. Bloch, *La société féodale: La formation des liens de dépendance* (Paris: Albin Michel, 1939), 95–115.

[7] Naturally, one cannot speak of homogeneous formulae here either. Regional factors, as well as the predominance now of the Western Latin, now of the Byzantine Orthodox poles in the process of this welding together, all produced a number of variations. What follows refers primarily to the East Central European region (cf. note 3), and more narrowly to Hungary.

concentrated form and at accelerated speed, and in the course of the thirteenth century these dramatically transformed the region and set up the structural "common denominators" of feudal Europe. In a few short decades the royal domain and the earlier administrative system based on royal castellanies disintegrates and is replaced in the economic sphere by the preponderance of large estates, either in secular or clerical hands, and in the political arena by the ascendancy of the upper clergy and the aristocracy vis-à-vis the king. Knighthood and certain forms of feudal relationships come into being, while the "free" middle social strata disappears. New forces of integration forge from a variety of social elements the nucleus of a new stratum, the nobility, enjoying uniform prerogatives, their "golden liberty," while others lead to the progressive merging of people in a variety of conditions of bondage and to the gradual cessation of servitude, from which a unified class of dependant peasantry emerged with its own property and freedom of movement. Concomitantly, the region's agrarian base was transformed: there is large-scale internal colonialisation, the area of cultivated land expands, agrarian technology changes with the introduction of the heavy plough and the three-crop rotation system, while the old manorial system with a domestic economy worked by servants disappears. With more vital internal and external trade the first privileged towns appear and the figure of the burgher emerges on the scene. All these features, now arising in the course of little more than a single century, had taken five hundred years (from the ninth to the thirteenth centuries) to develop in Europe's primary regions, the fruits of a protracted and more deeply structured historical development.

For the rapidity of the historical processes in the newer regions was characterised by a certain "superficiality." In spite of the changed relationship between the king and the barons and between the big landowning *domini* and their *familiares*, vasallage, fief, and feudal law did not evolve in the sense they did in the West. The nature of personal dependency represented by *servitium* and *fidelitas* merged characteristics of the archaic retinue relationship with certain superficial and inorganic quasi-feudal elements. Knighthood was generally an exclusive and circumscribed phenomenon. The knightly ethos, its ideals, and the way of life it involved touched the nobility only superficially; neither then nor later were *miles* and *nobilis* correlative concepts. The nobility itself is much more broadly based—more "peasant-like"—than in the West. The free and autonomous *civitates* were differentiated both in their size and in their subordinate importance from western towns; already at this time there is a burgeoning of that peculiar half-agrarian, half-industrial "peasant-town" form of urbanisation, the *oppidum*. All these elements and characteristics follow the European model but differ from it in their inorganic superficiality, in their archaic peculiarities, in a certain gross lack of differentiation or in differences of magnitude.

Thus, by around 1250–1300 Europe's structural unity, the "synchronous" character of European history, is an evident fact discernible in many ways. This unity, however, manifests itself in multifarious and in many respects "asynchronous" structures, which, however, does not alter the indisputable fact of its existence. The new regions had their own belated and consequently compressed "High Middle

Ages"—the term, indeed, becomes almost meaningless—
after which they become in the late Middle Ages and in
spite of all local variation organic participants of a homogeneous process to which the name "European history" is
commonly given.

A NEW HISTORICAL FRAME OF REFERENCE: THE NATION

It is not within the scope of this study to pursue this model
further. Rather, we will select one of many possible ap-
proaches—specifically, the history of ideas—and focus
on certain particulars. The thirteenth century was characterised among other things by the development of an in-
creasing "synchronicity" in intellectual structures; everywhere intellectual currents could now express objective
"common denominators" almost simultaneously and without the necessity of assuming direct transmission. At the
same time, however, in particular instances there still remains something peculiar in their appearance and in their
function, some characteristic "asynchronousness." In what
follows I shall try to delineate the nature of this dichotomy
through the analysis of a single literary work and to draw
some lessons in that field of intellectual endeavour most
closely related to social reality: the conception of history
and social theory—in short, in the field of the transformation of political thought.

The work in question is the *Gesta Hungarorum* of Master
Simon of Kéza, cleric at the court of Ladislas IV (the

Cuman), written between 1282 and 1285.[8] This *opuscu-lum*—the writer's own term for it—does not derive its significance from any inherent literary value—its style, in fact, is dry and rather monotonous—nor from claims to historical accuracy, but rather from the paradoxical fact that it is an ingenious historical fiction from start to finish. History for the author is a framework to be moulded at

[8] *Scriptores rerum Hungaricarum tempore ducum regumque stirpis Arpadianae gestarum*, ed. Emericus Szentpétery, vol. 1 (Budapest: MTA, 1937), 141–94 (the two volumes of this collection of texts will henceforth be referred to as *SRH*). The relationship between Simon's work and the so-called fourteenth-century chronicle redaction, which exists in a number of textual variations ("*Chronici Hungarici compositio saeculi XIV*," *SRH* 1: 239–505) has been debated ever since the beginning of critical historical scholarship in Hungary; see *Repertorium fontium historiae medii aevi* (Roma: Istituto Storico Italiano per il Medio Evo, 1970), 3: 301–2, 409–11. Some of the more recent studies include: S. Domanovszky, *Kézai Simon mester és krónikája* (Master Simon of Kéza and his chronicle) (Budapest: MTA, 1906); I. Madzsar, "A hun krónika szerzője" (The author of the Hun chronicle), *Történeti Szemle* 11 (1922): 75–103; J. Horváth, Jr., *Árpád-kori latinnyelvű irodalmunk stílusproblémái* (Stylistic problems in the Latin literature of the Árpád age) (Budapest: Akadémiai, 1954), 350–91; idem, "A hun történet és szerzője" (The history of the Huns and its author), *Irodalomtörténeti Közlemények* 67 (1963): 446–76; J. Gerics, "Adalékok a Kézai Krónika problémáinak megoldásához" (A contribution to the solution of the problems in Simon of Kéza's chronicle), *Annales Univ. Sc. Budapestinensis de R. Eötvös nominatae, Sectio Historica* 1 (1957): 106–34; J. Szűcs, "Társadalomelmélet, politikai teória és történetszemlélet Kézai Simon Gesta Hungarorumában" (Social theory, political theory, and the idea of history in Simon of Kéza's *Gesta Hungarorum*), *Századok* 107 (1973): 569–643, 823–78. (Wherever, in what follows, space does not allow more detailed analysis, I refer to this longer study of mine in Hungarian.)

will to serve theory. Within it he brings together a number of currents of thought common to all of Europe and adapts them to certain epistemological needs which were beginning to be felt in Hungary, and, indeed, does so in a way so "up-to-date" that for centuries historiography was unable to escape the spell of the picture he painted. Another paradox of the work is the fact that the "European" elements of its political thinking are located in a medium as originally "un-European" as the construct of the Hunnish origins and the prehistory of the Magyars. For it was Master Simon who identified a dualism in Hungary's past—Hunnish prehistory against Hungarian history—which was to persist from the late Middle Ages up to the beginnings of modern historiography.[9] And last but not least, it was Master Simon who assigned to the Magyars

[9] For the significance for intellectual history of Simon of Kéza's *Gesta Hungarorum*, see principally P. Váczy, "A népfelség elvének magyar hirdetője a XIII. században: Kézai Simon mester" (A Hungarian propagandist of the principle of the people's sovereignty in the thirteenth century: Master Simon of Kéza), in *Károlyi Árpád emlékkönyv* (Budapest: Sárkány, 1933), 546–63, as well as passim in the works of Horváth, Gerics, and Szűcs cited in the previous note, and Gy. Kristó, "Kézai Simon és a XIII. század végi köznemesi ideológia néhány vonása" (Simon of Kéza, and some features of the ideology of the gentry of the late thirteenth century), *Irodalomtörténeti Közlemények* 76 (1972): 1–22. For the "modernisations" of the Hunnish history in the fifteenth century see E. Mályusz, *A Thuróczy-krónika és forrásai* (The Thuróczy chronicle and its sources), Tudománytörténeti tanulmányok, no. 5 (Budapest: MTA, 1967), 105–24; P. Kulcsár, *Bonfini magyar történetének forrásai és keletkezése* (The sources and origin of Bonfini's Hungarian history), Humanizmus és reformáció 1 (Budapest: Akadémiai, 1973), 28–52.

their place within European history within the medieval world-picture.

The Hunnish origin of the Magyars is, of course, a fiction, just like the Trojan origin of the French or any of the other *origo gentis* theories fabricated at much the same time. The Magyars in fact originate from the Ugrian branch of the Finno–Ugrian peoples; in the course of their wanderings in the steppes of Eastern Europe they assimilated a variety of (especially Iranian and different Turkic) cultural and ethnic elements, but they had neither genetic nor historical links to the Huns.[10] There existed in ancient Magyar tradition an origin-saga (the saga of the magic hind) which in some of its motifs resembles the origin-sagas of the Hunnish and other steppe peoples, but even these elements preserve only trace memories of Onogur, Alan, and Khazar

---

[10] For a review of the question (with the earlier literature) see Gy. Györffy, *Krónikáink és a magyar őstörténet* (Hungarian chronicles and Magyar prehistory) (Budapest: Néptudományi Intézet, 1948; reprint Budapest: Balassi, 1993), 126–46. Some kind of Hun tradition could conceivably have been transmitted through Onogur–Bulgarian mediation, since this people was a part of the remnants of the Hun empire of Attila's sons in the Pontus region (at the head of the list of the Danubian Bulgars' earliest princes stands the name *Irnik* son of *Avitochol*, the Bulgarian form of *Hernac* son of *Attila*.) There is, however, no trace of such a motif in the Magyar tradition of ancient times. It is still an open question whether the Székely did or did not have their own Attila-tradition, and rests on the assumption that the Székely can be identified with the Bulgarian tribal fragment referred to in Muslim sources as *s.k.l* (*eskil, iskil*); cf. Gy. Györffy's article in *Századok* 92 (1958): 74–80. [The issue is still wide open and the identification seriously questioned by Turkologists.]

ties.[11] The historical memory of the Magyars in the middle of the tenth century reached back through their sagas to the Khazar Khaganate (seventh to ninth centuries).[12]

The belief in the identity of Huns and Magyars appears in the Christian West in the tenth century, although at first it coexisted with other theories. One source of this belief was the inclination to regard all the peoples who descended upon Europe from the fifth century onwards as the "scourge of God" against the Christians and as one and the same people. From here sprang, for example, the notion of an Avar–Magyar (or even a Hunnish–Avar–Magyar) iden-

[11] J. Berze Nagy, "A csodaszarvas mondája" (The saga of the magic hind), *Magyarságtudomány* 1 (1942): 157–75. For the literature on the question see Györffy, *Krónikáink*, 11–38. For more recent discussion see J. Szűcs, *"Gentilizmus": A barbár etnikai tudat kérdése* ("Gentilism": the question of barbarian ethnic consciousness), Diss. C.Sc. Budapest, 1970 (posthumously published in J. Szűcs, *A magyar nemzeti tudat kialakulása* [Budapest: Balassi–JATE–Osiris, 1997], 7–295); see now also, idem, "Zwei Fragmente," Studien zum Nationalbewusstsein: Mittelalter und Gegenwart, Hrsg. J. M. Bak, Special issue of *East Central Europe/ l'Europe du Centre-Est: Eine wissenschaftliche Zeitschrift*, vol. 20–23 [1993–96] 2: 55–90.)

[12] For the interpretation of Constantine Porphyrogenitus' reports (*De administrando imperio*, chs. 38–40), and for the chronological basis of the tradition, see esp. J. Deér, "A IX. századi magyar történet időrendjéhez" (A contribution to the chronology of ninth-century Magyar history), *Századok* 79–80 (1945–46): 3–20; K. Czeglédy, "A kangarok (besenyők) a VI. századi szír forrásokban" (The Kangars (Petchenegs) in sixth-century Syrian sources), *Magyar Tud. Akadémia Nyelv és Irodalomtudományi Osztályának Közleményei* 5 (1954): 243–76. For a summary of these problems see Szűcs, "Gentilizmus," ch. 3.

tification.[13] The other support for telescoping the two peoples into one was the fact that the name *Ungri~Ungari~Hungari* generally given to the Magyars in the West was reminiscent of the name *(H)unni*. In reality, it derives from the name of the Onogur confederation of tribes to which the ancestors of the Magyars once also belonged, and which entered Medieval Latin after transmission and transmutation through old Slavic and Byzantine sources (where it appears in forms like *Ongri~Ugri*).[14] The song of the Nibelungs established this identity and the prestige of the works of Godfrey of Viterbo confirmed it. Indeed, by around 1200 the Hunnish origin of the Magyars was taken for granted in the West.

Not so, however, with the Magyars themselves. To be sure, in this period certain ideological advantages of the identification had already been recognised by the so-called Anonymus (Magister P.), a Hungarian chronicler who had studied probably in Paris. Starting from the notion that Pannonia was once the land of *Athila rex*, he identified *Ecilburg* (the *Etzelen bürge* of the song of the Nibelungs;

---

[13] The *Annales Alemannici* (*MGH SS* 1: 40ff.) at the beginning of the tenth century are the first to refer to the Magyars as *gens Hunorum*. For the relevant sources see Györffy, *Krónikáink*, pp. 129–31. Certain seeds of this theory appear also in Widukind (*Rerum gestarum Saxonicarum libri tres, MGH SSrG* 60: 28–29), who identifies the Magyars with the Avars, and regards the latter as the remnants of the Huns, recounting also the Hun origin saga as told by Jordanes.

[14] B. Hóman, "A magyar nép neve a középkori latinságban" (The name of the Hungarian people in Medieval Latin), *Történeti Szemle* 6 (1917): 129–58, 240–58; E. Moór, "Die Benennung der Ungarn in den Quellen des IX. und X. Jahrhunderts," *Ural-Altaische Jahrbücher* 31 (1959): 191–229.

in Hungarian, Óbuda) as "Attila's town," and the Székely
as "the people of King Attila." He could then present the
legendary ruler of the Huns—some confusion and contradictions notwithstanding—as the ancestor of the Árpád
dynasty, so that the Magyar conquest could be seen simply
as the assertion of their "right of ownership" (or in modern
terms, their historical claims) over Pannonia. However,
these three motives are all that appear regarding the Huns
in his *Gesta Hungarorum*. How could he give the Magyar
people ancestors like the Huns, whose name still had such
hateful associations in the Christian West?[15] Even around
1250 the royal court of Béla IV still refused to countenance
any notions of his association with Attila.[16] Yet three
decades later, Ladislas' cleric had succeeded in promoting
the Hunnish origin theory to a central truth, and his account of Magyar history, which he culled from the chronicles of the previous two centuries, was preceded by a
separate "book" of similar length (*Hunnorum gesta*) containing a detailed account of the glorious ancient past of
the "Hun–Hungarians."

Now it would be quite wrong to picture Simon as an
isolated dreamer preoccupied with some novel vision of
history at odds both with ideas current in contemporary
Europe and with the Christian conception of history earlier
prevalent in Hungary. On the contrary, as philological
research and source examination progress, there emerges
clear evidence for the many interconnections between his

---

[15] *Anonymi (P. magistri) Gesta Hungarorum, SRH* 1: 33–117; cf. Györffy, *Krónikáink*, 134–36.

[16] *Vetera monumenta historica Hungariam sacram illustrantia*, ed. A.
Theiner (Rome: Vatican, 1859), 1: 230.

sources and for the extent to which the work is embedded in the contemporary intellectual world, the author's idiosyncratic ideas notwithstanding. It has long been recognised that the epic materials that form the basis of his Hunnish history derive not only from Jordanes's *Getica* (551) and Godfrey of Viterbo's *Pantheon* (1189) but from a surprisingly broad range of reading. For example, while visiting Venice he studied a lost history of the city containing numerous references to the Huns (which might, in fact, be identical to a *Historia Attilae* known to us only from references). His Italian shows the influence of the Venetian dialect, and it seems clear that he studied Roman and canon law in nearby Padua. He had been to France as well, and is the first Hungarian writer to record a French place-name in its French form (*Chalon*). What is more, he incorporated local French legends at certain points in his history of the Huns; for example, he located the site of the battle of Catalaunum near "Beauvoir" (*Campus Belvider*, one of a number of places so-called).[17] Research has also identified the two main theoretical foundations of the work, scholastic rationalism and Roman law (both of which can be connected with his north-Italian studies).[18] More recent studies suggest that we ought to give rather more credence to the author's assertion in his prologue that he gathered the materials and ideas for his work from far-flung sources *per Italiam, Franciam ac Germaniam*. For it can be shown

---

[17] The relationship to the written sources has already been clarified by Domanovszky, *Kézai*, 37–70, and S. Eckhardt, "A pannóniai hún történet keletkezése" (The origins of the Pannonian Hun history), *Századok* 62 (1928): 18–9, 30–1, and passim.

[18] For details see Horváth, *Árpád-kori*, 374–82; Gerics, "Adalékok," 111–12, 115ff.; Szűcs, "Társadalomelmélet," 589–95, 602–12.

that more than once he introduces memories of his own travels into his account of Attila's three expeditions against Western Europe. On one such journey, begun before 1269, he went to France as a member of a diplomatic mission and travelled down the Rhine valley, through Burgundy to Lyons, and from there home via northern Italy (see Map 1). Then between 1269 and 1271 in another diplomatic matter as Queen Elizabeth's cleric he twice traversed Charles of Anjou's southern Italian kingdoms of Naples and Sicily, travelling as far as Messina (see Map 2). It must have been during the 1270s (or at any rate between 1272–1283) that he studied at the university of Padua and earned his degree of *magister*. Returning home, and now the king's cleric, he set down at the beginning of the 1280s to draft his newly conceived "Hun–Magyar" history, based on his readings, experiences, and adventures.[19]

Much relies here on his experiences and adventures! His reading of literature could provide no support for his Hunnish–Hungarian identification nor sufficiently satisfying details of Hunnish glory. This he remedied in two ways. First, he simply transferred to the Huns a whole series of events he had read of in old Hungarian chronicles regarding the Magyar conquest of Pannonia and the Hungarians' assaults on the West in the tenth century. This account was then enriched with colourful material from his varied personal experiences. Ancient ruins at home or abroad he imagined to preserve some vestiges of the Huns; names of places which could be linked with the Huns according to the "etymological" methods fashionable at

---

[19] For details see Szűcs, "Társadalomelmélet," 573–80, 836–67.

the time were worked up into "historical" episodes; every
turn of phrase, every legend which he had picked up at
home or abroad was put to good use. His literary sources
were often terse in their discussion of the Hunnish expeditions, but as he had himself been to most of the areas
mentioned in Jordanes and Godfrey of Viterbo he did not
scruple to fill in the details from his own travel experiences
and his knowledge of geography. The history of the Huns
thus unfolded on a field of action which embraced not only
Pannonia but Western Europe as well, and their deeds
became legendary epics in which almost every actor, motif,
and turn of events is a unique fusion of literary sources,
oral traditions, etymological deductions, and personal experiences. What bound them together was "logic," and
what conferred authenticity was the repeatedly-expressed
conviction that present-day realities—a ruin, a name of a
town, a turn of speech, any element of the world of experience—can be used to deduce the past from the present
if one proceeds reasonably, matching contemporary elements with references in the written sources. Everything
hinges on ingenious but rational combinations. This is valid
not only for the epic but also for the theoretical content of
the work.[20]

This approach to the past and the methodology it involved
was very much "up-to-date" and fashionable at this time.
Just as writers of history in the course of the twelfth and
thirteenth centuries increasingly strove to free themselves

[20] The peculiar mechanism of Simon's historiographical method was
discussed by Eckhardt, "A pannóniai," particularly pp. 17ff., 47–56. See
also Horváth, "A hun történet," 466–76; Szűcs, "Társadalomelmélet,"
863–64, 869–72.

from the rigid formulas of ecclesiastical historiography, so too they tried to distance themselves from the dry rhetoric of the annals and chronicles. The gesta, with their attempt at a coherent, even "novelistic" narration, proved a suitable literary medium for setting the "once-off" deeds of kings, magnates, bishops, and abbots in a new historical perspective within the larger groupings of peoples now taking shape, Europe's emerging nations. Between the old, overly broad perspective of the world chronicles and the excessively narrow horizons of monastic, provincial, or town records, the middle of the twelfth century saw the beginnings of medieval "national" historiography (Abbot Suger, William of Malmesbury, Henry of Huntingdon, Geoffrey of Monmouth), which after 1200 spread to Europe's new peoples too (the Danes Sven Aggeson and Saxo Grammaticus, the Norwegian Snorri Sturluson, the Polish Vincent Kadłubek, the Hungarian Anonymus, etc.), which was to find its most striking vernacular expression in the mid-thirteenth century continuation of the *Grandes Chroniques de France.* It was a time of feverish activity and competition among men of letters throughout Europe as they sought to find in the past ancient, admirable, and glorious persons (preferably ones who had also played a conspicuous role in antiquity) whom they could make into the ancestors of their own *gens* or *natio* by the application of "scientific" methods—the combination of historical, logical, and etymological arguments—and with the aid of oral traditions and legends which were becoming fashionable in his time. A number of peoples vie in the claim to Trojan descent (the English, the Celts of Wales, the French, the Germans, and some Italian towns), with the French emerging as undisputed victors. In other cases, etymological

inspiration was furnished by the Greek Danaids (for the
Danes) or the Greeks themselves (e.g. *Graccus* the founder
of *Cracus*/Cracow for the Poles); and so on.[21] The climate
was, therefore, already ripe when Master Simon, roaming
per Italiam, Germaniam, Franciam during the 1260s and
70s, meditated on his future work. At home, too, the
precedents had been set by Master P.'s first somewhat timid
initiatives.

The ancestor question was, in fact, already settled. For
Christian Europe had by then agreed to agree on the
Hunnish descent of the Magyars. And once a Hun–Hungarian identity was accepted in the West, other combinations could hardly be given serious consideration, nor was
there need to. It is customary to seek an explanation for
the genesis of the Hunnish theory in the "pagan" Cuman
environment of Ladislas IV's court toward the end of the
1270s (Ladislas being Cuman on his mother's side). But
while this doubtlessly contributed to the acceptance on the
king's part of an affinity with Attila (which, as we have
seen, his grandfather Béla IV had still refused to countenance), this is in iself insufficient explanation for Simon's

---

[21] H. Grundmann, *Geschichtsschreibung im Mittelalter: Gattungen-Epo-
chen-Eigenart* (Göttingen: Vandenhoeck & Ruprecht, 1965), 15–17; A.
Grau, *Der Gedanke der Herkunft in der deutschen Geschichtsschreibung
des Mittelalters* (Leipzig: Vandenhoeck & Ruprecht, 1938); M. Klippel,
*Die Darstellung der fränkischen Trojanersage in Geschichtsschreibung
und Dichtung vom Mittelalter bis zur Renaissance in Frankreich* (Mar-
burg: Hausknecht, 1936); H. Koht, "The Dawn of Nationalism in
Europe," *American Historical Review* 52 (1947), esp. 270–77; H. He-
impel, "Alexander von Roes und das deutsche Selbstbewusstsein des
13. Jahrhunderts," *Archiv für Kulturgeschichte* 26 (1930): 50–55; Borst,
Turmbau, 2: 700ff., 767ff., 912ff.

adoption of the notion. The king's cleric did not in fact share his master's pagan leanings; indeed, he tactfully ignored them in his writings, even presenting the king as the loyal son of the Holy Mother Church with which Ladislas was, in fact, forever quarreling. The significant fact is that by the thirteenth century European public opinion was so far reassured of the general consolidation of Christianity that it was prepared to consign the horrors associated with Attila and the Huns to past history. This swing is reflected in the report quoted above which Humbertus de Romanis delivered at the Synod of Lyons (1274): the conversion of the formerly terrifying "barbarians" was pronounced a great victory of the Christian Cause, and the Hungarians—now unquestionably of Hunnish descent (*Huni qui et Hungari*)—were received into the family of Europe's peoples.[22] By now Master Simon, if anyone, was in the position to know that in elaborating his theory he would be working well within the consensus of European public opinion.

The advantages were obvious. In their own way, the Huns, too, were an "ancient" people, and of their glorious and conquering past there could obviously be no doubt. Moreover, the Hunnish descent completely fulfilled an important ideological criterion of all such theories: the ability to support claims of historical right. It demonstrated that the Magyar conquest was nothing other than the assertion of

---

[22] Cap. V: *Quod ista septem genera persecutorum iam pene enervata sunt praeter Saracenos. . . . Barbari non comparent praeter Tartaros, qui etsi solos Hungaros persequuntur*"; Cap. VI: "*Nam Wandali qui et Poloni, et Huni qui et Hungari, Gothi qui et Daci sunt effecti Catholici*" (Mansi, *Sacrorum conciliorum nova et amplissima collectio* (Venice, 1780), 24: 110).

the rights of the Hun–Hungarians "returning" to Pannonia (so Master Simon's second book, on Hungarian history proper, is entitled *Liber de reditu*). What is more, the Hunnish past could, with a twist, be fitted into the Christian view of history which required that a people should have fulfilled even in ancient times a certain function in the evolution of Christianity. Already in the first *Vita* of St. Stephen there occurs the notion of the still pagan Hungarians as the *flagellum Dei*, the instruments of the Almighty in chastising Christendom for its sins. Of course in the earlier Christian view of history it was primarily Attila who was "the scourge of God." But Master Simon was able to revive this *topos* and go a step further. In his account of the famous meeting at Ravenna (ch. 17) he has Attila, about to attack the pope, being turned back by a vision which enjoins on him instead to massacre the Arian heretics in the interests of the papacy. With this innovation, Attila is exalted to the position of a defender of the Church; he has attained a function within, so to say, the *ecclesia militans.*[23]

---

[23] *Vita Sancti Stephani regis* ("Legenda maior"): *Unde contigit divine pietatis intuitu in filios perditionis et ignorantie . . . Ungaros videlicet . . . clementi visu de celo prospicere, ut quos ad ulciscendas prevaricationes Christianorum de sedibus naturalibus in occiduas partes occulto perpetuitatis consilio prius destinaverat, hos . . . de via iniquitatis ad iustitie semitam ad spem in eternum permanentis perduceret retributionis"* (SRH 2: 378). — For the notion of "function," see E. Sestan, *Stato e nazione nell'alto medioevo: Ricerche sulle origini nazionali in Francia, Italia, Germania* (Naples: Edizioni Scientifiche Italiane, 1952), 33; Fr. Hertz, *Nationality in History and Politics: A Study of the Psychology and Sociology of National Sentiment and Character* (London: Kegan Paul, Trench, Trubner, 1945), 280; D. Kurze, "Nationale Regungen in der spätmittelalterlichen Prophetie," *Historische Zeitschrift* 202 (1966): 3, 10, 23.

Proving the Hunnish origin itself did not cause much difficulty. European public taste had not only rehabilitated the formerly despised world of oral traditions and sagas (*fabulae*) but had assigned to them a definite "theoretical" role. Simon was clearly familiar, on the one hand, with the ancient Magyar descent-saga preserved in oral tradition (which by around 1200, as Anonymus indicates, one could hear only in "the false stories of the peasants and foolish songs of the minstrals," *ex falsis fabulis rusticorum vel a garrulo cantu ioculatorum*); on the other hand, he discovered an early saga concerning the Huns in Jordanes' *Getica.* The two were related in certain motifs (the pursuit of the hind and the abduction of women). The names of the two eponymous brothers in the Hungarian saga, *Hunor* and *Mogor*—in fact, the legendary personification of the Onogur–Magyar—offered tempting possibilities, the name of the former resembling as it did the name of the Hun people.[24] This provided Simon with his key argument for the Hun–Hungarian identity, which he was thus able to support with western "literary" authority. In fact it was his sole piece of "historical" evidence, but his exemplary scholastic argument in the prologue appeals to the author-

---

[24] For the growing value of oral tradition, see J. Honti, *Anonymus és a hagyomány* (The Anonymus and tradition), Minerva 60/1 (Budapest: Danubia Kiadó, 1942), esp. 14–5, 21ff. Nevertheless, even the Anonymus, around 1200, was reluctant to write down the Magyar origin saga. That this legend was written down only in the thirteenth century was proven by Horváth, *Árpád-kori*, 13–29, 297–98, 317; cf. Szűcs, "Társadalomelmélet," 615–16. For the probable transformation of *onour-unour-unor*, see Györffy, *Krónikáink*, 30–31. [This etymology has been seriously challenged lately, e.g. by A. Róna-Tas, "Ugor, ogur, or ugur: Remarks on the name 'Finno-Ugrian,'" in *Emlékkönyv Mikola Tibor tiszteletére* (Szeged, 1996), 265–69.]

ity of Holy Writ (*per textum comprobatur*) and the natural order (*natura rerum*) to confirm "rationally" that the origin of the Magyars resembles that of the "other nations of the world" (*sicut mundi nationes alias*).

However, this "proof" in itself can hardly be said to be his most important achievement, even though he managed at the beginning of his work (ch. 4) to give it canonical validity by tying it to the Biblical genesis of peoples and to the building of the Tower of Babel, thus finally locating the *natio* in the family tree of Europe's peoples on Japheth's branch. For this was essentially a routine task, fitted into a prepared scheme. The significant point is that Simon was able to present the historical identity of the Hun–Hungarian "nation" as an unbroken entity "from ancient times to our own days." Proceeding from this, he effectively overthrew previous historical viewpoints.

In order to appreciate the significance of this, one must glance at the preceding state of affairs. Historiography began early in the Middle Ages with the "*Volksgeschichte*" (the *origo* or *historia gentis*), which reached its flower in the sixth to eighth centuries (Jordanes, Gregory of Tours, the so-called "Fredegar," Isidore of Seville, Paul the Deacon, Bede, etc.). This form attempted to co-ordinate the "barbarian" traditions of the new peoples just stepping onto the stage of history—Western and Eastern Goths, Franks, Lombards, Anglo-Saxons, etc.—with the universal viewpoint of Christianity, but in such an "ethnocentric" way as to still preserve the framework of each people's history, with their individual origins and their own heroic past (*acta regum et bella gentium*). The productive epoch for this kind of historiography came to an end with the eighth century (Widukind's Saxon history in the tenth century is but an epilogue). After the dispersal of the original peoples themselves, the horizon of history on the one hand expanded, as testified by the appearance of world-chronicles, and on the other, contracted into localism. Thus, that which starts in the twelfth and thirteenth centuries is (as has already been said) a new kind of phenomenon reflecting the new integrating currents: it is the seed of "national" historiography.[25] But all this developed in the old Europe. When after the millennium a series of new peoples confronted the task of reconciling their own "barbarian" traditions with the norms of Christendom, the altered historical situation left little scope for the kind of compromise observable earlier. In form the Christian chronicle-literature that was now produced is also of the "history of the people" genre (as shown by the title *Gesta Ungarorum* of its first-fruits in Hungary, written around 1060 and reconstructable from fragments). Its content, however, is very much less so. The fully developed system of values of Europe's Christian feudal system demanded the stifling of the pagan, "barbarian" past. The early Hungarian *Gesta* accepted the artificial literary theory of "Scythian" origins which took shape in the monasteries of the West and was first conceived of by Abbot Regino of Prüm (in 908). The real *origo gentis* and real past of the pagan Magyars lived on until the thirteenth century, but only in the "false tales of the peasants" and slowly reduced to the level of folktales. This *Gesta* discussed as much of the preconversion past as its author could glean from the annals of Altaich and from Regino,

---

[25] Grundmann, *Geschichtsschreibung*, 12ff.

and discussed it with the same prejudices, being none too sparing in denunciatory epithets and judgements.[26]

In this respect, the attitude of the early Hungarian chronicles differs but little from the historiography of the other "new barbarians" of Eastern and Northern Europe. The goal was assimilation at any price, so that, as has been aptly said by Amo Borst, "each country could feel like a Christian microcosm."[27] The pagan past, the ancient past itself was considered a kind of genealogical antecedent of secondary importance. For according to the Pauline teaching passed on by the Church Fathers, through the mystery of baptism man becomes "a new creation" (*nova creatura*), born again through the waters of baptism (*renascitur homo ex aqua*). He wins, therefore, his true human essence, his *humanitas*, only through becoming a Christian, a *fidelis Christianus*, in contradistinction to his original "natural" self (*homo naturalis seu animalis*). What was true of the individual was also true of peoples. The term "people," *populus* or *gens*, refers in this view not to some immanent and *naturalis* entity but, from the ecclesiastical point of view, to the masses of believers, or from the lay point of view, to the mass of subjects (*fideles subditi*), whom Divine Providence had subjected to the power of the rulers (the *populus subiectus* or *subditus*).[28]

[26] E. Mályusz, "Krónika-problémák" (Chronicle problems), *Századok* 100 (1966): 714, 725.

[27] Borst, *Turmbau*, 2: 701–3.

[28] W. Ullmann, *The Individual and Society in the Middle Ages* (Baltimore: Johns Hopkins Press, 1966), 7–24.

So in the sources of the eleventh and twelfth centuries, in the chronicles and legends, in the charters and decrees, the "people" of Hungary appear simply as *gens regis* or *populus regni*, the people of the Christian monarchy, in other words, the great mass of the subjects of the realm. In the thirteenth century, *Hungarus* is a mere derivative of *regnum Hungariae*; a "Hungarian" is one who is the subject of the king, who was born in this country, or, as a contemporary (1205) definition unambiguously states, a *persona que originem de regno Ungarie duceret.*[29] Genuine *historia* is viewed as beginning with Baptism, when, as King Stephen's Greater Legend (ca. 1083) expressed it with biblical sonority, "the sons of perdition and ignorance," this "wild and roaming people, the Magyars," who had, in the pagan past "been lost in darkness, saw a great light."[30] The fundamental historical watershed in this view of history comes with the acceptance of Christianity, and with the increasingly mythicised Saint Stephen; everything that came before is degraded to insignificance and damned as "prehistoric." Otherwise, the Hungarian chronicles of the eleventh and twelfth centuries are mostly preoccupied with the past of the members of the Christianised Árpád dynasty. Of "so-

[29] For the terminology, see J. Deér, "Közösségérzés és nemzettudat a XI-XIII. századi Magyarországon" (The sense of community and national self-consciousness in the Hungary of the 11th to 13th centuries), *A Gróf Klebelsberg Kuno Magyar Történetkutató Intézet Évkönyve,* 4 (Budapest: Kertész, 1934), 97–100 [see now also idem, "Entstehung des ungarischen Nationalbewusstseins," in Studien zum Nationalbewusstsein (as n. 11, above), 11–54], and Szűcs, "Gentilizmus," 181–98. The charter of 1205 is published in *Monumenta ecclesiae Strigoniensis*, ed. F. Knauz (Esztergom: Horák, 1874), 1: 181.

[30] *SRH* 2: 378, 380.

ciety" proper only the notable personages who appear in
the historical picture are those who play an active role in
the fortunes of the dynasty.

This formula begins to loosen around 1200. The Anonymus specially did much to free it up as he searched for a
continuity between the pagan past and the *nobilissima gens
Hungarie*, turning his attention not only to the ancestors
of the dynasty (*gesta regum*) but also to the antecedents of
the contemporary noble families (*gesta nobilium*), whose
existence he traced back to the time of the original conquest.[31] It was Master Simon, however, who finally dispensed with the formula in the interests of the emerging
esprit laique and "national" historiography.[32] With this,
historical consciousness undergoes a fundamental transformation. The theme of Christianity as a turning-point
that marked an epochal change does not disappear, but
what was previously considered lacking in interest, what
indeed was denied expression as mere prehistory, "the
wanderings in darkness," now expanded and became the
critical point of historical consciousness and a focus of
social-political debate.

According to the new *gesta Hungarorum*, from the genesis
of languages and peoples at Babel through the migration of
the Magyar ancestors from their legendary seat at Meotis
to Scythia, where the "multiplied" people were divided into

[31] J. Győry, *Gesta regum—gesta nobilium* (Budapest: OSzK, 1948).

[32] See O. Brunner's instructive analyses in *Adeliges Landleben und
europäischer Geist* (Salzburg: Otto Müller, 1949), 62–90, as well as
Ullmann, *Individual*, 104–16.

108 clans, the Hungarian *natio* was "until today" (*usque hodie*) a close kinship of blood. This ethnic unity was disturbed neither by their wanderings from Scythia until they "first" conquered Pannonia; nor as they subjugated half the world from the Don to the Rhine under the leadership of Attila; nor on their return to Scythia, only to rally their strength for their "return" to Pannonia in 872 (!) and for its conclusive occupation. There is, therefore, no break from the Flood to the thirteenth century, in spite of the various vicissitudes in the life of this people and in spite of the variability of fate, of its "fortunate and unfortunate" turnings, the account of which fills the 23 chapters which make up the "Deeds of the Huns."

The major category of historical thought, as well as the agent of history's transmission, is the *natio* itself, whose historical continuity is ensured primarily by its common origin. The number 108, projected back into antiquity, is probably nothing other than the historicisation of the number of the *genera* (loosely related groups of aristocratic and noble families all claiming descent from common eleventh and twelfth century ancestors) which could be counted around 1280.[33] The second criterion of a people's historical existence is the identity of its language. The Huns, in our author's view, spoke Hungarian, for Hun and Magyar were not two related peoples but one and the same, which at one time just happened to be referred to principally as "Hun" but later was called *Hungarus*. Just one illustration of the

---

[33] Györffy, "A magyar nemzetségtől a vármegyéig, a törzstől az országig" (From the Hungarian clan to the county, from tribe to country), *Századok* 92 (1958): 26.

kind of tortured etymological deductions which such rea-
soning permitted is the notion that *Ispania* derived its name
from the Magyar *ispán* (head of a royal county).[34]

It has been customary to regard Simon's work as a unity
which can be divided structurally into two basic components, the Hun and the Hungarian *gesta*, with two more or
less inorganically attached "appendices" (a so-called "Ad-
vena-catalogue," and a "second appendix"). These, however, are artificial demarcations, based on structure and
genre, and manage to ignore the essential fact that the basis
of the work is the origin-fiction and that the structure of
the work is dictated by the logic of this. The writer himself
gives us the key in a short digression at the end of ch. 6.
According to this, "pure Hungary" (*pura Hungaria*) con-
sists of the descendants of the 108 clans established in
ancient times "without any intermixing" (*absque omni
missitalia*); those who subsequently became part of it were
either newcomers (*advenae*) or the descendants of prisoners of war (*ex captivis oriundi*). These categories mirror the
structure of the work as a whole. A synonym for the
history of the Huns is "the first book of the entry" *(liber
primus de introitu)*, while Hungarian history from the
conquest to 1282 is subsumed in "the second book of the

---

[34] . . . *capitanei . . . qui Hunorum lingua spani vocabantur, ex quorum
nominibus tota Ispania postmodum est vocata* (ch. 12). Similarly, it was
after Attila's brother *Buda* that Attila's town *Oubuda* was named (ch.
13), and a number of the Hun captains got their names, "etymologically,"
from thirteenth-century Hungarian toponyms (Cuwe, Erd, Turda, etc.),
cf. Horváth, "A hun történet," 467–71. The concept of "kindred peoples"
is also formed on the basis of kindred languages: thus a group separated
from the nation in antiquity *statura et colore Hunis similes, tantummodo
parum differunt in loquela, sicut Saxones et Turingi* (ch. 14).

return" *(secundus liber de reditu)*. The conceptual unit of the first two books, as the author expresses it in ch. 76, tacitly referring to the common content of both, is the history of "pure Hungary" *(pura Hungaria)*. What follow are not "appendices" but two further "books"; for to these, too, the author assigns the name *liber*. The first deals with the noble newcomers of foreign origin *(De nobilibus advenis)*; the other is a dissertation on the non-noble social elements—those of foreign origin, and those descended from prisoners of war *(conditionarii . . . ex captivis oriundi)*. The conceptual unit of these latter two books is the "mixed" elements *(missitalia)*. The fourfold construction is, therefore, conceived in a conceptual dualism, according to which even within the kingdom of Hungary there are "pure Magyars" as well as "mixtures." This conceptual dualism forms the main historical organising principle of Simon's *Gesta*.[35]

It would be a mistake to interpret this unhistorical origin-fiction, asserted with such consistent logic, as the seed of some racial theory. Note that not one word is said against

[35] For the details of the construction and the constructional principles of the work, see Szűcs, "Társadalomelmélet," 616–20. The pairs of conceptual opposites in Simon's *Gesta* are clear: *pura Hungaria~missitalia; verus alumnus regni Scitiae~missitalius exterae nationis; de Scitia oriundi~missitalia* (chs. 6, 22, 55). This peculiar word is a derivative of *miscitare* 'to mix, to mingle' (cf. Du Cange, *Glossarium*, 5:176) corresponding to the medieval Italian forms *mischiare, meschiare* (Florentine *mestiare*) and derivatives (e.g. *mischiato, mistamente*)—see C. Battisti and G. Alessio, *Dizionario etimologico Italiano* (Florence: G. Barbera, 1954), 4:86. The forms *missitalium* or *missitalius* demonstrate the same characteristic Venetian phonetic peculiarity as Simon's name for Venice, *Venesia* (ch. 15); cf. Eckhardt, "A pannóniai," 4. This is one of the linguistic proofs of Simon's Venetian sojourn.

the "mixtures." Rather, in a somewhat clumsy way it serves to counterbalance the rigid Christian conception of history. Moreover, this historical principle, as suggested above, is intersected by an other. Socially, both groups are divided into nobles and non-nobles (*ignobiles*). Thus even as the work concludes with a social-theoretical discussion, the history of the Huns is introduced by a similar dissertation on the ancient origins of social inequality in the "pure" Hun–Magyar society. We shall have more to say of this later. It is enough here to note that the agent of history is the "true" or "pure" (*vera, pura*) *natio*, whose conceptual opposite is every foreign (*extera*) *natio*.

The above is not merely a conceptual principle; it is an ordering principle in the Hunnish history as well. For in this fanciful construct Pannonia before the Huns was a kind of historicised Holy Roman Empire, whose ruler was the German (*Alamannus natione*) king *Detricus*—a figure created from elements of the Dietrich of Bern legend—whose people were a peculiar Roman–German–Lombard (!) hotch-potch. The "pure" Huns were, therefore, in danger of "admixing" with this product of the author's imagination, especially when, under Attila, their empire extended from Cologne in the West to the *Lithuani* in the North and Zadar in the South. It is for this reason that the author scrupulously separates the Huns even in their institutions from every *extera natio*, and the latter are given a separate governor in the person of Attila's brother Buda (ch. 10). In lifestyles, too, the two elements diverged (ibid.), as well as in their military organisations (chs. 10, 12, 15). After Attila's death it was the *extera natio* which caused the outbreak of factionalism (ch. 19); and so on.

It is instructive to compare in verbal detail Master Simon's *Gesta* with the version of Hunnish history by an unknown compiler of a few decades later (the so-called fourteenth-century chronicle composition),[36] as it draws attention to an important development in the history of ideas. For the compiler was evidently at a loss for what to do with the details we have been discussing above. Either he left them out or he distorted their meaning, using extracts of the text only where *"extera natio"* could be interpreted as referring also to some "foreign" individual, and he nowhere uses the word *"natio"* as Simon does to refer to the Hun–Hungarians themselves. It is worth noting that Simon was the first to use the word *natio* to refer to his own people, and moreover with a highly positive connotation. Indeed, in his conceptual system peoples or "nationalities" are generally referred to as *nationes*. But in the earlier chronicles of Hungary, in legends and in legal writings, the writer's own people are always referred to as *gens*. The term *"natio"* either simply meant "descent," or referred to foreign, largely barbarian and pagan tribes, with some pejorative connotation.[37]

This eleventh and twelfth century usage is consonant with the contemporary European use of concepts which stretched back to antiquity. The word *natio* preserved its etymological and semantic affiliation with the notion of

[36] This lost construction became the basis of the late medieval chronicles of Hungary (*SRH* 1: 239–505); cf. note 8.

[37] See note 29. The concept *natio Hungarica* first appears in Hungary in 1298 in a charter (*ÁUO/Codex diplomaticus Arpadianus continuatus*, ed. G. Wenzel, Mon. Hung. Hist. I. Diplomataria (Budapest: MTA, 1874), 22: XII, 619).

"birth" (*nascor*), in close relationship with the concept of *natura*; and "natural origin" counted as a value neither in later antiquity nor in the Middle Ages. It is, therefore, understandable that the word *natio* in its more comprehensive sense referred both in classical and medieval Latin principally to unorganised, barbarian, or pagan tribes, somewhat analogous to the modern ethnographic concept of *Naturvolk*.[38] The word begins to express a higher value in Europe in the thirteenth century, as the conceptual offshoot of the renaissance of the idea of origin which marked the beginnings of the early "national" outlook. Around 1250 we find *natio regni Angliae* (its vernacular form, *nacion: inglis man par in commun*, appears around 1300). The French *nation* enters French literature in the 1260s and '70s, where it refers to the totality of "the French." At about the same time the concept emerges within the Italian urban setting in the forms *natio, nazione*. The "ideological" character of the theories of origin emphasises the notion that a people (*gens*) belongs together principally through its common "birth, descent, origin," and in virtue of this forms one and the same *natio*. And, as the latter has by now acquired value, the word itself comes increasingly to express a specific value.[39] So in this respect,

[38] *Thesaurus linguae Latinae* (Leipzig: Teubner, 1925–34), 6/2: 1842–65 (G. Meyer); K. Heissenbüttel, *Die Bedeutung der Bezeichnungen für "Volk" und "Nation" bei den Geschichtsschreibern des 10. bis 13. Jahrhunderts* (Göttingen: Dieterich, 1920); K. Bierbach, *Kurie und nationale Staaten im früheren Mittelalter (bis 1245)* (Dresden: M. Dittert, 1938), esp. 10–37. See also Fr. W. Müller's basic study referred to in the following note.

[39] *The Oxford English Dictionary* (Oxford, 1933), 7:30; Fr. Godefroy, *Dictionnaire de l'ancienne langue française du IXᵉ au XVᵉ siècle* (Paris, 1888), 5:462; Fr. W. Müller, "Zur Geschichte des Wortes und Begriffs

too, Master Simon joins the mainstream in his "up to date" way, for a time confusing, even dumbfounding his near contemporaries, as the reaction of the fourteenth century compiler strikingly illustrates.[40]

It is not the intention of this study to delve into the multifaceted subject of the genesis of "nationalism" in the Middle Ages.[41] Let two concrete examples suffice to demonstrate through what intellectual contradictions and historiographical debates the new concept had to fight to gain recognition.

Simon tells how after the death of Attila and the dissolution of his empire his legitimate son, Csaba, returned to the "nation of his father" (*ad patris nationem*) in Scythia and

'nation' im altfranzösischen Schrifttum des Mittelalters bis zur Mitte des 15. Jahrhunderts," *Romanische Forschungen* 58/59 (1947): 247–321. For the Italian use of the words see N. Tommaseo and B. Bernardo, *Dizionario della lingua Italiana* 3/1: 451; Heissenbüttel, *Bedeutung*, 78–90. For the German terminology see W. Müller, "Deutsches Volk und deutsches Land im späteren Mittelalter," *Historische Zeitschrift* 132 (1925): 460ff. The use of the French "*nation*" is rooted in a conception already formulated around 1300 in a legal dissertation: *gens . . . qui sont nez hors du royaume*, in other words, the entire people "born" within the French kingdom form one and the same "nation"; see B. Guenée, "État et nation en France au Moyen-Age," *Revue Historique* 237 (1967): 25.

[40] For a detailed account of the sources see Szűcs, "Társadalomelmélet," 626–31.

[41] For some theoretical aspects of this complex of questions, see J. Szűcs, "'Nationalität' und 'Nationalbewusstsein' im Mittelalter: Versuch einer einheitlichen Begriffssprache," *Acta Historica Acad. Sc. Hungaricae* 18 (1972): 1–38, 245–66, now also in his *Nation und Geschichte* (Budapest: Corvina, 1981), 161–243.

began at once to agitate for a return "in order to take vengeance on the Germans." The later chronicler predictably baulked at the first phrase: in his version Csaba returns to "the abode of his father" (*ad paternam sedem*). The rest he omits: Csaba merely encouraged the return with his "admonitions."

Another episode is of even more interest. Master Simon, although evidently fond of Csaba, nevertheless condemns him at one point. He recounts how Csaba, on returning to Scythia, "boasted of his mother's nobility" (*nobilitate genitricis in communi se iactaret*—Csaba's mother was supposedly the daughter of a Greek emperor). For this the Hunnish nobility "held him in contempt" (*ipsum contemnebat*), saying that he was "not a true scion" (*non verus alumnus*) of Scythia but "a mixture from an alien nation" (*missitalius exterae nationis*), and in consequence, he was not given a wife in Scythia. Two generations later the compiler of the fourteenth century chronicle still does not understand this conception, or does not accept it. He replaces the entire account with the brief statement that "on his grandfather's advice" Csaba sought a wife elsewhere. This trivialisation effectively glosses over the significance of the claims implicit in Simon's original version about origins and "public opinion" among the Hunnish nobility. Nothing could better highlight the difference in outlook of the two authors.[42]

[42] Chs. 20 and 22. Specifically, in the thirteen cases where the two versions can be examined in parallel we find six cases where the later chronicler either left out or substituted something else for the word *natio*; in certain places, failure to comprehend the word's new value has led to the misinterpretation of the action of the epic itself.

This is all the more significant because Csaba is the only figure in Hunnish history whom Master Simon links genealogically with one of the prominent baronial families of his own time (viz. the Aba clan). All the other heroes and Hun captains owe their names to etymological inventions. For the author consciously avoided giving any contemporary baronial family the pretext for deducing "rights" from the history of the Huns. As we shall see later, what Master Simon strove to deduce from Hunnish antiquity was, apart from the Hungarian "nation," the principles of "constitutional law," and this precisely in defiance of the high-born of his times. Thus even his sole "actualisable" hero, the putative ancestor of the Aba clan, is found to have a blemish: he is a "mixture," not a "real" Hun![43] What is striking in this story is the transformation in attitude. The social prominence conferred by descent is no longer, in itself, an absolute value (could one, after all, imagine a greater claim to prominence in those days than the blood of emperors?); if it is not conjoined with the "purity" of the *natio*, it can only have a lower place in the scale of values.

Master Simon's other latent debate is conducted with his predecessor in historiography, Master Ákos, who a decade earlier, around 1272, had rewritten the earlier Hungarian chronicles. What inspired Master Ákos, a descendant of the well-born Ákos kindred, was the idea of a unified aristocracy. He, too, accepts the "Scythian origin"; nevertheless, he saw the new nobles who arrived in the course of the establishment of the kingdom of Hungary as the social

[43] The important ideological and chronological character of this work has already been pointed out by Horváth, *Árpád-kori*, 447–49.

equals of the Hungarians (*nobilitate pares Ungaris*). He gives three criteria for *nobilitas*: settlement of relatively long duration in the realm; intermixing and intermarriage with the Hungarians (*Ungaris inmixti*); and, finally, the acquisition of land.[44] When it comes to discussing the same principle, Simon, without directly arguing against his predecessor, gives a different order of preconditions for noble status. First in importance is service to the king; second, the possession of a grant of land; and only last, a longer term of residence in the country. It is particularly characteristic of our author that regarding the second precondition he uses the term fief (*pheudum*), thus attributing to Hungary a feudal system it did not have, and so faithfully "ordering" Hungarian reality according to the European model.[45] For present purposes, however, the decisive difference between them is this: Master Ákos regards as positive the "intermixing" of foreigners and Magyars (*Ungaris inmixti*), whereas Simon would see this as negative (cf. *missitalius exterae nationis*). In the long run, belonging to a "nation" comes to take precedence in the system of values over being well-born.

---

[44] *SRH* 1: 303–4; cf. E. Mályusz, *Az V. István-kori Gesta* (The gesta of the time of Stephen V), Értekezések a történeti tudományok köréből (Studies in Historical Sciences) 58 (Budapest: Akadémiai Kiadó, 1971), 53ff., esp. 61–64.

[45] Ch. 94: *qui servientes regibus vel caeteris regni dominis ex ipsis pheuda acquirendo nobilitatem processu temporis sunt adepti*; ch. 90: *latisque et amplis pheudis in diversis Hungariae partibus noscitur investisse*, whereas the fourteenth century chronicle version has: *latis et amplis hereditatibus* (*SRH* 1: 192, 297); *iobagiones vero castri . . . ad regem venientes, terram eis tribuit de castri terris, ut pheuda castri* (*SRH* 1: 193). Hungarian legal terminology had hardly ever employed the term *pheudum*.

Simon's historical conception was quick to influence the attitudes of the nobility. It undermined the notion of the mythicised St. Stephen as the point of departure of Hungarian history—that it was he who "redeemed" the nation and led it out of the "darkness"—although this had been the guiding principle of the early chronicles and legends and was still present in a charter of Béla IV of 1231: only through the holy king's merits "did this land pass from sorrow to joy, from slavery to liberty."[46] In 1290 the Styrian Ottokar von Horneck already bore witness to the rejection of this theory in favour of the claim of the nobility that "it was their ancestors who vanquished the pagans with their mighty strength, suffering the loss of so many lives."[47] In much the same way Matthew of Paris recounts the French nobility boasted but a little earlier that it was they who were "the principal members of the kingdom," and that the establishment of the kingdom can be "attributed to the sweetness of battle," in other words, to their ancestors, the glorious descendants of the Trojans.[48] Overall, in spite of dissonant chords which accompanied the process, the genesis of medieval nationalism advances irreversibly throughout all of Europe in the thirteenth century. One of

[46] Fr. Zimmermann and C. Werner, *Urkundenbuch zur Geschichte der Deutschen in Siebenbürgen* (Hermannstadt: Michaelis, 1882), 1: 54.

[47] *Si (Ungarn arm und rich) jahen . . . ir vordern hetenz mit grozen kraft den heiden erstriten und heten ouch darumb erliten vil manigen bloutes guz . . . Oesterreichische Reimchronik,* lines 40771–40779 (*MGH Dt. Chr.* V/1); cf. E. Bartoniek, "A magyar királlyáavatáshoz" (On the inauguration of the Hungarian kings), *Századok* 57 (1923): 279. For the demonstrable effect of Simon's *Gesta* in the 1280s and 1290s, see Szűcs, "Társadalomelmélet," 635–36.

[48] Hertz, *Nationality*, 215.

its most far-reaching consequences was undoubtedly to prepare the way for the laicisation and secularisation of thought, and, in particular, of attitudes toward history.

SIMON'S SOCIAL THEORY:
THE ORIGINS OF HUMAN INEQUALITY

As long as the ecclesiastical conception of history was unchallenged and the "descending theme of government and law" prevailed in the social and political spheres,[49] little theoretical explanation was required to explain the facts of the "social structure." The Fathers of the Church had already justified human inequality in terms of the theological thesis of original sin,[50] while "society", at least as regarded from above, seemed relatively homogeneous, since Divine Providence had placed the mass of humanity predetermined for subjection, the *populus subiectus*, under some or other lay authority. Differences within each such social unit and "people" were similarly explained in terms of the "functional" scheme of the World Order, which preordained for each and every person a place in the field of prayer, war, or work (*oratores, bellatores, laboratores*).

[49] W. Ullmann, *Principles of Government and Politics in the Middle Ages* (London: Methuen, 1961), 20ff.

[50] For a historical survey of the question, cf. R. W. and A. J. Carlyle, *A History of Medieval Political Theory in the West* (Edinburgh and London: W. Blackwood, 1928), 5: 21–26; H. von Voltelini, "Der Gedanke der allgemeinen Freiheit in den deutschen Rechtsbüchern," *Zeitschrift der Savigny-Stiftung für Rechtsgeschichte, Germ. Abt.* 57 (1937): 189–207; Fr. Graus, *Volk, Herrscher und Heiliger im Reich der Merowinger* (Prague: Tschechoslowakische Akademie der Wissenschaften, 1965), 282ff.

Should, however, a more "historical" explanation of social inequalities be sought, that, too, was offered in terms of the predominating viewpoint. The acceptance of Christianity was not only the starting-point of history in this view, but in Hungary as elsewhere some mythical legislator became the source of all right and all liberty. By the turn of the eleventh to the twelfth century the ancestral hereditary estates were already spoken of as "the donation of St. Stephen," so by the thirteenth century every freedom (*libertas*, i.e. socio-legal *conditio*) was considered as something instituted by the holy king (*instituta a sancto Stephano*). And because the concept of freedom was itself relative, it was viewed essentially as the grant of privilege from above. Thus in the relatively unsettled and mobile social structure of the eleventh and twelfth centuries there existed as many "liberties" between the two extremes of servitude and the evolving "golden liberty" of the nobility as there were social strata, groups, and statuses.[51] A "historical" explanation of the origin of servitude, we have cause to believe, had already been given in the lost eleventh-century primary *Gesta*: the occupying Magyars had reduced all the people they found in Pannonia to servitude.[52]

[51] P. Váczy, *A szimbolikus államszemlélet kora Magyarországon* (The era of the symbolic view of the state in Hungary), Minerva Könyvtár 40 (Pécs: Dunántúl Egyetemi Nyomda, 1932), esp. 35–38, 54ff.

[52] The relevant text of the eleventh century *Gesta Ungarorum* as far as one can reconstruct it from the unanimous testimony of the texts of the Anonymus, Riccardus, Alberic of Trois-Fontaines, and Thomas of Spalato, was probably the following: . . . *totum populum* (*Pannonie*) *in servitutem redegerunt*; cf. B. Hóman, *A Szt. László-kori Gesta Ungarorum és XII.–XIII. századi leszármazói* (The *Gesta Ungarorum* of the time of St. Ladislas and its 12th and 13th century derivatives) (Budapest: MTA, 1925), 15–32; Szűcs, "Társadalomelmélet," 586–89.

Only the highest social stratum, the well-born, were able to shake off the influence of the canonically sanctioned *a sancto rege* conception. The evidence suggests that by the eleventh century there existed a "seven Magyars" theory, according to which true *nobilitas* consisted in being descended from one of the seven chieftains who led the Magyars in the conquest of Pannonia. This idea was extended around 1272 by the same Master Ákos referred to above to include all the great families of his times.[53]

These embryonic "social-theoretical" ideas, however, became increasingly obsolete as the earlier heterogeneity of statuses and "freedoms" gave way in the course of the decisive thirteenth century to new structures more in line with contemporary Europe: a unified nobility on the one hand, and an integrated dependent peasantry on the other. By the 1260s and 70s, the concept of *nobilis* broadened to include all the nobility, while by the end of the century the Hungarian term for tenant peasant, *jobbágy* (Latinised as *iobagio*), became a common term to include the diverse "non-noble" (*ignobilis*) and dependent strata of society.[54]

[53] For the contention that the text fragment *qui autem de istis septem nati sunt, ipsi sunt modo viri nobiles in terra Ungariae*, which appears in Alberic of Trois-Fontaines' world chronicle, originated in the 11th-century Hungarian Gesta, see Szűcs, "Társadalomelmélet," 587. For the hidden debate of Master Ákos with the ancient Hungarian Chronicles, see *SRH* 1: 292–93; cf. E. Mályusz, *Az V. István-kori*, 53ff.

[54] The formulae for ennoblement have been carefully collected by P. Váczy, "A királyi serviensek és a patrimoniális királyság" (The royal *servientes* and the patrimonial kingship), *Századok* 61 (1927): 253–62. — E. Mályusz, "A magyar köznemesség kialakulása" (The evolution of the Hungarian lesser nobility), *Századok* 76 (1942): 272–305, 407–34. For the concept of *jobbágy*, see I. Szabó, "Jobbágyság-parasztság" (*Jobbágy*-status and peasantry), *Ethnographia* 76 (1965): 10–31.

But the earlier "historical" notions became similarly obsolete, especially after Master Simon radically broke through the traditional historical limits and set up the *natio* as the basic historical point of reference. In doing so, however, even he could hardly ignore the fact that the mass of the peasantry were predominantly *natione Hungarus*, which naturally raised problems for the old theory of the subjugation of the "peoples of Pannonia." In any case, as a cleric who had studied Roman law he had at his disposal more modern techniques for explaining the origins of the foreigners. The fourth section of his work is given over to a historical account of the status of these diverse elements, presented in terms of the *ius gentium* (or as he calls it, *mos gentium*) of Roman law, on the premise that these persons were originally prisoners of war.[55] Within his view of history, however, this could refer only to the foreign and "mixed" (*missitalia*) elements of the population. It left open the question of the origin of the peasant masses within the "pure" (*pura*) Hun–Hungarian nation, for, as he notes himself, "if every Hungarian descended from one and the same mother and one and the same father, how can one be called noble and the other non-noble?"[56]

The question is, in fact, anticipated in the theoretical analysis near the beginning of his work (ch. 7), where he recounts the Biblical and legendary stories of the genesis of peoples and the "Scythian" epoch—in short, among his account of "ancient times" marking the beginnings of

[55] *SRH* 1: 192–94. For the Roman legal background, see Horváth, *Árpád-kori*, 374–77.

[56] Ch. 7.

Hunnish history proper in "the sixth age of the world." In the medieval conception of time this was more or less equivalent to the end of "prehistory" and to the beginning of "history." In Master Simon's account each Hun was originally the equal member of a free and self-governing *communitas*, and it was customary to call to arms "in the name of God and the people" each man capable of bearing arms "to hear the counsel and precept of the *communitas*." There were some, however, who refused to comply with this order, who "treated it with contempt" (*contempsissent*), without being unable to justify their absence. The punishment of these, as prescribed by the *lex Scitica*, was either to be cut in two with a sword, "exposed to hopeless situations" (*exponi in causas desperatas*), or cast into servitude. He concludes that "it was these kinds of crimes and excesses (*vitia et excessus*) which separated one Hungarian from another." The state of non-nobility is the consequence of this "crime" (*casus criminis*).[57]

This account differs decisively from the two explanations current at that time regarding the origins of human inequality, both the Christian-patristic theory of *peccatum* and the Roman legal concept of *ius gentium*. *Ignobilitas* is here the consequence of a specific "crime," the legal result of the refusal to obey the call to arms embodied in a concrete "judgement." Historians have heretofore been unable to account for the source of this idea. Yet there was

---

[57] Ibidem: *Vitia itaque et excessus huiusmodi unum Hungarum ab alio separavit, alias cum unus pater et una mater omnes Hungaros procreavit, quomodo unus nobilis, alter innobilis diceretur, nisi victus per tales casus criminis haberetur.*

a country where the idea appeared in the same century, first as an epic motif, and later as a mode of theoretical argumentation: France. In 1315, when Louis X sent out commissioners to examine the legal status of the serfs, the ordinance identified as the origin of their condition of servitude the crimes of their ancestors, their "misdeed" (*mesfait* = *méfait*). As Marc Bloch has already noted, the nature of this "historical sin" was then familiar to all; it required no further explanation.[58]

And, indeed, its prehistory stretched back at least a century. One first finds it in the *Chanson de Gui de Bourgogne*, written after 1211. Charlemagne had been fighting for three decades against the Moors when a group of his men, 4,700 soldiers, deserted from the war, in punishment for which they and all their descendants were reduced to servitude; these were the first *serfs*. This motif then transcends its local bounds and is modified in the course of the thirteenth century. Those concerned are no longer deserters from battle but "cowards" who had refused the call to arms (*couards d'Apremont*); moreover, Charlemagne decides on their punishment not after but before the campaign. It was in this form that the story found its way into the *Roman de Renart le Contrefait*, a poem written at the beginning of the fourteenth century, which even informs us that the story is a common subject of discussion.[59] From the

---

[58] M. Bloch, *Rois et serfs: un chapitre d'histoire Capétienne* (Paris, 1920; reprint Geneva: Slatkine-Magariotis, 1976), 132, 142–52.

[59] H. Lemaître, "Le refus de servage d'ost et l'origine du servage," *Bibliothèque de l'École des Chartes* 75 (1914): 231–38; cf. Bloch, *Rois et serfs*, 151.

epics it found its way into jurisprudence, indeed, into one of the most notable collections of French customary law, the *Coutumes de Beauvaisis* of Philippe de Beaumanoir, written between 1279 and 1282. Here the motif has already lost its connection with the epic context and has been built into a wider socio-political theory. According to this, in the beginning every man was free, but as people "multiplied," pride and envy led to dissensions and wars. At this point the communities of the people (*la communetés du peuple*) elected for themselves kings, transferring to them jurisdictional authority, leadership in war, and the right to promulgate edicts. And so that there should be someone to protect the people from "bad judges," the bravest and wisest men were granted *seignouries.* It is their descendants who are the nobles. The origin of the *serfs* is more diversified: some had been prisoners of war, others had chosen servitude voluntarily, and so on. Many, however, were the descendants of those who, when the king had sent out a general call to arms, had been reluctant to appear. All those who had refused the call to arms without good reason were reduced to servitude.[60]

These motifs have clear parallels in Master Simon's account, which also, as we shall see later, discusses this issue in terms of "constitutional law" (they differ in this, that in Philippe de Beaumanoir's theory the focus is on providing a theoretical underpinning for the position of the *rois de*

---

[60] Lemaître, "Le refus," 235, cf. Fr. Olivier-Martin, *Histoire du droit française des origines à la Révolution* (Paris: Domat Montchrestien, 1948; reprint Paris: CNRS, 1984), 248. Philippe de Beaumanoir's work treats the origins of servitude in two places (c. 1453 and 1438): *Coutumes de Beauvaisis* (Paris: A. Salmon, 1900), 2: 235–36, 218.

France, whereas Simon of Kéza is concerned to do the same for a self-governing *communitas*, though at a later stage, he, too, introduces the notion of the election of a king). The common motifs are the following: (1) the original equality of the human community; (2) the interrelationship of the "multiplication" of people and the move toward the delegation of authority;[61] (3) the separation of the judicial, military, and legislative aspects of authority;[62] (4) the emphasis on the provisions made for the control of "bad judges" and for the nullification of inappropriate sentences;[63] (5) finally, the explanation of the origins of servitude as the consequence of the disobedience of the call to arms. In the French version, of course, the decision is the king's, while with the Huns the judgement is passed by the community.

Nevertheless, it is not the parallelisms that are of decisive significance. Master Simon was too much in command of his material to resort to mere copying from his sources. In

---

[61] Beaumanoir: *quant li peuples commenca a croistre*; Simon of Kéza: *multiplicati Huni in Scitia habitando . . .* ; whereupon there follows in both the "historical" deduction.

[62] Beaumanoir: *. . . si eslurent roi et le firent seigneur d'aus et li donnerent le pouoir d'aus justicier de leur mesfés, de fere commandemens et establissemens seur aus . . .*; Simon of Kéza: *. . . capitaneos inter se scilicet duces vel principes praefecerunt. . . . Constituerunt quoque inter se rectorem unum . . . qui communem exercitum iudicaret, dissidentium lites sopiret, castigaret malefactores, fures et latrones*. In the case of the call to arms, *unusquisque armatus . . . debeat comparere communitatis consilium praeceptumque auditurus. . . .*

[63] Beaumanoir: *. . . et pour ce qu'il peut le peuple garantir contre . . . les mauves justiciers*; Simon of Kéza: *si rector idem immoderatam sententiam definiret, communitas in irritum revocaret. . . .*

any case we cannot be sure that the source here was Philippe de Beaumanoir's text. But clearly we are dealing with a widespread tradition. We can read in the Renart novel that it was a matter of common discussion that there lived in Paris alone at least a thousand *serfs* of such origins at the time the novel was written.[64] We do not know whether or not Simon had travelled in Northern France, but we do know that he travelled through Burgundy, where the conception had received its first literary formulation at the beginning of the century. Knowing Master Simon's predilection for incorporating into his work bits of information culled from here and there, we need hardly be surprised that epic and later legal elements of the Charlemagne tradition became embedded in his notion of the historicised Hun *communitas*. In essence, therefore, the idea seems to be another of those motifs deriving from *Francia* which are hinted at by the author in his prologue.

Italia, too, provided its contribution, in the form of the threefold mode of punishment prescribed by "Scythian law" as the consequence of the "crime." The three kinds of punishment mentioned above could not have arisen from the historicisation of contemporary Hungarian legal practice. They are, however, similar to those three modes of punishment (*publica iudicia*) prescribed by Roman law for common crimes.[65] The first, as we have seen, was the execution by sword of those who had refused to obey the edict of the community. In Roman law, too, in the case of the

---

[64] Lemaître, "Le refus," 233.

[65] This has been pointed out by Gerics, "Adalékok," 112ff., cf. Szűcs, "Társadalomelmélet," 589–95.

most serious common crimes, the first capital punishment (*poena capitalis*) was death, in the case of high treason, execution by the sword.[66] The second sentence seems obscure if one does not know that in the expression *exponi in causas desperatas* the word *causa* is being used in a specific sense, as a technical term of Roman law meaning "legal status."[67] It is not a matter, therefore, of generally exposing the condemned to some hopeless situation, but rather of reducing him to one of many such "legal statuses" or conditions. Neither is the use of the plural merely coincidental. For although in Roman law the second sentence was banishment, its severity was of several degrees, varying from a specified length of time of punishment (*relegatio in tempus*) to deportation with the loss of civic rights or banishment to some island (*relegatio in perpetuum, in insulam deportatio*).[68] Hungarian criminal law contained no analogues; it was, therefore, enough to reproduce the essence of the mode of punishment. Finally, one finds that the third mode of punishment also has analogies in Roman criminal law, for the more serious instance of "civic death" (*mors civilis*) was condemnation to forced labour in the mines, as a consequence of which the condemned became a slave (*servus poenae*). In fact, the commentaries (e.g.

[66] *Dig.* 37.1.13; 48.1.2; 48.13.6, pr. etc.; often simply *poena mors*. The *capitis amputatio* referred to political crimes, e.g. *Dig.* 48.19.8; 48.19.38; *Cod.* 9.8.5 (*gladio feriatur*).

[67] *Thesaurus linguae Latinae* (Leipzig: Teubner, 1906–12), 3:687–88, e.g. "*in servilem causam deductus*" (*Dig.* 4.5.3.1).

[68] H. Heumann-E. Seckel, *Handlexikon zu den Quellen des römischen Rechts* (Jena, 1909; reprint Graz: Akademische Druck- und Verlagsanstalt, 1958), 191. For the relevant parts of the *Digesta*, see Szűcs, "Társadalomelmélet," 592.

Accursius) speak simply of "servitude" rather than specifically "slavery in the mines."[69] Thus, Simon's *detrudi in servitutem* precisely matches the term in Roman law.[70]

But what of the *lex Scitica* itself—the notion of the legal combination of judgement and servitude being the enforcement of a definite "law"? Is this perhaps another case of Roman law in Hun-Scythian garb? In Roman law specific *leges* applied to various common crimes, and high treason was dealt with under the so-called *lex Julia maiestatis*; this covered every kind of conspiracy, rebellion, treachery, "everything perpetrated against the *populus Romanus* or its security."[71] The notion that the model of the *lex Scitica* was the *lex Julia* certainly fits with what we know of our author. We have seen that he tells how the call to arms was issued in the name of *Vox Dei et populi Hungarici*; he refers to the persons who give the call to arms as *praecones*, just as in ancient Rome professional criers or *praecones* called the armies to the *censura*; and as a lawyer, he could well have regarded the refusal of the call to arms, on the Roman analogy, as a "criminal case" (*casus criminis*), a crime against the *populus Hungaricus*.

---

[69] For example, already *in Dig.* 48.19.2. pr. (Ulpianus) the punishment is simply *servitus*; Accursius *gl. ad Dig.* 48.19.28 (Callistratus) sv. *metalli coercitio:* "Haec inducit servitutem, ut supra eo 1. *aut damnatum*" (= *Dig.* 48.19.8).

[70] E.g. *in carcere detrudere, in metallum detrudi per sententiam, in servilem conditionem esse detrusi*, etc. (*Dig.* 4.2.22; *Cod.* 5.5.3; *Cod.* 8.51.2). Cf. Heumann-Seckel, *Handlexikon*, 143.

[71] *Dig.* 48.1.1 (Ulpianus); *Inst.* 4.18.3–11.

So the *ignobilitas* that resulted from the refusal of the call to arms, originally a French motif, is set in a Roman legal framework as "criminal law." The explanation for the existence of servitude thereby acquires a contemporary "scientific" aura. In France, the historical framework was provided by the Charlemagne tradition; in Hungary, by the history of the Huns. In fact, what we are seeing in both cases is the evolving self-consciousness of the nobility inventing a myth for itself. For the theory expressed a definite need of the times, providing a "historical" explanation for a particular social attitude. The story of the *couards d'Apremont* had actually no historical basis even in France; the historical Charlemagne had been concerned to protect rather than to repress the free social elements.[72] What is being justified is the boundary which sought to divide nobles and peasants into two separate groups on the basis of their participation or non-participation in military service. The fact is that in thirteenth century Hungary the most diverse elements were still going to battle together, including large numbers of "non-nobles";[73] but the nobility was by now feeling that it needed to present itself as the sole warrior class. The identification of *bellator* and *nobilis* had already begun to appear in the diploma-formulae from the middle of the century, where the nobility are characterised as the community of warriors (*bellantium collegium*).[74] Concurrently, the "true" or "golden liberty" of the

---

[72] Lemaître, "Le refus," 237–38.

[73] J. Molnár, "A királyi megye katonai szervezete a tatárjárás korában" (The military organisation of the royal counties at the time of the Tartar invasions), *Hadtörténeti Közlemények* 6 (1959): 222ff.

[74] Váczy, *Államelmélet*, p. 22.

nobility was rising ever higher above the diverse other
"liberties" distributed through society.

This self-concept was supported by attitudes common
throughout Europe. The primary one was the increasingly
popular theory of "functionalism," which perceived secular
society in terms of the dualism of warriors and workers
(*bellatores~laboratores*).[75] This view was given support in
turn by the glossators to the newly revived Roman law,
who defined two basic "species" of mankind, freemen and
servants (*liberi~servi*)[76]—the necessary corollary throughout medieval Europe being that the *nobilis* is the only
"truly" free man.[77] As we have seen, Simon had already
overthrown one traditional historical obstacle, the *a sancto
rege* division point. Having done so, he was then able to
present the social divisions of mankind—nobility and non-
nobility—not as the creation of the "holy king" but as a
development from ancient times. The origin of human
inequality was thus given not only "historical" and "legal"
underpinnings but also received a boost in "moral" status.
For the refusal to answer the call to arms had been a

[75] J. Batany, "Des 'Trois Fonctions' aux 'Trois États'?" *Annales E.S.C.*
18 (1963): 933–38.

[76] Originally, for example, *Dig.* 1.1.4 (Ulpianus): *iure gentium tria
hominum genera esse coeperunt. . .* But see also the glossa of Accursius:
*Item quomodo sunt tria genera? Imo tantum duo, scilicet liberi et servi,
quia liberti liberi sunt.*

[77] It is in the thirteenth century that there takes root in Western
Europe, too, the idea that the *militaris* service is identical to the *nobilis
et bellicosa* way of life, therefore also with the concept of *libera conditio*;
see L. Genicot, "La noblesse dans la société médiévale," *Le Moyen Age*
71 (1965): 557.

repudiation not only of martial *virtus* but also of the major political virtue, loyalty;[78] those, therefore, who had preserved this virtue, the nobility, rose above the peasantry even in "moral" stature.

THE NEW CENTRE OF POLITICAL THOUGHT: THE *COMMUNITAS*

When Simon begins his discourse on social theory with "*Igitur in aetate sexta saeculi . . . ,*" this was not a random choice of words. In the medieval conception of time, the "sixth world epoch" indicates not only that "pre-history" has given way to "history," but that we are dealing with what in modern terminology we would call identical "structures": within this epoch there already operate identical norms and regularities, and "history" itself with its own causality is now a mere chain of events. So for the author the *aetas sexta saeculi* is in a certain sense already the here-and-now, *nunc*, the present.[79] Certainly his wider historical horizon stretches back to biblical and legendary times, and in this perspective the "nation" is an uninterrupted continuity from the beginning of the world "until now"; but the social and political norms which are valid

[78] For *fidelitas* as the highest *virtus politica*, see A. Kurcz, "Arenga und Narratio ungarischer Urkunden des 13. Jahrhunderts," *Mitteilungen des Instituts für Österreichische Geschichtsforschung* 70 (1962): 337–41.

[79] Simon of Kéza, ch. 3: *olim in veteri testamento, et nunc sub aetate sexta saeculi . . .* (*SRH* 1: 142). For the attitude to time, see E. Bernheim's great work *Mittelalterliche Zeitanschauungen in ihrem Einfluss auf Politik und Geschichtsschreibung* (Tübingen: J. C. B. Mohr, 1918); also H. Grundmann, "Die Grundzüge der mittelalterlichen Geschichtsanschauungen," *Archiv für Kulturgeschichte* 24 (1931): 326–36.

"even until today" developed later, in the "sixth world epoch". He therefore makes clear at the beginning that although the Hun–Hungarian *natio* "descended from one father and one mother" in antiquity, as far as social organisation is concerned "today" also provides a valid structure. The *separatio* of the people into nobles and non-nobles, although it occurred secondarily, nevertheless also occurred long ago.

At the same time, he clarifies the basic principles of "constitutional law," which centres on the theory of the ancient *communitas*. Naturally, he says, in "historical times" it was already an "isolated" *communitas* which was the agent of history, for already in the days of the Huns there existed a nobility (*Hunnorum nobilitas*; ch. 22). It has long been recognised that this theory of *communitas* expresses nothing other than the demand of the "general congregations of the realm" (if not "Diets") of the assembled lower nobility in the 1270s and '80s[80] to acquire a share in power, to ally themselves with the king against the anarchical government of baronial groups and factions.[81] This is an instance of the needs of a "premature corporatism"[82] being articulated in a historicised manner, for in actuality it was

[80] S. E. Kiss, "A királyi generális kongregáció kialakulásának történetéhez" (On the evolution of the royal "generalis congregatio"), *Acta Universitatis Szegediensis: Acta Historica* 39 (1971).

[81] Cf. esp. the works of Váczy, Horváth, Gerics, and Kristó listed in notes 8–9.

[82] Gy. Bónis, *Hűbériség és rendiség a középkori magyar jogban* (Feudalism and corporatism in medieval Hungarian law) (Kolozsvár: Erdélyi Tudományos Intézet, n.d. [1947?]), 170.

still the baronial groups and factions which ruled the political scene at the time.

In this field, too, Simon was ahead of his times. For, although the concept of *universitas regni* appears in a diploma as early as 1299 it is only after 1330 that the expression *"universae nobilitatis communitas"* is incorporated into the Hungarian politico-legal conceptual system.[83] The nobility as a "body" (*consortium, collegium, coetus, societas*) does, indeed, appear from the middle of the thirteenth century in the formulae of the patents of nobility, but only as the "body of warriors", not as a "body politic," *corpus politicum*, in the organism of the kingdom. What is more, it is only in these decades that there is a movement away from the archaic outlook which saw the emerging nobility as, metaphorically speaking, the king's broader retinue (*Gefolgschaft*). To the middle of the century a member of the lower nobility is referred to as the "servant of the king" (*serviens regis*), a member of the king's *familia*. Ennoblement meant that the new noble could, so to speak, feel at home in the king's court, in his house (*in domo regia*); his liberty to do so was the expression of royal

---

[83] 1299: *universitas nobilium Ungarorum, Saxonum et Cumanorum; nostre universitatis coetus = universi barones et nobiles regni Ungarie (Codex diplomaticus Hungariae ecclesiasticus ac civilis,* ed. G. Fejér (Buda: Regia Universitas, 1841), 7/5: 502–4); 1330: *universe nobilitatis communitas* (M. G. Kovachich, *Supplementum ad Vestigia comitiorum apud Hungaros . . . celebratorum* (Buda: Regia Universitas, 1798), 1: 268). For a survey of these questions see J. Holub, "La Représentation politique en Hongrie au Moyen-Age," in *Xe Congrès International des Sciences Historiques, Rome, 1955: Études présentées à la Commission Internationale pour l'histoire des Assemblées d'États* (Louvain and Paris, 1958), esp. 88–89.

favour (*gratia*), which he was bound to recompense with loyal service (*servitium*).[84] It is in the course of a transitional period (1266–83) that the nobleman becomes unqualifiedly and unequivocally *nobilis*, at a time when the letters of patent still refer to him in the intermediate terms of *serviens seu nobilis, nobilis serviens.* Thus, until the 1280s there is lacking the conceptual foundation which could transform an essentially vertical viewpoint into a horizontal one, in other words, which would establish that *nobilitas* is neither solely the creation of the Holy King (as still in the Golden Bull of 1222, referring to the liberty of the "royal servants"), nor a manifestation of the grace of the existing monarch (as the diplomas imply), but rather is an ancient development, with a very old "historical existence." This change, too, was Simon's work.

According to the fictional history of the Huns, in the sixth world epoch the *communitas* chose for itself six captains (*capitaneos* or *duces*). They also appointed a *rector* charged with judicial duties, but with the proviso that the community could at any time revoke its decision and discharge any such *capitaneum et rectorem* guilty of a "lapse" (*errantem*). At the start Attila himself was also just one of the captains; it was only after the "first" conquest of Pannonia that the Huns elected him as king (*rex*). However, this transitional "monarchical" age came to an end with Attila's death, whereupon power returned to the hands of the *communitas.* So from the time of the return to Scythia, throughout the "second" conquest, and up to the time of St. Stephen's father Prince Géza, it was again the "communal" constitu-

[84] Váczy, *Államelmélet,* 9–23.

tion that was operative (*dum se regerent pro communi*, ch. 10). This multi-functional notion contains several elements: self-government through replaceable officials elected *pro tempore* for a specified time (chs. 7, 42); the legislative function of the *communitas* and its ability to promulgate an *edictum*; the passing of sentences and the bringing of decisions in military matters (this is held to apply as much to the western campaigns of the tenth century as to the earlier period; e.g. ch. 40); the composition of the army (chs. 8, 26); decisions in matters regarding settlement (ch. 8); and so on. But since those who had refused to obey the edict of the *communitas*, the call to arms, had been reduced to servitude, it was a distinct *communitas* who already in the Hun epoch exercised all these rights.

Historians have exhibited considerable uncertainty regarding the source of the *communitas*-theory. On the domestic scene, certainly, it was unprecedented.[85] Thomas Aquinas' political theory might suggest itself, given Simon's scholastic training.[86] However, this can scarcely be the direct or sole source, for we find that Aquinas regarded the ideal constitution (*optima politia*) to be that form of mixed government (*regimen commixtum*) which somehow blends these elements: royal authority (*ex regno*), the will of the

[85] For details of the proof that Simon introduced the concept of *communitas* into the chronicle literature, and that the occurrence of this concept in the later chronicles is derivative, see Szűcs, "Társadalomelmélet," 598–601.

[86] Váczy, "Népfelség," 557–59.

well-born (*ex aristocratia*), and the power of the people (*ex democratia id est potestate populi*).[87] However, in Master Simon's primitive constitution it is only Aquinas' third component which explicitly appears (i.e. democracy, meaning at this time, of course, no more than what Aquinas defined it to be: "the people have the right to choose the prince"). Even the mixed *politia* he envisions as a later development has only two components: the *rex* and the *communitas*.

Here again a closer look at the language used by the writer to express his conceptual system provides us with the key to the problem. It becomes evident that he imagines that in the smaller component units of the Hun "communal" system and in their military groupings there are operative "corporative" principles and elements of self-government analogous to those existing in the larger unit; the synonymous expressions *communitas* (occasionally in its Italian form *commune*), *caetus, consortium, societas* apply to these as well. These terms, the conception itself, the characteristic linking of the Whole and the Part, and in particular the term first appearing in ch. 19, *"pars sanior"* (a significant technical term referring to the "qualitative" principle in corporate constitutionalism), all point unequivocally to one and the same conceptual system: the corporate doctrine unified into a theoretical system by the middle of the thirteenth century.[88]

[87] *De regimine principum* 1.2.105.l. See Th. Eschmann, "Studies on the Notion of Society in St. Thomas Aquinas," *Mediaeval Studies* 8 (1946): 1–42; Fr. M. Schmölz, "Societas civilis sive Respublica sive Populus," *Österreichische Zeitschrift für Öffentliches Recht* 14 (1964): 28–50.

[88] For details, see Szűcs, "Társadalomelmélet," 602–4.

Thanks to Otto Gierke's fundamental studies,[89] we now recognise that this theory-cluster, though it had its roots in Roman and canon law, was a particular result of thirteenth-century jurisprudence, and introduced a new conceptual model of "society" which revolutionised European political thought. In its original role, the "corporation" was a social unit (*societas publica*) owing its purely internal autonomy (the election of superiors, the administration of justice, the principle of representation, self-government) to the grant of a privilege by some superior authority. In time, however, the theory came to recognise the "sovereignty" of the *societas*: in other words, to maintain that such an organised social unit can have legitimate existence without the permission of a superior authority (*sine licentia superioris, absque authoritate principis*).[90] This new model had the potential to transform the vertical, descending concept of social and political relationships in a horizontal direction. For on this basis the individual was no longer primarily the subordinate (*fidelis subditus*) of some lay or ecclesiastical authority but the member of an overarching association, of an autonomous society (*membrum univer-*

---

[89] O. Gierke, *Das deutsche Genossenschaftsrecht*, 3: *Die Staats- und Korporationslehre des Alterthums und des Mittelalters und ihre Aufnahme in Deutschland* (Berlin: Weidmann, 1881), 188–478.

[90] The glossators had already deduced a multitude of rights from the essence of the corporation, "durch welche dieselbe als ein gesellschaftlicher Organismus mit einer eigenen und selbständigen Sphäre des Gemeinlebens, als eine Macht über seine Glieder ausgestattetes Gemeinwesen charakterisiert wird" (Gierke, *Genossenschaftsrecht*, p. 215) and "Indem sie (die Juristen) die alten Definitionen wiederholen, unterstellen sie die Summe aller menschlichen Verbandseinheiten einem gemeinsamen Gattungsbegriff und einer gemeinsamen Theorie" (*ibid.*, 355).

sitatis or *communitatis*). Similarly, no longer could each mass of people be comprehended only as a "people" of subjects (*populus subditus*), but rather as a legal personality (*persona repraesentata* or *politica*), "represented" by certain individuals or certain groups capable of confronting even the ruler himself. For here as elsewhere in medieval philosophical thought the principle of unity asserted itself, which saw analogous principles governing the internal structure of each element of human society from its smallest units to its broadest, the Universal Church. According to this model there existed a variety of social units within the continuum ranging from the village community (*communitas vici*) to the universal Christian community, all functioning according to similar common "corporative" principles. From this there developed an intermediate stage, the nucleus of the later *Ständestaat*, the concept of *universitas* or *communitas regni*. This represented one pole in a dualistic theory of the state (the *status regni*), standing in contradistinction to the "king's state" (*status regis*) and participating in government as a body politic through "representation." Its members might be mortal, but as a self-sustaining legal personality, it maintains its identity; it "never dies" (*nunquam moritur*).

At the same time, it followed that the individual, too, was liberated from his exclusively subordinate political status. The thirteenth century was thus a time of the "rebirth of the citizen,"[91] although of course within strict bounds, as a member of a corporative "society" fortified on all sides with prerogatives. The Italian city-states excepted, it was

[91] Ullmann, *Individual*, 104ff.

still only the nobleman at best who could, within the structures of monarchy, sense something of the status of the citizen of antiquity (the *civis*) and of "civil" political relations. In fact, the circle could be even narrower; in England, for example, the *communitas regni* was identical with the aristocracy even at the end of the thirteenth century.[92] Nevertheless, all this did not alter the fact that a model of a "political society" had emerged whose cohesion were determined not "from above" but from within— as Thomas Aquinas summed it up, "within the unity of law and public utility" (*unitas iuris et communis utilitatis—De Regimine Principum* 11, 2, 42, 4).

That Simon's political theory was conceived in this climate of ideas is suggested both by his terminology and by the familiar analogy of Whole and Part. Corporate self-government is the "organisational principle" of the fictitious ancient Hun society. Again, the immediate source of his theory could hardly have been Thomas Aquinas. For Aquinas, the *communitas* could not exist without the sanction of higher authority,[93] whereas in Master Simon's fiction the *communitas* is already a given. It antecedes the monarchy (the election of Attila as king) and remains in sole possession and exercise of power until the very beginning of the Christian monarchy. It thus reflects the view of contemporary jurisprudence which sees *communitas* as capable of existing without higher authority.

---

[92] W. A. Morris, "Magnates and Community of the Realm in Parliament, 1264–1327," *Mediaevalia et Humanistica* 1 (1943): 58–94.

[93] *Societas publica . . . non potest constitui, nisi ex superioris auctoritate* (*Contra Impugn.*, ch. 3); *Omnis communitas aliqua lege ordinatur* (*Sent.* 27.1.1); see Eschmann, "Studies," 8.

This model also owed much to another political theory
newly evolving in the thirteenth century from Roman law,
the theory of the delegation of power. According to this,
the *populus* was the original source of law and power,
and only subsequently and secondarily did it delegate its
authority to the ruler.[94] At Simon's historical starting point
in the "sixth world epoch" the Hun *communitas* is the
ancient "constitutional form" of the *populus Hungaricus*,
and this state of affairs is altered only when the Huns
elected Attila to be "king over them," *Romano more* (ch.
10), after the conquest of Pannonia. This has given rise to
a view that Simon was a sort of noble-republican propagandist: as if, confronted with the Western style monarchy
of his day, he looked back with nostalgia to an ancient
"Hun–Scythia" utopia which, in Váczy's words, "is cast up
by the waves of time, and therein disappears again after its
years of glory and greatness."[95] But this misses the point.
In contemporary European theories the *populus* is never

[94] It is more accurate to speak here of the theory of the delegation of
power than of the "sovereignty of the people," which would tend to
give rise to anachronistic notions. For a summary of this and related
questions see M. Wilks, *The Problem of Sovereignty in the Later Middle
Ages*, Cambridge Studies in Medieval Life and Thought, n.s. 9 (Cambridge: Cambridge University Press, 1963), esp. 184–226; e.g. "The
idea of separation of powers whose invention is sometimes attributed
to Locke and Montesquieu can therefore be said to be quite clearly
envisaged in the political thought of the later Middle Ages. Sovereignty
does not reside in any one part of the political community, ruler or
people, but is shared between them. Strictly speaking, the term cannot
be applied to either."

[95] Váczy, "Népfelség," 560–61; for a critique of this, cf. Gerics, "Adalékok," 107–9.

"sovereign" in the modern sense, it merely provides, in the wake of the ruler's assumption of its original power, a kind of limited "historical" source for the present. This is what Simon meant, too.

The "historically" fluctuating relationship of *communitas* and *rex* is portrayed quite anachronistically but in a manner consistent with the author's theory. The ancient form of self-government changes in Attila's time. But the expression "in the Roman manner" referring to the manner of the election of the king is not meant to censure as "foreign" or Western the monarchical form of government. "*Romano more*" is here simply a synonym for the word *voluntarie* used elsewhere;[96] in other words, the election of a king "in the Roman manner" means the voluntary and free delegation of power, in medieval technical language *voluntaria subiectio ac consensus*.[97] And although the earlier "communal" functions and jurisdictions became vested in the ruler during Attila's monarchical rule, the *communitas* does not disappear. Rather, a kind of "mixed" *politia* comes into existence, for power is not Attila's alone but belongs both to the Huns and their ruler (*Hunnorum dominium et Ethelae*, ch. 14). Thereafter, from the death of Attila to Prince Géza, the original constitution of the *communitas* again becomes operative, and it is only the Christian monarchy which again brings about a fresh change. Master Simon is careful, however, to leave the *communitas* some

---

[96] Simon of Kéza, ch. 10: . . . *Romano more Huni super se Ethelam regem praeficiunt*; ch. 8: *Tunc Romani Ditricum Veronensem Alamannum natione . . . super se praefecerant voluntarie* (*SRH* 1: 149, 150).

[97] Gierke, *Genossenschaftsrecht*, 571.

degree of participation in power even after this time—in
fact, continuously to his own days. Thus, for instance, still
in the time of Géza and St. Stephen the agreement of the
communitas tota, its *assensus*, was necessary for the acceptance of the pope's decree (ch. 95). Similarly, after the
death of St. Stephen it was not only the aristocracy, as the
texts of the old chronicles maintain, who strove to settle
the nation's disorders, but the aristocracy and the nobility
together (*principes et nobiles regni*, ch. 46). King Coloman,
too, modified his measures out of respect for the *communitas nobilium*.[98] These and similar explanations and inter-
polations establish the continuing presence of the *communitas* throughout the developments of the eleventh and
twelfth centuries.

The author's concept of *communitas* not only has roots in
his corporate theory and the theory of the delegation of
power, but aligns itself with particular trends in legal thinking. For there were two schools of thought in contemporary jurisprudence. According to the first (whose repre-
sentatives included Irnerius, the founder of the Bologna
school, and Placentinus, the distinguished master of the
French school of Montpellier at the end of the twelfth
century) the will of the *populus*, once expressed, is a unique,
irrevocable historical event, and as such had no present
political consequences at all. For, if the Roman legal maxim
is taken at face value, the people vested "all their power"
(*omne suum imperium et potestatem*) in the ruler, and so

[98] For details, see Szűcs, "Társadalomelmélet," 608–9; Kristó, "Kézai,"
14–16.

retained none of it.[99] However, according to a second viewpoint developed among others by Azo, the pre-eminent master of the Bologna school around 1200, the delegation of power does not mean that the people had totally renounced their power, for, in fact, they retained something of it subsequently. Therefore, although certain individuals can be excluded from legislating, the entire *universitas seu populus* cannot. Authorities like Bulgarus and Johannes Bassianus in the twelfth century, and Odofredus in the thirteenth, concurred with the second interpretation. In debate with Placentinus, Hugolinus insisted that the people did not delegate power in such a way as to retain nothing of it (*non transtulit sic, ut non remaneret apud eum*); rather, they made the ruler merely "the custodian, so to speak" (*quasi procuratorem*) of power.[100]

[99] Irnerius (*gl. ad Dig.* 1.3.32, *de legibus*): *Loquitur hec lex secundum sua tempora, quibus populus habebat potestatem condendi leges. . . . Sed quia hodie potestas translata est in imperatorem, nihil faceret desuetudo populi*; Placentinus (*Summa Inst.* 1.2): *Nam populus in principem transferendo communem potestatem, nullam sibi reservavit, ergo potestatem leges scriptas condendi, interpretandi et abrogandi* (Fr. Calasso, *I Glossatori e la teoria della sovranità: Studio di diritto commune pubblico* (Milan: Giuffré, 1951), 72).

[100] Azo (*Summa Codicis*): *Dicitur enim translata id est concessa* [sc. *potestas*] *non quod populus omnino a se abdicaverit eam. . . . Nam et olim transtulerat, sed tamen postea revocavit*; idem, *Lectura Codicis* 1.14.12: *Dic ergo, quod hic non excluditur populus, sed singuli de populo . . . quia plus fecit ipse, quam aliquis aliorum. Ideo singuli excluduntur, non universitas sive populus*; Odofredus (*Comm. in Dig.* 1.3.32): *Nam populus bene potest hodie legem condere, sicut olim poterat. . . . Item non obstat, quod alibi dicitur, quod populus omne imperium legis condere transtulit in principem . . . quia intelligo transtulit id est concessit, non tamen a se abdicando*; Hugolinus (*Distinctiones*): *Sed certe non transtulit sic, ut non remaneret apud eum, sed constituit eum quasi procuratorem*

It was essentially the latter school of thought on contemporary constitutional theory which guided Simon.
The ideas which inspired him originated in the *scartabel-
los*—that characteristically Italianate word he used for the
sources he found scattered *per Italiam, Franciam ac Germaniam* (Prol.)—which included not only his books on
Roman law but also contemporary tracts on jurisprudence
which he read in Padua. In fact, these works were also
available at home; the library of one of his colleagues at the
royal court, Master Ladislas (fl. 1277), had not only the
complete *Corpus Iuris Civilis* but other books on Roman
and canon law like Azo's *Summa*.[101] Simon did not seek a
cultural "ideal" in the ancient past of the Huns. On the
contrary, he emphasises the positive turning point that
came about at the time of Prince Géza and King Stephen
with the renunciation of their nomadic, "despoiling" mode
of life. He accepts the dualism of *gens Christiana* and
populus barbarus (ch. 99), and, far from being an opponent
of the Christian monarchy, can be seen as the "king's
propagandist."[102] Rather, the purpose of his political theory is to prove that the ancient Hun–Hungarian *communitas* did not disappear with the coming of the monarchy,
that it did not vest its power in the kings without (in

---

ad hoc. For the entire complex of questions, see Gierke, *Genossenschaftsrecht*, 566ff.; Carlyle, *Medieval Political Theory*, 2: 56–67; Calasso, *I Glossatori*, 72–78; Wilks, *Problem of Sovereignty*, 184–86.

[101] *Mon. Eccl. Strigon.* 2:71–72; cf. E. Ivánka, "László mester esztergomi
prépost könyvtára" (The library of Master Ladislas, provost of Esztergom), *Theologia* 4 (1937): 216–26.

[102] For details, see Gerics, "Adalékok," 122–30.

Hugolinus' succinct phrase) "some of it remaining with it."
Thus, the theoretical burden of his work ties in closely with
one particular trend in contemporary jurisprudence and in
the political theories just then finding definition. At the
same time, it expresses within a colourful and eminently
readable epic framework a political claim beginning to
make itself heard around 1280 in Hungary, that the king
should grant to the body of the nobility assembled in the
generales congregationes a part in the exercise of power and
legislature, even as, in its turn, the *communitas nobilium*
(who find a spokesman for the first time in this work)
shows itself willing to support and strengthen the royal
power in the face of those "inclined to an indolent life," the
aristocracy (*vivere volentes otiose*, ch. 96).

TWO AUTHORS,
TWO HISTORIES WITHIN ONE EUROPE

In December of 1270, a group of four men were heading
southward on horseback from Naples toward Catona at
the tip of Calabria, intending to cross by boat to Messina
in Sicily in order to convey the greetings of the new king
of Hungary, Stephen V, to Charles of Anjou on his return
from Tunis and the last Crusade. Besides the leader of the
diplomatic mission, the canon of Esztergom Master Sixtus,
we know of two other figures in the group, the clerics
Master Simon of Kéza and Master Andrew. Master Andrew (known as Andrew of Hungary) was soon to enter
the service of the son of Louis IX, Count Peter of Alençon,
and went with his new master to France, where around
1272 he wrote an account of Charles of Anjou's rise to

power, the *Descriptio victoriae . . . Karoli regis Siciliae.*[103]
Simon of Kéza returned home, and a decade later in Buda,
as he was writing his *Gesta Hungarorum*, he wove details
of his adventures on this voyage into the story. For example, in one colourful episode of the events at Ravenna (ch.
17) we learn that the Hun captain Zovárd roamed through
Apulia to Calabria as far as the area around Catona and
Reggio di Calabria and, on his return journey, laid waste
southern Italy to Monte Cassino. In reality, of course, the
Huns never reached southern Italy; the inspiration for this
whole episode is the author's own journey through Apulia
and Calabria in the autumn and winter of 1270. On the
return journey Simon crossed from Messina to Catona, and
from January 27 to February 27 of 1271 travelled through
Calabria, detouring through Apulia to Monte Cassino, in
order to accompany Charles of Anjou to Rome.[104] Catona,
in the tip of Italy, inspired the author to another of his
wonted etymological fancies: "Cato was born and lived
here," he later wrote. Even if Cato was not really born there
but in Tusculum, one might still attribute a certain symbolic significance to this quaint association of words. It is
unlikely to have been a display of classical learning. Cato's
name at this time was principally known from the popular
late-antique collection of sayings, the *Dicta Catonis*, which
had served as textbook of grammar since the "Dark Ages".
It is, nevertheless, connected with a new interest in the
Roman past which arose in the northern Italian universities

---

[103] Published in *MGH SS* 24 (Hannover, 1882), 559–80. For a reconstruction of this diplomatic mission, see Szűcs, "Társadalomelmélet,"
841ff., esp. 847–55.

[104] Szűcs, *ibid.* 853–55.

through the study of Roman law, an interest to which Cato's "sayings" were the more closely relevant in that the most widely used textbook, Accursius' *Glossa Ordinaria*, frequently called attention to them (*ut dixit Cato*).[105] This, in turn, links with the reviving interest in ancient ruins, something which, as we have already seen, served the author as a mine of ideas for characters and episodes in Hunnish history. Many things coalesce, therefore, in this historical moment around the turn of 1270–71, when in the tip of Calabria, the Hungarian cleric, preoccupied with his vision of a glorious Hunnish past, lets his thoughts and fancies roam back to antiquity. The new conceptions of history writing and the revived study of Roman law, the arising interest in antiquity, and the need for a glorious national past mingle to form the peculiar "Roman–Hun" mixture, transported into the world of contemporary "Europe," which provided the epic and theoretical basis for the *Gesta Hungarorum*. And let us not forget that as the idea was taking shape in our author's head, he had before his eyes on the ferry-boat the flower of French, Spanish, and southern-Italian knighthood returning from the last Crusade.

The two Hungarian clerics on the scene both left a single work for posterity; both works preserve the memory of personal experience with contemporary Europe. But here their paths diverged. *Andreas Hungarus* did not return home, but continued to wield his pen in the service of one

---

[105] W. J. Chase, *The Distichs of Cato: A Famous Medieval Textbook* (Madison: University of Wisconsin Press, 1922). Accursius *gl. ad Dig.* 1.1.2 sv. *et patriae*; cf. *gl. Dig.* 9.2.7.4 and 32.1.101.

of the most interesting and dynamic rulers of the time, Charles of Anjou: he also upheld a theory of empire which interestingly combined the universalism of the Middle Ages with the nascent new theory of the state.[106] Simon of Kéza returned home to write a work which was to influence his nation's historical consciousness for centuries. It was not only their paths which diverged; the spirit of their works diverged as well. On the one hand, there is Master Simon's fantastic historical construct, in which even his memories of southern Italy serve to enhance the Hun–Magyar glory, and in the theoretical tone of which every bit of knowledge gathered abroad is reflected in the *hic et nunc* of social and political realities and the claims of the emerging "estates" in contemporary Hungary. On the other hand, there is Master Andrew's *Descriptio*, undoubtedly at a higher level both in organisation and literary merit, which used its sources to present a basically authentic account of contemporary history, but with a biblical tone of universalism and a corresponding partisanship with the Guelph and hatred of the Ghibelline cause. These works represent the two diverging roads of the medieval spirit: the one seeks primarily, even within the universalism of Christianity, the particular place of his own nation; the other adopts unreservedly the "supranational" world of ideas. In the final analysis, however, both represent one and the same unity: the history of a Europe coalescing into one in the course of the thirteenth century.

---

[106] E. G. Léonard, *Les Angevins de Naples* (Paris: Presses Universitaires de France, 1954), esp. 103ff.; L. Boehm, "*De Carlingis imperator Karolus, princeps et monarcha totius Europae*: Zur Orientpolitik Karls I. von Anjou," *Historisches Jahrbuch* 88 (1968): 1–35.

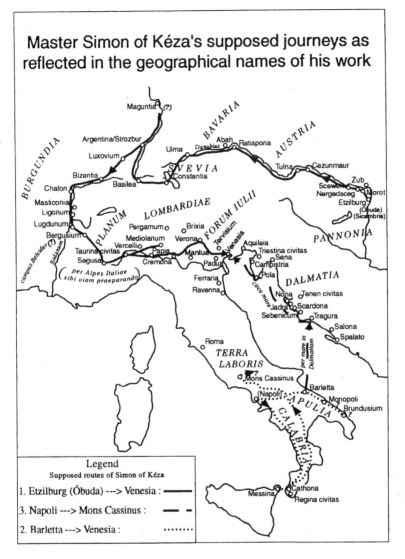

Master Simon of Kéza's supposed journeys as reflected in the geographical names of his work

Maguntia (?)

BAVARIA

Argentina/Strozbur
AUSTRIA
Abah
Ratispona
Ulma
Danubius
Luxovium
Tulna
Cezunmaur
BURGUNDIA
Bizentia
SVEVIA
Constantia
Scewen
Zub
Basilea
Nergedsceg
Morot
Chalon
Etzilburg
Masticonia
(Obuda)
Ligonum
LOMBARDIAE
(Sicambria)
Lugdunum
Pergamum
Brixia
FORUM IULII
Bergusium
Mediolanum
Verona
Tervisium
PANNONIA
Taurina civitas
Vercellio
Venesia
Segusa
Papia
Mantua
Aquileia
Per Alpes Italiae
Cremona
Triestina civitas
sibi viam praeparando
Padua
Sena
campus Belvider (?)
Ferraria
Campistria
Rodanum
Ravenna
Pola
DALMATIA
circa mare
Nona
Tenen civitas
Jadra
Scardona
Sebenicum
Tragura
Salona
per mare in Dalmatiam
Spalato
Roma
TERRA
LABORIS
Mons Cassinus
Barletta
(Napoli)
APULIA
Monopoli
Brundusium (?)
CALABRIA
Messina
Cathona
Regina civitas

Legend
Supposed routes of Simon of Kéza

1. Etzilburg (Óbuda) ---> Venesia : —————

3. Napoli ---> Mons Cassinus : — —

2. Barletta ---> Venesia : ·········

Map 1

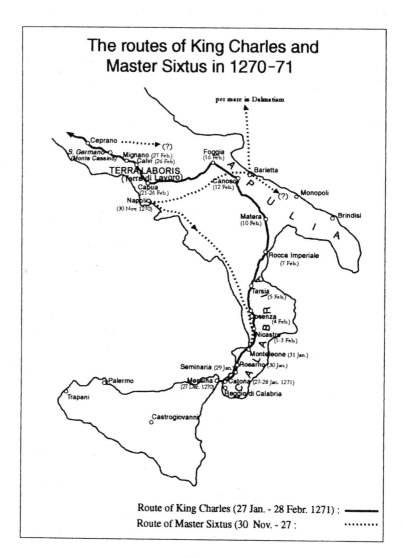

The routes of King Charles and
Master Sixtus in 1270-71

per mare in Dalmatiam

Ceprano .... (?)
S. Germano Mignano (27 Feb.)   Foggia
(Monte Cassino) Calvi (26 Feb)   (16 Feb.)
TERRA LABORIS   Barletta
(Terra di Lavoro)
Capua   Canosa   Monopoli
(21-26 Feb.) (12 Feb.)   (?)
Napoli
(30 Nov. 1270)   Brindisi
                     Matera
                     (10 Feb.)

                          Rocca Imperiale
                          (7 Feb.)

                     Tarsia
                       (5 Feb.)
                     Cosenza
                       (4 Feb.)
                     Nicastro
                       (1-3 Feb.)
                  Monteleone (31 Jan.)
              Seminaria (29 Jan.) Rosarno (30 Jan.)
Palermo   Messina   Catona (27-28 Jan. 1271)
                (27 Dec. 1270) Reggio di Calabria
Trapani

   Castrogiovanni

Route of King Charles (27 Jan. - 28 Febr. 1271) : ———
Route of Master Sixtus (30 Nov. - 27 :   ....

Map 2

SIMONIS DE KÉZA

GESTA HUNGARORUM

SIMON OF KÉZA

THE DEEDS OF THE HUNGARIANS

SIMONIS DE KÉZA

[GESTA HUNGARORUM]ᵃ

1.   Invictissimo et potentissimo domino Ladislao tertio[1] gloriosissimo regi Hungariaeᵇ magister[2] Simonᶜ de Keza, fidelis clericus eius, ad illum aspirare, *cuius pulchritudinem mirantur sol et luna*[3].

2.   Cum vestroᵈ cordi affectuose adiaceret Hungarorum gesta cognoscere, et id mihi veraciter constitisset, nationis eiusdem historiasᵉ, quae diversis scartabellisᶠ,[4] per Italiam, Franciam ac Germaniam[5] sparsae sunt et diffusae, in vo-

ᵃ Simonis de Keza Chronicon Hungaricum elegans opusculum *K*

ᵇ Hungarorum *K*

ᶜ Symon *K*

ᵈ nostro *K, H*

ᵉ historias *E*, ystorias *S*, victorias *K, H*

ᶠ scartabellis *E*, scartabelis *S*, sparsa bellis *H*, scartabris *K*

---

[1] Ladislas (László) IV "the Cuman," king of Hungary 1272–90. In calling him "the Third" the author disregards the infant Ladislas III, who died in 1205 soon after his coronation.

[2] Master: either because he was learned (he probably studied law in Northern Italy in the 1270s) or because of his office with the chancellery. He is mentioned as Queen Elizabeth's cleric in 1272, then as Ladislas IV's *aulae nostrae notarius* in 1283 (Szűcs, above, p. IL).

SIMON OF KÉZA

[THE DEEDS OF THE HUNGARIANS]

1.   To the most invincible and powerful lord Ladislas the Third, most glorious king of Hungary,[1] Master[2] Simon of Kéza, his faithful cleric: may he approach Him "whose beauty sun and moon marvel at."[3]

2.   As it was a matter dear to your heart to learn of the deeds of the Hungarians, and I had ascertained this fact for certain, I set about to bring together in one volume the stories of that nation scattered and spread in various sources[4] through Italy, France, and Germany.[5] However,

[3] From the "Antiphonarium in festo S. Agnetis et Comm. virginum" (Hesbert, *Corpus*, 3, no. 3407); a much quoted passage, cf. St. Bernard, *Opera omnia* 4: 321.

[4] The prologue is modelled after the *Pantheon* of Godfrey of Viterbo (ca. 1198) (*MGH SS* 22: 104). For an analysis of the prologue's prose rhythms see Horváth (*Stílusproblémák*, 386–87), who notes the contemporary Hungarian practice of employing mostly dispondaic and trispondaic sentence-endings. — The word *scartabellis*, from *scartabello* (*codex chartaceus*), is one of Simon's many Italicisms (see Szűcs, above p. LXIII etc.); Losonczi, *De latinitate*, 24–46).

[5] In the 1260s and between 1268 and 1271 he may have visited parts of Germany, France, and Italy as the king's envoy; see Szűcs, above p. IL, and Maps 1 and 2.

lumen unum redigere procuravi, non imitatus Orosium[1], qui favore Ottonis caesaris, cui Hungari in diversis suis praeliis confusiones plures intulerant[2], multa in libellis suis apochrifa confingens ex daemonibus incubis[3] Hungaros asseruit generatos. Scripsit enim quod Filimer, magni Aldarici regis Gottorum filius, dum fines Scitiae armis impeteret[4], mulieres, quae patrio[a] nomine Baltrame[b] nominantur, plures secum in exercito suo dicitur deduxisse[5]. Quae cum[c] essent militibus infestissimae, retrahentes plurimos per blandities a negotio militari, consilium regis ipsas fertur de consortio exercitus eapropter expulisse. Quae quidem pervagantes per deserta[d], litora paludis Meotidae[e]

[a] patrio *S*, alio *K*, *E*, generatio *H*,

[b] Baltrame *S*, *E*, Baltucme *H*, Baltranae *K*

[c] cum *S*, dum *K*

[d] loca sive *S add.*

[e] Meotidis *H*, Moeotidis *E*

---

[1] The name Orosius is taken from the main source of this passage, Jordanes *Getica* 24.121. But Simon may have used Orosius' *Historia contra paganos* (1.1 and 1.2) directly, especially for the description of Scythia.

[2] Simon anachronistically refers to the German Emperor Otto I "the Great" (936–73), who defeated the roving Hungarians in the battle of Lechfeld, close to Augsburg, in 955. The Hungarians led some forty raids against western Europe, from ca. 899 to 955, and around ten pillaging campaigns against the south and east of Europe.

[3] The story is borrowed from Jordanes *Getica* 24.121–22. The word *incubi* demonstrates the influence of the *Pantheon* (p. 183); for its meaning, cf. Isidore, *Etymologiarum libri* 8.11.103–4: *...Incubi appellantur sive Inui ab ineundo passim cum animalibus. Saepe enim inprobi*

I have not imitated the example of Orosius.[1] For he con-
cocted many apocryphal stories in his pages out of partial-
ity towards the Emperor Otto, on whom the Hungarians
had inflicted numerous discomfits in their various battles,[2]
and claimed that the Hungarians were begotten of demonic
incubi.[3] Thus he writes that when Filimer, son of Aldaric
the Great,[4] king of the Goths, was attacking the borders of
Scythia, he took away with him in his army numerous
women known in their own language as Baltrame.[5] These
women were a great menace to the soldiers as they drew
large numbers of them from their military duties with their
blandishments, so for this reason, the story goes, the king's
council expelled them from the company of the army.
Thereupon they wandered through the wilderness and

existunt etiam mulieribus, et earum peragunt concubitum "They are
called Incubi or Inui from their indiscriminate intercourse with animals; often they behave shamelessly to women and copulate with them
too." — From this point on, Simon equates the history of the Huns
with that of the later Hungarians, the two peoples being one and the
same in his eyes. By the tenth century some West-European Latin and
Byzantine chronicles had already taken for granted the identity of the
Huns and Hungarians. The first serious and detailed argument for their
common origin—not known to Simon—was written by Heriger of
Lobbes (abbot 990–1007), whose work was continued by Anselm of
Liège (d. 1056) in his *Gesta episcoporum Tungrensium, Traiectensium
et Leodiensium* (*PL* 139, cols. 1021–24), based on the same chapters of
Jordanes' *Getica* that Master Simon later made use of.

[4] In *Getica* 24.122 Filimer (or Filemer) king of the Goths is referred
to as the son of Gadaric (*Gadarici magni filius*) rather than as *magni
Aldarici regis filius*.

[5] The *Getica* (24.121) calls them "Haliurunnae"; glossed as *magas
mulieres* "magician women" (Maenchen-Helfen, "Legends").

tandem descenderunt[1]. Ibique diutius dum mansissent pri-
vatae solatio maritali, incubi daemones ad ipsas venientes
concubuisse cum eis[a] iuxta dictum Orosii[2] referuntur. Ex
qua quidem coniunctione dixit Hungaros oriundos. Sed ut
eius assertio palam fiat falsissima, [SRH, 142] primo per
textum comprobatur evangelicum, quod *spiritus carnem et
ossa non habeant,* et *quod est de carne, caro est, quod autem
de spiritu, spiritus est*[3]. Contrarium quoque naturis rerum
dixisse iudicatur et penitus adversatur veritati, ut spiritus
generare possint, quibus non sunt concessa naturalia in-
strumenta, quae virtutem ac officium dare possint gener-
andi valentes perficere veram formam embrionis[4]. Quo-
circa patet[b], sicut mundi nationes alias, de viro et faemi-
na Hungaros originem assumpsisse. In eo etiam idem
satis est transgressus veritatem, ubi solos sinistros prae-
liorum eventus videtur[c] meminisse ipsorum Hungarorum,
felices praeteriisse silentio perhibetur, quod odii mani-
festi materiam portendit evidenter. Volens itaque veritatem imitari, sic inprosperos ut felices interseram, scrip-
turus quoque ortum praefatae nationis, ubi et habitave-

---

[a] eis *S*, ipsis *K*

[b] quocitra patrem *K*

[c] videtur *K add.*

---

[1] The Sea of Azov. Simon takes the name from the description of
Scythia in earlier Hungarian chroniclers such as the Anonymus, who
in turn took it from the *Exordia Scythica*; see Harmatta, "Érudition."

finally settled on the shores of the Meotis marsh.[1] They remained there a long time, deprived of marital consolation, but then—according to Orosius[2]—demonic incubi are said to have come to them and had intercourse with them; and he maintains it was from this congress that the Hungarians sprang. However, that his assertion may be seen to be patently false is proved, in the first place, by the text of the gospels, which say that "a spirit has not flesh and bones," and "that which is born of the flesh is flesh, and that which is born of the Spirit is spirit."[3] One must dismiss it as against nature and quite contrary to the truth when he maintains that spirits can beget when they are not supplied with the natural organs which could provide the procreative ability and function capable of creating the true form of an embryo.[4] From these considerations it is obvious that like other peoples of the world, the Hungarians owe their origin to man and woman. There is another respect, too, in which he strays in no little way from the bounds of truth, in that he seems to recall only the battles lost by the Hungarians, while passing over in silence those with outcomes favourable to them. This is an unmistakeable sign of the overt bias in his writing. As I am concerned to reproduce the truth, I will include both the favourable and the unfavourable ones. I will also write about the origin of the aforementioned nation, where they lived, how many

[2] Jordanes (*Getica* 24.121) has instead: *ut Priscus istoricus refert* "as the historian Priscus"—or, "an ancient historian"—"relates."

[3] Luke 24:39, John 3:6.

[4] The passage employs the terminology of scholastic disputation: *assertio, comprobatur, contrarium, adversatur.*

rint, quot etiam regna occupaverint et quotiens[a] immutaverint sua loca. Illius tamen adiutorio ac gratia mini-
strante, qui rerum omnium, quae sub lunari circulo esse
habent et ultra[b], vita quoque fruuntur creatione habita, est
Deus opifex creator idem ac redemptor, *cui sit honor et
gloria in saecula* sempiterna[1].

EXPLICIT PROLOGUS

INCIPIUNT HUNNORUM GESTA[2]

3. [*M*]*ultifarie multisque modis olim* in veteri testamento[3], et nunc sub[c] aetate sexta saeculi diversas historias
diversi[d] descripserunt, prout Iosephus, Isidorus, Orosius
et Gotfridus[4] aliique quamplures, quorum nomina exprime-
re non est opus. Ego autem in illo tempore illius mundi
illud opus incoavi, quando *caritas refriguerat, iniquitas
abundaverat* et *omnis caro* ad malum quam ad bonum
pronior erat[e,5]. [SRH, 143]

[a] quoties *H*

[b] ultra *S, H, E*, ultro *K*

[c] in *S*

[d] diversi istorias *S*

[e] *K, H, E omit the last sentence. Henceforth we follow Ms K.*

---

[1] Rom. 16:27, 1 Tim. 1:17.

[2] Cf. *SRH* 1, ch. 2, 239–40. Henceforth chapters of the so-called
14th-century Hungarian chronicles, which may have used the same
sources as Simon or contained texts that were known to him, will be
referred to.

realms they occupied, and how many times they moved to new lands—but ever with His help and grace Who is craftsman God, Creator as well as Redeemer of all things which have their being under the lunar circle and beyond, and enjoy life since creation; to whom "be honour and glory for ever and ever"[1] eternally.

END OF THE PROLOGUE

BEGINNING OF THE DEEDS OF THE HUNS[2]

3.   "At sundry times and in divers manners in time past"[3] in the Old Testament, and now in the sixth age of the world,[4] different historians have written different histories, for example Josephus, Isidore, Orosius, and Godfrey, and others too numerous to mention. But I began this work at the time of the world when "love" had "waxed cold," and "iniquity" had "abounded," and "all flesh" was more prone to evil than to good.[5]

---

[3] Heb. 1:1.

[4] For the sixth age cf. *Pantheon* Introduction 105, and Rev. 20:10; also Isidore *Etymologiarum libri* 5.38. The chronological notion of the six ages follows the tradition in St. Augustine and Bede.

[5] Direct borrowing from Josephus is unlikely, though not impossible. His name appears together with Orosius in the introduction of the *Pantheon* (*MGH SS* 22: 103). Simon obviously consulted the latter, and apparently also the *Etymologiarum libri* and the *Historia Gotica* and *Chronica* of Isidore. — For "But I began . . . " cf. Matt. 24:12; but these phrases are commonplaces, cf. e.g. *De vita s. Geraldi comitis* (*PL* 133: 641).

4.   Porro cum per cladem diluvii praeter Noe et tres filios eius deleta esset omnis caro, tandem ex Sem, Kam et Iapfeth[a] LXX. duae tribus post diluvium sunt progressae[1]. De Sem XXII.[b], ex Kam XXXIII.[c], a Iafeth vero X. et septem[2]. Dum autem tribus istae, sicut refert Iosephus, lingua Hebraica uterentur[3], ducentesimo[d] primo anno post diluvium[4] Menrot[e,5] gigans filius Thana[6] ex semine Iafeth oriundus, turrem construere caepit cum omni cognatione sua, attendentes periculum praeteritum, ut si contingeret diluvium iterari, possent evitare ultionis iudicium turris interfugio[7]. Divini vero mysterii arbitrata sententia, cui

[a] Iapheth *E*, Iaphet et Kam *H*

[b] 25 *H*

[c] 37 *H*

[d] ducentesimo *S*, decimo *K*, deinde *H*, dicto *E*

[e] Nemroth *H*, Nemprot *S*

---

[1] Cf. *SRH* 1, ch. 4, 247–50. The scriptural basis is Gen. 7:21, 7:23, and 10:1.

[2] Cf. Isidore *Chronica* 429, where the numbers of tribes are: Japheth, 15; Ham, 30; Shem, 27. The other Hungarian chronicles (*SRH* 1: 243) have the same numbers as Simon.

[3] Simon probably did not use Josephus directly but cites him via perhaps one of the earlier Hungarian chroniclers, in which the Biblical introduction to the Hunnish and Hungarian history was already elaborated, or via Isidore (cf. *Chronica* 428: *ut refert Iosephus*).

[4] Simon's source had "ducentesimo uno," as in *SRH* 1: 247, written in full and not in Roman numerals. For the chronological problem see the note to Isidore, *Chronica*, *PL* 83, cols. 1019–22.

4.   After all flesh had been destroyed through the disaster of the Flood save Noah and his three sons,[1] finally seventy-two tribes came forth after the Flood from Shem, Ham, and Japheth: twenty-two from Shem, thirty-three from Ham, and seventeen from Japheth.[2] Now, as Josephus tells,[3] all these tribes spoke Hebrew. But in the two hundred and first[4] year after the flood the giant Ménrót,[5] son of Thana,[6] of the seed of Japheth, began to construct a tower. Ever mindful of their danger in the past, he and his kin hoped that if the flood came a second time they could escape judgement and retribution and take refuge in the tower.[7] But the mysterious judgement of God, which hu-

[5] It is hardly likely that our *Menrot* is a variant of the "Nimrod" of the biblical text. Rather, the biblical Nimrod has been identified with "Ménrót," a legendary figure in Hungarian historical tradition. The *Gesta* of the Anonymus records a personal name Ménmarót, cf. *men*, Bulgarian-Turkish for 'great,' and *marót*, Hung. for 'Moravian' (Györffy, *Krónikáink*, 207). In the Bible Japheth's son is Magog and not Nimrod. This suggests that the Magog who in the Anonymus (ch. 1, *SRH* 1: 35) gives his name to the Moger/Magyar was first conflated with Ménrót, and then identified with Nimrod. — Henceforth, as Simon's stories and especially names have often parallels or variations in the *gesta* of the Anonymus (P. Magister) of c. 1200—the use of which by our author has been amply demonstrated—we shall regularly refer to it for comparison.

[6] A Scythian king called Tanaus is mentioned in Justinus (*Epitoma Historiae Philippicae* 1.1) and Isidore (*Etymologiarum libri* 13.21.24). Regino of Prüm also mentions in his geographical description of Scythia (ad ann. 889) the river Thanais, which, according to Isidore as well, was named after Tanaus (Györffy, *Krónikáink*, 206).

[7] Gen. 11; Isidore *Etymologiarum libri* 5.39.6 and 15.1.4: . . . *post diluvium Nembroth gigans Babylonem urbem . . . fundavit. . . .* For the motive in building the tower see Josephus *Antiquitates* 1.4.2.

non sufficit resistere humanus intellectus, sic[a] illorum mu-
tavit loquelam ac confudit, ut dum proximus a proximo
non posset intelligi, tandem in diversas sunt dispersi regiones. Fecerant enim in turri memorata, sicut dicit Iosephus,
deorum templa ex auro purissimo, palatia lapidibus pretiosis fabricata, columnas aureas et plateas diversimode
petris coloratis diversiusque[b] astracatas[c]. Et erat turris ipsa
in quadrum sublevata, ab uno angulo ad alium habens
passuum longitudinis millia XV. et latitudinis totidem[1].
Altitudinis vero quantitas finita nondum erat, sed usque
lunarem circulum, quem diluvii unda non attigerat, illorum
cogitatu [SRH,144] debebat sublevari. Trecentorum autem passuum grassitudo[d] fuerat fundamenti, sublevata siquidem paulatim artabatur, quod grassities[e] inferior pon-
dus prominens[f] sustineret. Sita etenim erat inter Nubiam
et Aegyptum, cuius antiqualia[g] cernuntur usque hodie eun-
tibus de Menphis Alexandriam[2]. Dimissis ergo incidentiis,
quae caeptae materiae dant colorem, redeundum est ad
[M]enroth, qui[h] gigans post linguarum incepta[m][i] confusionem terram Eiulath[3] introivit, quae regio Perside isto

[a] sic *H, E*, sicut *K*

[b] diversiusque *H*, duusuusque *K*, ductibusque *E*, diversisque *S*. *The
editor of E mentions in notes, p. 29.: "in Membrana legam*: duusuusque
astracatas".

[c] abstractas *E*

[d] grossities *H, E*

[e] grossities *H, E*

[f] praeminens *K*

[g] antiqualia *H, E*, antiquilia *K*

[h] *lacuna in K*, qui *H, E*

[i] *lacuna in K*, inceptam *H, E*

man intellect is powerless to oppose, altered and confused their speech; no man could understand his neighbour, and they were finally scattered over different lands. Josephus tells that in this tower they had built temples of purest gold to the gods, palaces wrought of precious jewels, golden columns and streets decked with all manner of different coloured stones. The tower itself was built square, measuring 15,000 paces from one corner to the other, and in breadth the same.[1] Its precise height was never fixed, but in their minds it was to rise as high as the lunar circle where the waters of the Flood had never reached. The foundation was 300 paces thick, and as it rose it narrowed gradually so that the thickness underneath might support the huge weight resting upon it. The site of the tower was between Nubia and Egypt, and its ruins can still be seen today by travellers going from Memphis to Alexandria.[2] But regrettably, we must set aside these details which enliven our theme and return to the story of Ménrót. After the confusion of tongues the giant entered the land of Havilah,[3]

[1] For the judgement see Gen. 11:7; also Josephus *Antiquitates* 1.4.2. Simon, however, or the author of the earlier Hungarian Chronicle, borrowed the story from Jerome *Commentarium in Esaiam* 5.14.22–23, expanding it probably from Isidore *Chronica* 430: *hanc turrem Nebroth gigans construxit, qui post confusionem linguarum migravit inde in Persas.* — For "in quadrum" cf. Herodotus 1.178–79. — For *diversisque* see Agnellus of Ravenna, *Liber pontificalis ecclesiae Ravennatis*, 302. — The Italicism *astracatas* comes from *lastricare* 'to cover' (also used by Agnellus *Liber pontificalis* 328, 363 in the forms *lastra*, *lasta*).

[2] An allusion to the pyramids of antiquity. Many authors, for example Otto of Freising (*Gesta Friderici*, 2.15 = FvS 16: 132), identified Memphis with Babylon.

[3] Cf. Gen. 2:11, 25:18; 1 Kings 15:7 etc.

tempore appellatur[1], et ibi duos filios, Hunor scilicet et Mogor ex Eneth sua coniuge generavit[2], ex quibus Huni sive Hungari sunt exorti. Sed quia gigans Menroth uxores alias sine Eneth perhibetur habuisse, ex quibus absque Hunor et Mogor plures filios et filias generavit, hi sui filii et eorum posteritas Perside inhabitant regionem, statura et colore Hunis similes tantummodo parum differunt in loquela, sicut Saxones et Turingi[3]. Cum autem Hunor et Mogor Menroth essent primogeniti, a patre ipsorum tabernaculis separati incedebant.

5.   Accidit autem dierum una venandi causa ipsos perrexisse in paludes Meotidas, quibus in deserto cum cerva occurrisset, illam insequentes, fugiit ante eos. Cumque ibi ab oculis illorum prorsus vanuisset, diutius requisitam invenire ullo[a] modo potuerunt[4]. Peragratis tandem paludibus

[a] *used several times for "nullo"*

---

[1] Isidore *Chronica* 21.

[2] The progenitress of the Hungarians in gentile historical tradition, but probably also a totem animal: "ünő" or "inő" is Hungarian for hind. This seems to confirm that the legend of the deer hunt (below, ch. 5) is rooted in the ancient oral traditions of the Hungarians, and is not a mere borrowing from Jordanes (Györffy, *Krónikáink*, 35–38). A mythical hind is first mentioned in connection with the Huns by Sozomenos (mid-fifth century); a similar story is mentioned by Thietmar of Merseburg regarding the Saxons (*Chronicon* 2.37). Perhaps this hind also corresponds to the figure of "Emesu" mentioned by the Anonymus (ch. 3). — The name Hunor may come from "Onogur," the name of a people with whom the proto-Hungarians lived in close proximity in the eighth century (cf. *Getica* 5.37, where it appears in the form *Hunuguri*), or is simply an eponym made up from "Hun," just as Mogor is from "magyar" ('Hungarian'). — The suggested connection

which is now called Persia,[1] and there he begot two sons, Hunor and Mogor, by his wife Eneth.[2] It was from them that the Huns, or Hungarians, took their origins. However, it seems the giant Ménrót had other wives apart from Eneth, on whom he sired many sons and daughters besides Hunor and Mogor. These sons and their posterity inhabit the land of Persia and resemble the Huns in stature and colour, merely differing a little in speech, like the Saxons and the Thuringians.[3] But as Hunor and Mogor were Ménrót's first born, they journeyed separately from their father in tents.

5.   Now it happened one day when they had gone out hunting in the Meotis marshes that they encountered a hind in the wilderness. As they went in pursuit of it, it fled before them. Then it disappeared from their sight altogether, and they could not find it no matter how long they searched.[4] But as they were wandering through these

between the legendary Mén(ma)rót of Hungarian tradition (see above p. LV) and our *Menrot* is further supported by the fact that Ménmarót had several wives in the Anonymus as well (ch. 11) (Kristó, *History*, 119–28).

[3] Simon undoubtedly knew German (see chs. 10, 11). Riccardus (the Dominican who wrote down Julianus' travels in the east in the 1230s) makes a similar comment in linking the "Hungarians" he encountered in the Magyar's land of origin, *Hungaria magna* (somewhere in Bashkiria), with those in Hungary (Dörrie, "Texte", 157).

[4] Cf. *SRH* 1, ch. 5, 250–52. Simon's account is apparently based on Jordanes (*Getica* 24.123–24), where the hind leads the hunters to Scythia. The Hungarian deer hunt motif already turns up in the Anonymus (ch. 34), but it is Simon who gives the first detailed version (Kristó, *History*, 119–28). However, as the Hungarian traditions of the deer hunt and the abduction of women seem to have had nomadic, oriental origins, perhaps only the stylistic framework is here borrowed from Jordanes.

memoratis, pro armentis nutriendis ipsam conspexerunt
oportunam, ad patrem deinde redeuntes ab ipso licentia
impetrata cum rebus omnibus paludes Meotidas intraverunt moraturi. Regio quidem Meotida Perside patriae
est vicina[1], quam undique pontus praeter vadum unum
parvissimum giro vallat, fluminibus penitus carens, herbis,
lignis, volatilibus, piscibus et bestiis copiatur. Aditus illuc
[SRH, 145] difficilis et exitus. Paludes autem Meotidas
adeuntes annis V. immobiliter[a] permanserunt. Anno ergo
VI. exeuntes in deserto loco sine maribus in tabernaculis
permanentes uxores ac pueros filiorum Belar[2] casu repere-
runt, quos cum rebus eorum in paludes Meotidas cursu
celeri deduxerunt. Accidit autem principis Dulae Alanorum duas filias inter illos pueros comprehendi, quarum
unam Hunor et aliam Mogor sibi sumpsit in uxorem[3]. Ex
quibus mulieribus omnes Hunni originem assumpsere.
Factum est autem, cum diutius in ipsis paludibus perman-
sissent, in gentem validissimam succrescere inceperunt,
nec capere eos potuit ipsa regio et nutrire[4].

[a] ibidem *H add.*

---

[1] The word *patria* in Hungarian Latinity of the thirteenth century had
begun to acquire emotional overtones; see Deér, "Entstehung." — In
the original source the phrase *fluminibus penitus carens* probably read
fluviis currens, and was modified by Simon from the version in an earlier
chronicle.

[2] The abduction of women also features in Jordanes *Getica* 24.123. The
abduction of the bride, which the laws of the eleventh century Hungarian kings condemned, remained part of Hungarian folk custom,
even if only in a symbolic form in later times (cf. Stephen I:27 *DRMH*
1:6). — The name Belar in Hungarian tradition refers to the Bulgarians,

marshes, they saw that the land was well suited for grazing cattle. They then returned to their father, and after obtaining his permission they took all their possessions and went to live in the Meotis marshes. The Meotis region borders on their Persian homeland,[1] and except from one very small ford it is cut off on all sides by the sea; it has no rivers but abounds in grass, trees, birds, fish, and animals; access and exit to this land is difficult. So they entered the Meotis marshes and remained there for five years without leaving. Then in the sixth year they went out, and when by chance they discovered that the wives and children of the sons of Belar[2] were camped in tents in a lonely place without their menfolk, they carried them off with all their belongings as fast as they could into the Meotis marshes. Two daughters of Dula, prince of the Alans,[3] happened to be among the children who were seized. Hunor took one of them in marriage and Mogor the other, and to these women all the Huns owe their origin. And as they stayed on in the marshes, they gradually grew into a very powerful people, and the land was not large enough to contain them or to feed them.[4]

cf. the Anonymus, ch. 57 (*SRH* 1: 114): *de terra Bular* (referring to Bilyar, a city in the Volga region of Bulgaria).

[3] The Alans are mentioned in Jordanes *Getica* 24.126 and in Riccardus' report (Dörrie, "Texte," 153). The name Dula seems to derive from ancient Danubian Bulgar or Alan traditions. Groups of Alans known as *Jazonici* (Hung. *Jász*) settled in Hungary in the second half of the thirteenth century (Kristó, *History*, 121).

[4] The motive of "overpopulation" is frequently mentioned in reference to migrations (cf. Paul the Deacon *Historia* 1.1; Regino *Chronicon* ad ann. 889: . . . *ut eos genitale solum non sufficiat alere*), and is cited by all the Hungarian chronicles.

6. Exploratoribus igitur in Scitiam abinde destinatis, Scitiae regno explorato cum pueris et armentis ipsam patriam intravere permansuri. Regnum itaque ipsum dum adissent, Alpzuros et Prutenos in eo invenerunt habitantes[1], quibus deletis et expulsis usque hodie illud regnum pacifice dinoscuntur possidere[2]. Scitica enim regio in Europa situm habet, extenditur enim versus orientem, ab uno vero latere ponto Aquilonali, ab alio montibus Rifeis includitur a zona torrida distans, de oriente quidem Asiae iungitur. Oriuntur etiam in eodem duo magna flumina, uni nomen[a] Etul et alterius Togora[3]. Gentes siquidem in eo regno procreatae otia amplectuntur, vanitatibus deditae, naturae dedignantis, actibus venereis intendentes, rapinas cupiunt, generaliter plus nigrae colore quam albae. Scitico quoque regno de oriente iungitur regnum Iorianorum et post haec Tarsia et tandem Mangalia, ubi [SRH, 146] Europa terminatur[4]. Ex plaga vero aestivali subsolana gens iacet Corosmina, Aethiopia etiam, quae India Minor dicitur[5], ac post haec

[a] nomine *K*

---

[1] Cf. *SRH* 1, ch. 6, 252–55. The Alpidzuri (on their own) are mentioned in Jordanes *Getica* 24.126. The Prussians often appear in 13th-century historical sources (e.g. Bartholomaeus Anglicus *De proprietatibus rerum* 15.134 and 140).

[2] The route and chronology of the Hungarian migration is still disputed; for an up-to-date overview see Kristó, *History*, 85–203.

[3] For the description of Scythia cf. Justinus 2.2; Regino *Chronicon* ad ann. 889. The Rifean mountains formed an essential part of this traditional geographical concept. Etul literally means 'river' in Turkic languages, but Simon, like many medieval writers, identifies it with the Don; descriptions appear in the Anonymus (ch. 7), Riccardus (Dörrie, "Texte," 157), and Julianus (*ibid*. 173). The river Togora appears in Orosius *Historia* 1.2.44 in the form *Ottorogorrae*.

6. They therefore sent off scouts to Scythia, and after
reconnoitring the realm of Scythia they decided to move
to this new home with their children and cattle and settle.
But when they entered, they found it was inhabited by
Alpidzuri and Prussians;[1] we know that they wiped these
people out or expelled them, but thereafter held that kingdom in peace to this day.[2] The land of Scythia is situated
in Europe but extends towards the east. Far from the torrid
zone, it is bounded on one side by the Northern Sea and
on the other by the Rifean mountains, while on the east it
adjoins Asia. It is the source of two great rivers, one called
the Etul and the other the Togora.[3] The races this kingdom
breeds are devoted to leisure, given over to vanities, scorn-
ful by nature, libidinous, and delight in raiding; in general
they are more dark in colour than white. On the east the
realm of Scythia adjoins the kingdom of the Georgians, and
after this comes Tarsia, and then Mongolia, and there
Europe ends.[4] In the tropical zone, close to the sun, are
situated the Chorasminian people, as well as Ethiopia,
which is called India Minor.[5] Farther, south of the course

[4] *regnum Iorianorum* is "the kingdom of the Georgians," or perhaps
the land Russian annals refer to as *Yugra* (Monneret, *Leggende*, 160).
— The word *Tarsia* comes from the Persian *Tarsa*; in the 13th century
it was thought to be the land of the Tartars (Bezzola, *Mongolen*, 34–36).
— The reference to Mongolia is proof of the author's up-to-date
geographical knowledge.

[5] The Chorasminian people take their name from Khwarezm, a widely
known geographical name at the time, referring to the area between the
lower part of the river Volga and Lake Aral. Members of a Muslim
people from the region, the so-called "Káliz," lived in medieval Hungary, performing important military and financial services; see S. Balić,
"Islam," 19–35. — *India Minor* had been mentioned in John of Plano
Carpini's itinerary; for the origin of the notion see Monneret, *Leggende*,
219, and for *Ethiopia*, cf. Jordanes *Getica* 6.47.

inter meridiem et cursum Don fluvii desertum existit immeabile. Fluvius siquidem Don in Scitia oritur, qui ab Hungaris Etul nominatur, sed ut montes Rifeos transit diffluendo, Don est appellatus. Qui tandem in planum effluens currit terram Alanorum postea vero cadit in Rotundum mare ternis[a] ramusculis[1]. Togora autem fluvius discurrit de Scitia exiendo per desertas sylvas, paludes ac montes niveos, ubi nunquam sol lucet propter nebulas. Tandem intrat Yrcaniam vergens in mare Aquilonis[2]. Longitudo siquidem Sciticae regionis stadiis CCC. et LX. extendi perhibetur, latitudo vero CXC.[b] Situm enim naturalem habet tam munitum, ut in solo locello parvissimo ibi aditus reperitur. Propter quod nec Romani caesares, nec Magnus Alexander, quamvis attentassent, potuerunt in eam introire[3]. Scitia enim solo laeta est, nemoribus, sylvis, herbis venustata et bestiis diversi generis mirabiliter dives ac referta. Habet etiam de occidente vicinos Bessos et Comanos Albos[4]. Sed circa mare Aquilonis, quod eidem

[a] trinis *K*

[b] centum viginti *H*

---

[1] The Round Sea (*Rotundum mare*) refers to the Caspian Sea (Jordanes *Getica* 5).

[2] The Northern Sea together with the name Hyrcania and the term *plaga* come from Orosius *Historia* 1.1.2; cf. *SRH* 1, ch. 6, pp. 253–54. This fictitious sea is perhaps a bay of the North Sea; Fehér ("Beiträge") identifies it with the *Scythicum mare* of Orosius and the *Scythicus Oceanus* of Isidore (15.13.2). Simon's description was copied by later Hungarian chroniclers, cf. *SRH* 1, ch. 6, 252–55.

[3] According to Jordanes *Getica* 5.33 the territory (*circuitus*) of the Meotis marshes extended *passuum mil. cxliiii* ("144 miles"). — Roman emperors and Alexander the Great were mentioned in the *Exordia Scythica* (p.320) and by the Anonymus, ch. 1.

of the Don there is an impassable desert. The Don in fact rises in Scythia and is called Etul by the Hungarians, but when it makes its way through the Rifean mountains it is referred to as the Don; as it flows into the plains it crosses the lands of the Alans and then empties into the Round Sea by three branches.[1] The river Togora rises in Scythia and passes through wild forests, marshes, and snowy mountains where the sun never shines because of clouds; finally it enters Hyrcania, veering towards the Northern Sea.[2] The land of Scythia is reported to extend 360 stades in length and 190 in width. The region is well protected by nature and can only be entered by a very small approach. This is why neither the Roman emperors nor Alexander the Great were able to enter it, for all that they tried.[3] For the soil of Scythia is fertile, with lovely woods, forests, and grasslands, and an amazing richness and diversity of wildlife. Its neighbours to the west are the Pechenegs and the White Cumans.[4] But around the Northern Sea, which is on its

[4] The Pechenegs are also mentioned in the Anonymus, chs. 25 and 57. Before the Hungarians entered the Carpathian Basin, there had been a war between them and the Pechenegs in 895; the Pechenegs then invaded the land between the River Don and the Lower Danube and may have forced the Hungarians to move west. Later, in the second half of the tenth century, some of the Pechenegs came to settle in Hungary, performing military duties as a warrior people. — The White Cumans are mentioned in the Anonymus, ch. 8 etc. In the eleventh century, their territories were east of the Lower Danube. The Arab geographer al-Idrisi (1100–1166) located White and Black Cumania by the Northern and Eastern shores of the Black Sea respectively. In other languages the name given to some of the Cumans meant 'pale, light, yellowish,' in other words, something more or less "white" (Györffy, *Krónikáink*, 90).

vicinatur, usque regnum Susdaliae est desertum sylvestre humano generi immeabile, quod ad magnum spatium extendi perhibetur, ubi nubium densitas per novem menses iacet. Ibi nec sol cernitur, nisi tantummodo in Iunio, Iulio ac Augusto, et id in tanta diei hora, quantum a VI. est usque nonam. In montibus etenim deserti memorati cristallus invenitur et grifo nidum parat, avesque legerfalc, quae Hungarice kerechet appellantur, procreare pullos dinoscuntur[1].

Sciticum enim regnum comprehensione una cingitur, sed in regna tria dividitur principando, scilicet in Barsatiam, Denciam et Mogoriam[2]. Habet etiam provincias centum et octo propter centum et octo progenies, quae dudum per filios Hunor et Magor, quando Scitiam invaserunt, sunt divisae[3]. Centum enim et octo generationes pura tenet

[1] Susdal was a Russian principality east of Moscow which had gained considerable political significance by the end of the twelfth century. — As to the region with the limited periods of sunshine, similar remarks were made later by Marco Polo 3.44; see Macartney, *Early sources*, 125. — For the crystal see Solinus *Collectanea* 15.22, 15.29, 16.2. — For the griffon see Herodotus, books 3 and 4, and Pomponius Mela *De situ orbis* 2.1. — The name Simon uses for hunting falcons, *legerfalc*, comes from the German *Gerfalke* or *Jägerfalk*, apparently the bird of prey *falco venaticus*. The Hungarian equivalent, *kerecset*, of Slavic origin, survives in Hungarian geographical names referring to places where falconers were settled. The bird is also mentioned in the itinerarium of the Minorite Benedictus Polonus (fl. 1247) (*Sinica*, vol. 1, ch. 5).

[2] Fictitious kingdoms. Barsatia probably derives from Bascardia, land of the Bashkirs, east of Great Bulgaria, where thirteenth century travellers (Julianus, John of Plano Carpini, Benedictus Polonus, and William of Rubruck) found Hungarians in *Magna Hungaria*. For *Den-*

border, as far as the realm of Susdal there is a wilderness of forest impassable to human beings, which is believed to extend a vast distance; dense clouds cover it for nine months of the year, the sun being seen only in June, July, and August, and then only between the sixth and ninth hours of the day. In the mountains of this wilderness crystal is found, and there the griffon makes its nest, and the hunting falcons called in Hungarian *kerecset* raise their chicks.[1]

In fact the Scythian realm has a single border, but administratively it is divided into three kingdoms, namely Barsatia, Dencia, and Mogoria.[2] As well, it has 108 districts, representing 108 families, which were divided among the sons of Hunor and Mogor long ago when they had invaded Scythia.[3] For the pure Hungarian nation comprises a hun-

cia and *Mogoria* the probable source is the word *Dentumoger* in the Anonymus, ch. 1.

[3] There are different explanations for the number 108. According to Györffy (*Tanulmányok*, 14–15), it derives from a no longer extant register of the Hungarian kindreds in King Coloman's time. Others have maintained that it is the sum of 100 and the seven Hungarian tribes plus the Kabar people, who came to Hungary around A.D. 895, or (e.g. Kulcsár, "Magyar ősmonda") that as a multiple of 54 it is a magic number of Jewish cabalistic traditions. The number of Hungarian clans at the time of the conquest is estimated to have been around 35 to 50, varying with the estimates of the number of chieftains and tribes (Kristó, "Néhány megjegyzés", 963). From the Middle Ages as a whole some 200 kindreds are documented, about 40% of which are only mentioned once. Simon's estimate of 108 clans is therefore reasonable. Simon is at variance with the Anonymus here, because the latter believed that all the later Hungarian clans and kindreds descended from the seven conquering chieftains.

Hungaria et non plures[1]. Aliae autem, si quae ipsis sunt coniunctae, advenae sunt vel ex captivis oriundi, quoniam[a] ex Hunor et Mogor in palude Meotida centum et octo progenies absque omni missitalia fuere generatae. Quorum ergo advenarum generatio in fine huius libri apponetur seriatim[2]. [SRH, 147]

7.   Igitur in aetate sexta saeculi multiplicati Huni in Scitia habitando *ut arena*[3], anno Domini septingentesimo in unum congregati, capitaneos[4] inter se, scilicet duces vel principes praefecerunt, quorum unus Wela[b] fuit, Chele file[c] filius ex genere Zemem[d] oriundus, cuius fratres Cuwe[e] et Caducha ambo capitanei. Quarti vero ducis nomen Ethela fuit, Bendacuz filius, cuius fratres Reuwa[f] et Buda uterque

[a] quum *K*

[b] Vela *H*

[c] Thelae filiae *H*, Thele file *E*; file *est omittendum*

[d] Zemein *E*

[e] Cuve *H*

[f] Reuva *H*

---

[1] The expression "pure Hungarian nation" can be understood in the context of a common legal practice in Italian city-states at the time which made a distinction between original citizens (*cives veri, originarii*, etc.) and newly settled inhabitants. When talking about the mingling of these two groups, the verb *mischiare* was used, probably

dred and eight kindreds and no more;[1] any additional ones
are immigrants or the descendants of captives, for 108 clans
were begotten by Hunor and Mogor in the marsh of Meotis
without any admixture. The family histories of these newcomers will be listed at the end of this book.[2]

7.   In the sixth age of the world the Huns dwelling in
Scythia had "multiplied like the sand."[3] In the year of Our
Lord 700 they came together and put themselves under the
command of captains,[4] that is, leaders or princes. Vela, son
of Csele, of the clan of Szemény was one of these; his
brothers Keve and Kadocsa were also captains. The name
of the fourth was Attila, son of Bendegúz, and his brothers

the basis of Simon's strange term *missitalia* "admixture" (see Szűcs,
above p. LXIII; Riesenberg, "Citizenship"; Veszprémy, "Kézai"; Hoff-
mann, "Outsiders").

[2] Cf. chs. 76–94 below.

[3] Cf. *SRH* 1, ch. 7, 255–57. "Like the sand" is biblical, e.g. Gen. 22:18,
Ps. 138:17.

[4] The year 700 is fictitious, though 445 A.D. for the murder of Bleda
and 453 A.D. for Attila's death were known to medieval chroniclers
(see also note 1, pp. 78–79); the date may have been chosen to make
a closer chronological connection with the Hungarian conquest, in
which Attila's grandsons are alleged to have participated. — The term
"captain" may derive from Italian usage, where it applied to community
leaders in communes elected for a fixed period, but was not unknown
in Hungarian Latinity of Simon's time either; a charter from around
1280 uses the term *nobiles capitanei* for county magistrates (Györffy,
Krónikáink, 191–92).

duces extitere de genere Erd oriundi[1] ut simul uno corde occidentales occuparent regiones. Constituerunt quoque inter se rectorem unum nomine Kadar de genere

[1] There existed two forms in Hungarian for the leader of the Huns, Attila and Etela; the German equivalent of the latter is Etzel (*LexMA* 4: 61–63). The Attila tradition is for the first time linked to Hungary in the Annals of Lambert of Hersfeld (*Annales* ad ann. 1071, *MGH SS* 5:185 = *FvS* 13: 150), in which we are told that Attila's sword was presented to Otto of Nordheim by the widow of the Hungarian king Andrew I in 1063. On the basis of the *Nibelungenlied* Hungary was identified as the land of the Huns in the twelfth century. However, there was initially no mention of a specific town of Attila, *Etzelen bürge* (*LexMA* 4: 63–64). Before Simon all Hungarian chronicles, e.g. the Anonymus (ca. 1200), the *Chronicon Hungarico-Polonicum* (ca. the 1220s), and the History of Thomas of Spalato (d. 1268), assumed a relationship between Hun and Hungarian history. It is still a matter of debate whether the Hungarians learned of the legend of Attila from the Germans or whether they heard about it from other nomadic tribes while still roaming the steppes long before their conquest of the homeland (cf. Kulcsár, "Magyar ősmonda"; Kristó, *History*, 71–84). — Attila and Buda apart, the names of the Hunnish chieftains are fictitious. Of the clans named, no documents survive about the Érd; Érd is a settlement near present Budapest, mentioned in contemporary charters and notable for Roman ruins, but a clan of this name do not seem to have achieved distinction. — The identification of the Szemény clan or family is uncertain; a *Zemeyn centurio* appears in a legal suit about Tárnokvölgy in 1259 (Horváth, *Stílusproblémák*, 363; Mályusz-Kristó, *Commentarii*, 1: 87). Others suggested that they are identical with the Szemere, mentioned by the Anonymus (Bollók, "Kézai", 120). — The

Reva and Buda were also leaders; they were of the Érd clan.[1] And they were all united in their purpose to conquer the lands of the west. In addition, they chose from their number one judge, Kádár by name, of the kindred of

name Buda derives from the historical Bleda, mentioned in the *Getica*, the name of Attila's brother, but was influenced by that of the place commonly associated with Attila's headquarters in Hungary, Óbuda (now a district of Budapest). As a Hungarian personal name, Buda is documented from 1138 (Fehértói, *Személynévtár*, 66–67). — Vela could derive from a geographical name in Riccardus' itinerary (Dörrie, "Texte," 155): *venerunt in terram Sarracenorum, que vocatur Veda in civitatem Bundaz*. It has also been associated with a Hungarian given name, Béla, and with Veleg, a place in County Fejér (Horváth, "Hun-történet", 471, 475). — The name Csele also occurs as a geographical name. — Keve derives from Keveaszó or Keveháza (today Kajászószentpéter in County Fejér), mentioned in several contemporary charters (Györffy, *ÁMTF*, 2: 389–90); as a personal name Keve is documented from 1138 (Fehértói, *Személynévtár*, 192–93). — Kadocsa and Szovárd resemble the names recorded of Hungarians who, according to the Anonymus (ch. 7), stayed in the East. — Bendegúz, Attila's father, is called "Mundzuco" in the *Getica*, but the connection between the two forms is unclear. The name has also been associated with the "Bundaz" mentioned in Riccardus' itinerary (see above) and with a settlement between Érd and Százhalom (Horváth, "Hun történet", 469). — Reva is perhaps based on a name Roas in the *Getica* (35.180), or related to the word *rév*, Hungarian for 'ferry,' or is a corruption of the name Keve (Horváth, "Hun-történet", 469–70). Vela, Csele, Keve, Kadocsa, Bendegúz, Reva, and Buda are unique inventions of Simon (or of an earlier author of a Hungarian-Hunnish history), and do not appear outside Hungary.

Turda[1] oriundum, qui communem exercitum iudicaret, dissidentium lites sopiret, castigaret malefactores, fures ac latrones. Ita quidem, ut si rector idem immoderatam sententiam definiret, communitas[2] in irritum revocaret, errantem capitaneum et rectorem deponeret quando vellet. Consuetudo etenim ista legitima inter Hunos sive Hungaros usque ad tempora ducis Geyche filii Tocsun[3] inviolabiliter extitit observata. Antequam ergo baptizati fuissent Hungari et effecti Christiani, sub tali voce precones in castris ad exercitum Hungaros adunabant: "Vox Dei et populi Hungarici[4], quod die tali unusquisque armatus in

[1] The original source of the quotation "they chose . . . " is Lactantius *Institutiones* 1.1.12, borrowed by Isidore *Etymologiarum libri*. 5.14, and later verbatim into Gratian (*Decretum* 1, Dist. 2, ch. 5, ed. Friedberg, 4, 7); however, the immediate source seems to be the Anonymus (ch. 53) (see Gerics, "Domanovszky"). — Kádár is again a fictitious name. It could be associated with the word *karcha*, i.e. judge, used at the time of the conquest, or with the title of similar form referring to a Khazar dignitary. The author may well have encountered the word in Hungarian geographical names. The office of *karcha* was in many ways similar to the later Hungarian count palatine (Istványi, "Congregatio", 54). — The assertion of the rights of the *communitas* against the dignitaries is thought to derive partly from the Golden Bull of 1222 (1222:14, *DRMH* 1:35) and partly from the behaviour of Italian communes towards their *podestà*s (Horváth, "Hun-történet," 472; Gerics, "Krónikáink," 316–17). — The connection with the little known Torda (or Turda) clan is unclear; Simon was possibly inspired by a place-name Tordas or Turdas near Keveaszó (Györffy, *ÁMTF*, 2: 411).

[2] *Communitas* and *commune* are important technical terms in the *Gesta Hungarorum*, expressing Simon's political theories (see Szűcs, above pp. LXXXVI–XCVI).

Torda:[1] he was to mete out judgement among the rank and file of the host, to settle quarrels between those in dispute, and to punish wrongdoers, thieves, and brigands. But if the judge should hand down an inordinate sentence, the community[2] could declare it invalid and have the errant captain and judge removed whenever it wanted. This custom was the law and strictly observed among the Huns (that is, Hungarians) up to the times of their duke Géza, the son of Taksony.[3] Thus in the days before the Hungarians had been baptised and became Christians, the criers in the camp would summon together the Hungarian host with the following proclamation: "It is the word of God and of the Hungarian people[4] that on such-and-such a day every man

[3] Simon dates the end of the old tribal (pagan) world by reference to Grand Prince Géza (d. 997). Taksony was a Hungarian prince, the grandson of Árpád and father of Géza; he is also mentioned by Constantine Porphyrogenitos, (*De administrando imperio* 40, p. 179): ". . . Zaltas had a son Taxis." The pronunciation of the name Géza is reconstructed as *'Djeücha' or *'Djeüsha' in old Hungarian, and is preserved in geographical names like Décs, Decső. The decision to lead Hungary into the European Christian world was indeed made by Géza. In 973 he sent envoys to the imperial diet at Quedlinburg and requested missionary bishops. In the 990s Géza secured a marriage for his son Vajk/Stephen with the Bavarian princess Gisela, sister of the future emperor Henry II; see Szabolcs de Vajay, "Grossfürst Géza."

[4] Cf. *Vox populi vox Dei* (*Proverbia sententiaque latinitatis medii aevi*, 2: 5, No. 919, 34182); it also occurs in a charter of the Hungarian king Béla IV in 1253 (*RA* no. 991). — Royal criers are referred to in a letter of Charles IV, king of Sicily, dealing with Hungarian matters (Wenczel, *Diplomacziai emlékek*, 47–48).

tali loco praecise debeat comparere communitatis consilium praeceptumque auditurus". Quicunque ergo edictum contempsisset praetendere non valens [SRH, 148]
rationem, lex Scitica per medium cultro huiusmodi[a] de-
truncabat, vel exponi in causas desperatas, aut detrudi in
communium servitutem[1]. Vitia itaque et excessus huiusmodi[b] unum Hungarum ab alio separavit, alias cum unus
pater et una mater omnes Hungaros procreaverit, quomodo[c] unus nobilis, alter innobilis diceretur, nisi victus per
tales casus criminis haberetur[2].

8. Tunc de tribubus centum et octo elegerunt viros fortes
ad bellandum, assumentes de quolibet genere decem millia
armatorum, aliis in Scitia derelictis, qui eorum regnum ab
hostibus custodirent elevatisque baneriis[3] egredientes Bes-

[a] huius *K*

[b] huius *K*

[c] quorum *K*

---

[1] This "Scythian law" is perhaps based on a Roman law, the *Lex Iulia
maiestatis* (*Digesta* 48.1.1, *Institutiones* 4.18.3–11; see Szűcs, above
p. LXXX), or the customary law of the Székely; for, according to
16th-century tradition, participants in their folk assemblies had the
right to publicly kill by sword those persons who acted against their
liberties and privileges (Horváth, "Hun történet," 473). — "Hopeless
situations" corresponds to a technical term in Roman law referring to
serious cases of criminal offence (*capitalia in causas desperatas*), see
Szűcs, above p. LXXXI, and Gerics, "Adalékok", 112. Norman law in
Southern Italy (Assise di Ariano) inflicted the same punishment on
deserters (Cuozzo, *Normanni*, 71).

in arms shall present himself without fail in such-and-such a place to listen to the counsel of the community and to hear their instructions." If anyone dared to defy the command without being able to offer a reason, Scythian law decreed that he be cut in half, or exposed to hopeless situations, or degraded to communal enslavement.[1] Thus, it was such offences and excess that separated one Hungarian from another; otherwise, since one father and one mother were the ancestors of all the Hungarians, how could one be termed noble and the other not noble, unless he was judged to be proved so by such blameworthy behaviour?[2]

8. They next chose strong fighting men out of the 108 tribes, taking 10,000 men at arms from every kindred and leaving the others in Scythia to protect their land from enemies. Then the banners[3] were raised and they set out.

---

[2] Bondage as a punishment for dodging military duties has precedents in French (*Pseudo-Turpin Chronicle*; Philippe de Beaumanoir, *Coutumes de Beauvaisis*) and in Catalan legal practice (Spiegel, *Romancing the Past*, 86; Szűcs, above pp. LXXVII–LXXVIII; Freedman, "Cowardice," 6–14). It is an open question whether the remarks of the French chronicler Alberic de Troisfontaines on Hungarian historical events in 955 (*totum populum, qui non exierat cum eis ad bellum, in servitutem redigerunt* "the whole people, who had not gone out to war with them were reduced to servitude"), quoted in *Chronicon ab orbe condito usque ad a. 1241* (*MGH SS* 23, ad ann. 957), are based on authentic information from Hungary or on the same legendary traditions as in France (Györffy, *Krónikáink*, 191).

[3] Cf. *SRH* 1, ch. 8, 257–59. This is the first datable occurrence of *ban(d)erium* in Hungarian Latinity, a borrowing from Italian. In the 14th century the term came to refer to the major part of the Hungarian armed forces, units (*banderia*) consisting of 50–400 men serving under the banners of the king, the queen, and the great lords lay and spiritual.

sorum et Comanorum Alborum terras transirent. Deinde
Sosdaliam Rutheniam[1] et Nigrorum Comanorum terras
ingressi tandem usque Tize fluvium salvis rebus[2], invitis
gentibus praefatis pervenerunt. Qua quidem regione circumspecta omni caetui complacuit non incedere ulterius
cum armentis et familia. Cum uxoribus etenim tabernaculis
et bigis descenderant de eorum terra. Cumque eo tempore
Pannoniam, Panfiliam, Frigiam, Macedoniam, Dalma-
tiamque tetrarcha Macrinus[a], natione Longobardus, urbe
[SRH, 149] Sabaria oriundus gubernaret armis bellicis in-
formatus[3], audito, quod Hunni super Tizam resedissent et
de die in diem lacerarent regnum eius, cum alumnis regni
sui[4] ipsos aggredi reformidans, ad Romanos suos nuncios

[a] Macritius *K*

---

[1] The Hungarians' route through the lands of the Pechenegs, the White
Cumans, and Susdal follows the Anonymus (chs. 7 and 8). The Black
Cumans and the White Cumans are both mentioned by al-Idrisi (see
note 4, p. 21).

[2] The author denies the losses of the advancing Hungarians. According
to Constantine Porphyrogenitus (*De administrando imperio* 40, p.
177), "the Petchenegs with Symeon [of Bulgaria] came against the
Turks [i.e. the Hungarians] and completely destroyed their families
and miserably expelled thence the Turks who were guarding their
country."

[3] The name Macrinus possibly derives from the name of the Caesar
Marcianus (450–57), mentioned in the *Getica* (49.255) as *princeps
orientis*; in some manuscripts Marcianus is a variant for Macrinus.
Another explanation is that it was taken from Roman inscriptions
bearing the names *Macrin(i)us* referring to *legati augusti* and *praefecti*

They crossed the lands of the Pechenegs and the White Cumans, passed through Susdal,[1] Ruthenia, and the lands of the Black Cumans, and in spite of the hostility of these peoples finally reached the river Tisza without loss of their possessions.[2] After surveying the region all the clans came to a decision not to advance farther with their herds and their people; for they had brought their wives, tents, and carts with them when they left their land. At that time Pannonia, Pamphylia, Phrygia, Macedonia, and Dalmatia were under the administration of the tetrarch Macrinus, a Lombard from the city of Sabaria experienced in military matters.[3] On learning that the Huns had halted by the river Tisza and were daily plundering his territory, he was reluctant to retaliate with forces recruited only from his fellow-countrymen.[4] Instead, he sent messengers to the Romans

of Pannonia Superior and Pannonia Inferior respectively in the 2nd and 3rd centuries (Mócsy-Fitz, *Pannonia*, 56–57, 75). On the other hand, Orosius (*Historia* 7.18) records the name *Macrinus* in a different context in connection with a geographic name (*apud*) *Archelaidem*; and Simon mentions a similar personal name later, cf. note 4, p. 59 — Simon connects Macrinus with Sabaria (modern Szombathely) perhaps because of the Roman ruins there or because he had read the Life of St. Martin, which mention that Martin was born in that city. These ruins were impressive even in the fifteenth century: ...*Sabaria vetusta olim civitas, cuius apparent adhuc multa vestigia, inter quae spectantur columnae eximiae magnitudinis...* (Ransanus, *Epithoma*, 64–65). The source for the list of provinces ruled by Macrinus is the *Exordia Scythica* (p. 318), which lists: "Asia, Grecia, Macedonia, Syria, Iudea, Arabia, Dalmacia, Frigia, Pamphilia, Damascus."

[4] For this use of *alumni* ("fellow-countrymen"), cf. the Legend of St. Stephen, *SRH* 2: 380, 405, and below ch. 60.

destinavit, contra Hunnos petiturus gentem et auxilium commodari. Ex parte etenim Romanorum in praedictis patriis imperabat. Tunc Romani Ditricum Veronensem, Alamannum nacione[1], illo in tempore super se regem praefecerant voluntarie, quem petentes, ut Macrino subsidium importaret; Ditrico ergo animo gratanti[a] annuente egressus cum exercitu Italico, Germanico ac caeteris mixtis gentibus occidentis, pervenit ad[b] Zazholm, ubi ipsi Longobardi convenerant, ad Potentianam civitatem[2], pertractans cum Macrino consilium, utrum Hunos in eorum descensu, Danubium transiendo, vel in alio loco congruenti invadere oporteret.

9.   In istis itaque tractatibus Ditrico Macrinoque residentibus, noctis silentio super utres Huni Danubium in Sicambria transierunt[3], exercitum Macrini et Ditrici, quem

[a] constanti *H*

[b] in *H, E*

---

[1] Simon conflates the Dietrich of Bern of the *Nibelungenlied* with the historical Gothic king Theodoric, just as the legendary cycles of Dietrich and Attila mingled in epics like the mid-12th century *Kaiserchronik* (Williams, *Etzel*, 149–50; *Gesta Theodorici regis, MGH SSrerMerov* 2: 202)). Attila and Dietrich of Bern are linked from the eleventh century on (Williams, *Etzel*, 205). Possibly Simon was also inspired by a contemporary *ispán* Detricus (1243–75), whose reckless deeds of valour were commemorated in Hungarian royal charters (Györffy, *Krónikáink*, 190).

[2] Százhalom: modern Százhalombatta. The name means 'one hundred hills,' referring to burial hills of Celtic origin. There was a Roman settlement called Matrica between Érd and Százhalom, whose remains were still visible in Simon's time. Százhalom is also mentioned by the Anonymus, ch. 46. — Potentia (modern Polenza) was the site of a

asking them to provide people and help against the Huns; for Macrinus was governing the aforementioned countries on the authority of the Romans. At that time the Romans of their free will had chosen Dietrich of Bern, of the German nation,[1] to be their king, and they asked him to take aid to Macrinus. Dietrich agreed willingly. Setting out with a mixed army of Italians, Germans, and other Western peoples, he reached Százhalom, where the Lombards themselves had gathered, and the city of Potentia.[2] He and Macrinus debated their strategy: whether to cross the Danube and fall upon the Huns in their settlement, or whether to attack them in some other more suitable place.

9. While Dietrich and Macrinus sat and deliberated, the Huns crossed the Danube at Sicambria in the silence of the night, swimming over on inflated bladders.[3] The army of

famous battle in 402 between the Romans and the Goths (Jordanes *Getica* 30.154); the eleventh-century *Chronicon Novaliciense* 5.29 (*MGH SS* 7: 117) speaks of the Huns but confuses Potentia with Aquileia; while for Pollentia as a site in Hunnish history see Cordt, *Attila*, 18.

[3] Cf. *SRH* 1, ch. 9, 259–60. The Anonymus, ch. 7 also refers to the use of inflated bladders by nomads (cf. Eckhardt, "Pannóniai hun történet", 611–12). — In the legends of the Trojan origin of the Franks, Sicambria was a place near the marshland of Meotis, in the area of *Pannoniarum*, where the roaming Franks sojourned for a time (Gerberding, *Rise of Carolingians*, 11–30, 173; Eckhardt, "Sicambria", 166–97). In the 12th century, historical sources still identified Sicambria with Scythia—Godfrey of Viterbo describes it as *Ungaria Vetus* (*Pantheon*, 201)—but the same writer in his *Speculum regum* and *Memoria seculorum* already locates it in Hungary (*MGH SS* 22: 61, 104). From the fourteenth century (and in Simon) it is identified with modern Óbuda (e.g. *Anonymi Descriptio Europae Orientalis*, 44).

capere Potentia non potuit, in tentoriis campis commorantem crudeliter trucidarunt. Pro qua enim invasione Ditricus acerbatus in campum Tawarnucweg[a] exivit[1] cum Hunnis committens praelium cum suorum et Macrini maximo interitu ac periculo. Fertur tamen Hunnos in hoc loco potenter devicisse. Hunnorum autem residuum [SRH, 150] in sua est reversum arrepta fuga tabernacula. In eo enim praelio ex Hunnis virorum centum millia et XXV. millia corruerunt, Cuwe[b,2] etiam capitaneo ibidem interfecto. De militia vero Ditrici et Macrini, exceptis illis, qui in suis tentoriis ante urbem memoratam fuerant trucidati, ducentena millia et decem millia perierunt. Videns ergo Ditricus tantam caedem suorum accidisse, die altera post congressum praelii perrexit versus Tulnam civitatem[3] cum Macrino. Tunc Huni intellecto, quod Macrinus et Ditricus de loco certaminis removissent sua castra, reversi ad locum certaminis, sociorum cadavera, quae[c] poterant invenire, Cuwemque[d] capitaneum prope stratam, ubi statua est erecta lapidea, more Scitico solemniter terrae commendarunt, partesque illius territorii Cuwe-Azoa[e,4] post

---

[a] Tavarnucveg *H*

[b] Cuve *H*

[c] qui *K*

[d] Cuvemque *H*

[e] Cuve Azoa *H*

---

[1] *Tárnokvölgy* (from Hung. *tárnok* 'a royal servitor in charge of supplies' and *völgy* 'valley'), 25 km South of Budapest. Mentioned in contemporary charters.

[2] For Keve see note 1, p. 27.

Macrinus and Dietrich was camped out in the fields, since Potentia was too small to hold them. The Huns fell upon their tents and massacred them without mercy. Incensed at this raid, Dietrich marched out to the field of Tárnokvölgy[1] to engage the Huns, and in spite of the peril and heavy losses to his and Macrinus's forces he is nevertheless said to have won a decisive victory. The remainder of the Huns fled back to their tents. 125,000 Hunnish warriors fell in the battle, including their captain Keve;[2] but 210,000 men perished from the forces of Dietrich and Macrinus, not counting those butchered in their tents before Sicambria. Seeing the massacre his men had suffered, Dietrich set out with Macrinus the day after the battle for the city of Tulln.[3] When the Huns were sure that Macrinus and Dietrich had broken camp and quit the battlefield, they returned to the battlefield and gathered the bodies of the companions they could find, and then solemnly buried them and their captain Keve according to Scythian rites at a place by the highway where a stone statue is erected. Thereafter they referred to that part of their territory as Keveaszó.[4] Having now experienced the fighting spirit and

[3] Tulln: a city by the Danube north of Vienna; mentioned as *Tulne* in the *Nibelungenlied*. Simon probably visited it during his travels.

[4] Till 1928 there was a two meter high altar stone with a dedication to Jupiter in Keveaszó; this, or some similar impressive Roman statue or milestone, possibly gave rise to a local historical tradition (Juhász, "Baracskai kő"). The stone statute is mentioned in the *Anonymi Descriptio Europae Orientalis* (44): *Ungari... pugnaverunt in campo magno . . . et in signum uictoriae perpetuum erexerunt ibi lapidem marmoreum permaximum, ubi est scripta prefata uictoria, qui adhuc perseuerat usque in hodiernum diem*. *Keve* happens to mean in old Hungarian 'stone,' but this is a coincidence.

hac[a] vocaverunt. Cognita itaque armorum et animi occidentis nationis qualitate et quantitate, Huni animum resummendo, exercitu resarcito adversus Ditricum et Macrinum versus Tulnam pugnaturi perrexerunt. Quorum adventum Ditricus ut cognovit, in Cezunmaur[1] eis contravenit[b], et a mane usque nonam praelium est commissum tam vehemens ac hostile, ut Wela[c], Rewa[d] et Caducha, Hunnorum illustres capitanei cum aliis XL. millibus in ipso certamine interirent[2]. Quorum etiam cadavera abinde removentes apud statuam memoratam cum caeteris sociis subterrarunt. Occubuit quoque Macrinus ex Romano exercitu ipso die et quamplures principes Germanorum Ditrico per iaculum in fronte lethaliter vulnerato et quasi toto exercitu occidentis interempto ac fugato.

10. Postquam vero exercitus se dispersit, Romano more[3] Huni super se Ethelam regem praeficiunt, ipseque Budam fratrem suum de flumine Tize[e] usque Don super diversas exteras nationes principem constituit ac rectorem. Ipse autem seipsum Hunorum [SRH, 151] regem metum orbis, flagellum Dei a subiectis suis fecit appellari. Erat enim rex

---

[a] hoc *H, E*

[b] convenit *H, E*

[c] Vela *H*

[d] Reva *H*

[e] Tiza *H*

---

[1] Zieselmauer: between Vienna and Tulln, a settlement of Roman origin, *Zeizenmure* in the *Nibelungenlied* (Ploss, "Zeizenmure", 12).

strength of the Westerners in quality and numbers alike, the Huns found fresh courage, replenished their host, and set out for Tulln to do battle with Dietrich and Macrinus. Learning of their approach Dietrich marched out to meet them at Zieselmauer.[1] The battle lasted from morning to the ninth hour and was so furious and bitter that the illustrious captains of the Huns Vela, Reva, and Kadocsa were killed in the fighting along with forty thousand of their men.[2] Again they removed the bodies of the slain and buried them near the aforementioned statue with their comrades. The Roman army, too, suffered hugely that day: Macrinus perished along with a number of German princes, Dietrich was fatally wounded in the forehead by a javelin, and virtually the whole of the Western army was killed or put to flight.

10. After the dispersal of the army the Huns, following Roman custom,[3] made Attila their king, and Attila named his brother Buda prince and arbiter over the different foreign nations from the river Tisza to the Don. Attila had his subjects address him as King of the Huns, the Terror of the World, and the Scourge of God. Attila's skin was an

---

[2] In ch. 11 we find the expression *a mane usque noctem* "from morning to night"; but the present reading is supported by Jordanes' account: *circa nonam diei horam proelium sub trepidatione committit* (*Getica* 37.196). — As historical references to these three captains were non-existent, they are killed off at this point in the story. They were originally created to make up the number of the Hungarian chieftains, which together with Kádár was held to be seven.

[3] Cf. *SRH* 1, ch. 10, 260–63. The meaning of "following Roman custom" is explained by the parallel in ch. 8: *Romani . . . super se regem prefecerant voluntarie*; see Szűcs, above p. XCV.

Ethela colore teter, oculis nigris et furiosis, pectore lato, elatus incessu, statura brevis, barbam prolixam cum Hunnis deferebat. Audaciae quidem temperantis erat, in praeliis astutus et solicitus, suo corpore competentis fortitudinis habebatur. In voluntate siquidem magnanimus, politis armis, mundis tabernaculis cultuque utebatur. Erat enim venereus ultra modum. In archa sua aes tenere contemnebat, propter quod ab extera natione amabatur, eo quod liberalis esset ac communis. Ex natura vero severitas[a], quam habebat, a suis Hunnis mirabiliter timebatur. Nationes ideoque regnorum diversorum ad ipsum de finibus orbis terrae confluebant, quibus pro posse liberaliter affluebat. Decem enim millia curruum falcatorum in suo exercitu deferri faciebat cum diversis generibus machinarum, quibus urbes et castra destrui faciebat. Tabernacula etiam variis modis regnorum diversorum habere consueverat operata. Unum habebat sic celebre et solemne, ut ex laminis aureis mirifice coniunctim solidatum, modo solvi et nunc reconiungi ad tendentium staret voluntatem. Columnae cuius ex auro laboratae habentes iunctiones, opera ductilia, in medio tamen vacuae, in iuncturis suis pretiosis lapidibus iungebantur mirabiliter fabricatae. Sed etiam sua maristalla, dum pergeret in exercitum, equis diversarum patriarum replebatur, quos, quamvis visus esset habuisse [caros][b], largiter egentibus tribuebat, ita quidem, ut vix duos haberet aliquando pro usu equitandi. Istae ergo maristallae ex purpura et bisso habebant paraturam. Sellae vero regales ex auro et lapidibus pretiosis fuerant laboratae. Mensa autem eius erat tota aurea, vasa etiam coquinarum. Thalamus

[a] severitatem *K*, ex nimia vero severitate *E*

[b] caros *add. Domanovszky in editione*

ugly colour; his eyes were dark and wild, his chest wide, his gait proud; he was short of stature, and he wore a long beard in the Hunnish fashion. He was daring but tempered in courage, with a reputation for astuteness and caution in battle and physical strength to match. He was magnanimous in the expression of his will. His arms were polished, his tents and his clothing clean. He was, in fact, inordinately lustful. Money he scorned to hoard, and on this account he was loved by foreign peoples, for being open-handed and free; whereas his own people marvellously feared the severity of his temperament. The people of different realms therefore journeyed to him from the ends of the world, and he dispensed to them freely of whatever he owned. In his army he had ten thousand scythed chariots as well as diverse kinds of engines of war for bringing down cities and castles. He had a variety of tents in the styles of different nations. One he often used was fitted with gold plates linked together in a wonderful way which could be taken apart and put together again as the persons putting it up desired; its poles were of gold and had finely-worked metal junctures but were empty in their middle, and were marvellously crafted and linked, with precious stones at their joins. When he went on campaign he filled his stable with horses from different countries; he evidently treasured them, but bestowed them freely on whoever had need of them, so that at times he barely had two to ride on. These stables were decked in velvet and fine linen. The king's chairs were wrought of gold and precious stones; his table and even his kitchen equipment were completely of gold; his bed was of the

quidem eius ex auro purissimo laboratu mirifico in exercitu secum ferebatur. Expeditio autem eius praeter exteras nationes decies centenis armatorum millibus replebatur, ita quidem, ut si unum Sciticum decedere [SRH, 152] contigisset, alter pro ipso confestim ponebatur. Sed arma gentis eius ex corio maxime et etiam metallis variis diversimode fuerant laborata, ferens arcus, cultros et lanceas[1]. Banerium quoque regis Ethelae, quod in proprio scuto gestare consueverat, similitudinem avis habebat, quae Hungarice turul dicitur, in capite cum corona. Istud[a] enim banerium Hunni usque tempora ducis Geichae[b], dum se regerent pro communi, in exercitu semper secum gestavere[2]. In istis itaque et aliis pompis huiusmodi Ethela rex Hunnorum prae caeteris regibus sui temporis gloriosior erat in hoc mundo. Civitatum, castrorum et urbium dominus fieri cupiebat et super illas dominari, habitare vero in ipsis contemnebat. Cum gente enim sua in campis cum tabernaculis et bigis

[a] illud *H, E*

[b] Geiche *H*

---

[1] The description of Attila is based on *Getica*, ch. 35, and *Pantheon*, ch. 17. Other details may come from a putative Hungarian version of the Alexander romance, which survived in a South Slavic translation (Hadrovics, "Nagy Sándor-regény"). The description of Attila's court— which according to Jordanes was plain and modest—may have been influenced by German epic tradition as in the *Nibelungenlied* (Williams, *Etzel*, 257). — The phrase "Scourge of God" is biblical (cf. Isa. 10:26) and was first used of Alarich's Goths in 410 by St. Augustine (*De civitate Dei* 1.8). — For *nationes...* ("the people of different realms . . . ") cf. the Anonymus, ch. 43: *nationes . . . confluebant ad ducem Arpad.* A similar description occurs in the 13th *Liber Attila* (p. 111; see Cordt, *Attila*, 24–26). — The word *maristalla* ("stable") is from Middle

purest gold and of wonderful workmanship, and he carried
it with him on his campaigns. His host consisted of fully a
million men-at-arms not counting foreign nations, and if
one Scythian happened to die he was immediately replaced
by another. The armour of his soldiers, however, was of
different materials, chiefly of hide but of various metals as
well, and they carried bows, knives, and lances.[1] King
Attila's banner bore the image of the bird the Hungarians
call *turul*, with a crown on its head, and this emblem he
carried on his own shield. In fact, until the time of Duke
Géza this flag was always carried with the Hunnish army,
as long as they had a communal style of government.[2] In
all, in this and every kind of pomp and glory King Attila of
the Huns surpassed all the monarchs of the earth in his
days. His ambition was to become master of cities, castles,
and towns, and to be lord over them; however, he scorned
to live in them. Instead, he and his people travelled through

High German *marhstall* (modern German *Marstall*) (*LexMA* 6: 325).
— The *expeditio* ("his host") recalls the ten thousand immortals of
Herodotus (7.83) and Quintus Curtius Rufus (3.3.13); this passage is
only included in the Greek and Serbian versions of the Alexander
romance (cf. *Historia de preliis J2*, 182, Ps.-Kallistenes 1.41; Hadrovics,
"Nagy Sándor-regény," 288–89), but a similar sentence, *elegit C acies
de viris probissimis*, appears in the Attila-story of the *Chronicon Hungarico-Polonicum* (*SRH* 2: 300–301). — The description of the "arma
gentis" ("the armour of his soldiers") comes from Herodotus (7.61),
most likely through the Alexander tradition.

[2] The "turul" bird (commonly identified with a breed of falcon, *falco
rusticolus altaicus*), was probably the totem of the Árpád clan. Unlike
the Anonymus (ch. 3) Simon subtly avoids making an overt genealogical connection between the house of Árpád and Attila the Hun, but
the common totem suggests close relationship.

incedebat, extera natio, quae eum sequebatur, in civitatibus et in villis. Indumentorum vero modus et forma sibi et genti[a] modum Medorum continebat[1].

11. Postquam vero in praelio Cezunmaur Romani corruissent et fuissent dispersi usquequaque, rex Ethela est conversus in castra gentis suae et ibi in descensu ultra Tizam paucis diebus habitavit, tandem in Scewen[b,2] curiam solemnem celebrare procuravit. Ad quam Ditricus de Verona cum principibus Germaniae accedens omne homagium Ethelae et Hunis fecisse perhibetur. Suggessit regi, ut invadere debeat regna occidentis. Cuius quidem consilium amplectendo exercitum statim proclamari iussit. Egressus de Sicambria primo Illiricos subiiciens, deinde Renum Constantiae [SRH, 153] pertransivit[3]. Abinde vero Renum inferius descendendo, rex Sigismundus[4] apud Basileam cum ingenti exercitu eis[c] contravenit[d] quem devincens cum impetu, suo fecit imperio obedire. A loco autem illo egressus obsedit Argentinam civitatem, quam primitus Ro-

[a] sibi et gente *K*, sua et gentis *H*

[b] Sceven *H*, Scewem *E*

[c] suo *H, E*

[d] convenit *H, E*

---

[1] Cf. *Getica* ch. 34, and also the first paragraph of the 1279 law on the Cumans of Hungary: . . . *descendent et recedent a tabernaculis suis et domibus filtrinis, et habitabunt ac morabuntur in villis more Christianorum in edificiis et domibus solo fixis* "from now on they shall settle down and leave their tents and houses made of felt. They shall reside and remain in villages of the Christian sort with buildings and houses attached to the ground" (*DRMH* 1: 69). Similar phrasing regarding the

the open country with their tents and carts, while the foreign nations who followed him occupied the towns and villages. The type and style of clothing worn by Attila and his people followed the style of the Medes.[1]

11. After the Romans were crushed at the battle of Zieselmauer and dispersed in all directions, King Attila returned to the camp of his people and spent a few days there at his settlement beyond the river Tisza. At length he called a formal court in Szőny.[2] History relates that Dietrich of Bern and the princes of Germany attended this court and did all homage to Attila and the Huns. Dietrich suggested to the king that he should invade the kingdoms of the west. Attila seized upon this proposal, ordering his army to be called out at once. Setting out from Sicambria, he first subdued the Illyrians, then crossed the Rhine at Constance.[3] As they moved further down the Rhine their advance was opposed by King Sigismund[4] with a huge army not far from Basle, but Attila fell upon him and defeated him, forcing him to acknowledge his overlordship. He then set out from there to lay siege to the city of Argentina. No

Goths occurs in Rodericus de Rada, *Historia*, 23. — The reference to the Medes may go back to the Alexander matter; see note 1, pp. 42–3.

[2] Szőny: on the Danube West of Esztergom; in Roman times Brigetio, but the Latin name was unknown in the Middle Ages.

[3] The itinerary of the Hun army follows the settlements mentioned in the historical sources on the one hand and the itinerary of Simon's travels on the other (see Map 1).

[4] For Attila's attack on Burgundy, cf. Paul the Deacon *Historia Romana* 14.5. — As king of Burgundy (reigned 516–23), Sigismund is mentioned in a different context in the *Getica* (58.298).

manorum caesar[a] nullus potuit expugnare metus orbis expugnavit diruendo murum eius, ut cunctis adeuntibus via libera haberetur, edictum faciens, ne vivente eo muraretur. Propter quod eadem civitas postmodum Strozbur[b], non Argentina usque hodie est vocata[1]. Amoto autem de loco illo suo exercitu[c] Luxovium, Bizantiam, Chalon, Masticoniam, Lingonensem et Lugdulum Burgundiae destruxit civitates. Descendens tandem iuxta Rodanum adversus Cathalaunos[2], ubi etiam diviso suo exercitu tertiam partem suae gentis contra Miranniamonam[d], soldanum scilicet Marroquiae[3] cum electis capitaneis destinavit. Quo audito Miranniamonia[e] de urbe Sibiliae fugiit ante Hunnos in Marroquiam brachio Sibiliae transpassato[4]. Tunc interea regem Ethelam Romanorum patricius dictus Ecius cum X. regibus [SRH, 154] occidentis invasit ex abrupto. Et dum subitum insultum niterentur facere super Ethelam, per nuncios praeliandi inducias ab ipsis postulavit, ut copia suae gentis, quae absens fuerat, iungeretur. Sed illis renuentibus inter utrosque exercitus a mane usque noctem in campo Belvider praelium est commissum. Erat enim inter

[a] caesarum *E*

[b] Strozburc *E*

[c] exercitu suo *H*

[d] Miramam Monam *H*, Miramammonam *E*

[e] Mirama *H*, *E*

---

[1] The author connects the name with German *Strasse* (= Latin *via*) and *Burg*: there was *libera via* "free access" to it. Simon might have picked up a local legend on his travels, as similar stories about Strasbourg appear after his time (Bleyer, "Hun-monda," 820).

Roman emperor had ever before been able to conquer this city, but the Terror of the World took it by storm, demolishing its walls so that all those passing by would have free access to the city and issuing a proclamation that it should not be walled as long as he lived. For this reason the city was renamed Strasbourg instead of Argentina, and is so called to this day.[1] He then led his army from there against the Burgundian cities of Luxeuil, Besançon, Chalon-sur-Saône, Mâcon, Langres, and Lyons, destroying all of them. Finally the Huns came to a halt on the banks of the Rhone by the lands of the Catalans.[2] Here Attila divided his army, sending a third of his forces under chosen captains against Amīr al-mu'nimīn, the sultan of Morocco.[3] When Amīr al-mu'nimīn learnt the news he fled before the Huns from the town of Seville to Morocco, crossing the straits at Seville.[4] In the meantime, the Patrician of Rome, Aetius, with ten western kings made a surprise move against King Attila. While they were planning to fall upon him unexpectedly, Attila sent envoys to negotiate a truce in the hope of winning time until those of his troops who were absent could join him. However, his overture was rejected. So the two armies joined battle on the field of Beauvoir. The

---

[2] Simon may have meant something like "by the lands of" or "against the Catalans," for the battle of Catalaunum is described in other terms (*in campo Belvider*), see note 1, p. 48 (Déri, "Marmorinus," 306). For a literary parallel for Attila's conquest of Spain, cf. Cordt, *Attila*, 48.

[3] Amīr al-mu'nimīn, that is, prince of all believers, in Arabic an honorary title of caliphs and sultans. It occurs in different variants in contemporary Latin historical texts to denote Muslim rulers.

[4] Knowledge of the Arab defeat at Las Navas de Tolosa in 1212 possibly inspired the author's reference to the flight to Morocco.

utrosque exercitus fluvius discurrens tam parvissimus, ut
si capellum in ipso quis iactasset, fluvii plano cursu vix
poterat inferius removeri, praelio autem iam confecto animalium sanguine et humano talis torrens efficitur, ut auri-
gam cum curru introtraheret et armatos, fieretque mor-
talitas per torrentem in exercitu valde magna. Istud ergo
praelium, quod commissum extitit inter Hunnos ac reges occidentis in loco memorato, omnibus praeliis huius
mundi, quae commissa sunt uno loco et uno die, per veteres
maius esse perhibetur[1]. In quo quidem conflictu Gottorum
rex Aldaricus miserabiliter intercipitur[2]. Cuius quidem obi-
tum alii reges ut cognoscunt, in fugam [SRH, 155] conver-
tuntur. Ab illo itaque die elevatum est cor Hunnorum et
regis Ethelae, timorque percussit orbem terrae et plura
regna hoc audito censu ac tributo eis servierunt[3].

12.　Tertia vero exercitus societas, quae fuerat contra Miranniamonam[a] destinata, propter moram interesse non valens in praelio, remansit usque vitam Ethelae Katalaunis,
habitatores tandem Katalauniae sunt effecti. Erant enim
soli Hunni praeter exteras nationes CCC. millia XXX.

[a] Miramammonam *H, E*

---

[1] Aetius (d. 454) was *patricius, consul,* and *magister utriusque militae.*
The *Getica* calls the kings *auxiliares,* without mention of number. The
battle took place at *campi Catalauni qui et Mauriaci,* according to
Jordanes (*Getica* 36). Our author generally follows Jordanes, but is
unique in calling the battlefield Belvider/Beauvoir (which must have
been south of Lyons, in the vicinity of Vienne, but is not identifiable;
cf. Szűcs, above p. XLVIII. To add to the confusion, he associates
Catalaunum with Catalonia (cf. note 1, p. 50 on *Hispania~ispán*). —

fighting raged from morning till nightfall. Between the two hosts there ran a river so small that if someone threw a hat into it, the shallow stream would scarcely move it. But by the time the battle was over, the blood of men and animals had swollen it to such a torrent that it could sweep away a chariot and its driver or men in full armour and there was a great loss of life from the army in it. Ancient writers say that this battle between the Huns and the western kings in that place was greater than any other battle in this world fought on one day and in one place.[1] Moreover, Aldaric king of the Goths died wretchedly in this battle.[2] When the other kings got to know of his death, they turned and fled. Accordingly, from that day on the heart of the Huns and King Attila was lifted, and fear struck the lands of the earth, and on hearing the tidings many realms submitted to them and offered to pay taxes and tribute.[3]

12. However, the third section of the army, which had been sent against Amīr al-mu'nimīn and which had been delayed from taking part in the battle, remained in the land of the Catalans for the rest of Attila's life and finally settled down in Catalonia. Not counting the other nations, these Huns numbered 330,032. Many of the Huns held office in

For the description of the torrent cf. *Getica*, ch. 40; Paul the Deacon *Historia Romana* 14.6 (*parvulus . . . rivulus*). — The translation of *capellum* as "hat" is uncertain, but no known medieval meaning of the word makes good sense here.

[2] In fact it was the king of the Visigoths, Theodoric I, who died in this battle (so *Getica* 40.209).

[3] "From that day on" recalls the wording in the *Chronicon Hungarico-Polonicum* (*SRH* 2: 300) and the Anonymus, ch. 44 (echoing Jth. 1.7).

millia et XXXII. Hunni. Ex his etiam Hunis plures fuerant
in exercitu capitanei constituti, qui Hunorum lingua spani
vocabantur, ex quorum nominibus tota Ispania postmodum est vocata, cum primo vocati essent Catalauni[1].

13.   Demorantibus siquidem Ethela et Hunnis in Belvider
aliquamdiu, tandem regressi cum victoria intraverunt To-
losanam civitatem, ubi a civibus cum laude summa sunt
suscepti. Indeque recedentes Remensem civitatem Galli-
corum, quae Ethelae in eundo restiterat, igne concrema-
runt, militia et civibus, qui[a] se in ea recluserant[a], omnibus trucidatis. Taliterque Francia et Flandria demolita[2] Renum Coloniae pertransivit, ubi Sanctam Ursulam, Brit-
tanorum regis filiam cum XI. millibus virginum Hunorum feritas crudeliter iugulavit[3]. Abinde Turingiam intro-
gressus [SRH, 156] in Isnaco curia celebrata super Da-
cos, Norvagios, Frisones, Litvanos et Prutenos exercitum magnum destinavit, quibus devictis et humiliatis sibi
fecit subiugari[4]. Ab Isnaco autem curia celebrata egrediens

[a] quae *K*

[b] recluserat *K*

---

[1] Cf. *SRH* 1, ch. 12, 267. A fantastic etymology, based on the homoph-
ony between (*H*)*ispania* and the Hungarian *ispán* (in the author's time
the head of a county or other royal officer).

[2] Cf. *SRH* 1, ch. 13. 267–69. For Toulouse and Reims cf. *Pantheon* ch.
17, 187–88.

[3] St. Ursula is also mentioned in the *Pantheon*, but not specifically as
the daughter of the king of the Britons. Simon's account reflects the

the army as captain, or *ispán* in the Hunnish language, and afterwards the whole of Spain [*Hispania*], which was previously known as the land of the Catalans, took its name from this title.[1]

13.   Attila and the Huns remained for some time in Beauvoir; then at length they started for home. They entered the city of Toulouse victoriously and were received with paeans of praise by the citizens. Then they left and came to Reims, a city of the Gauls. Because the city had offered resistance to Attila during his advance, he had it burnt to the ground, massacring the soldiers and all the civilians who had shut themselves up in it. They then devastated France and Flanders in similar wise.[2] Next they crossed the Rhine at Cologne, where the Huns in their savagery mercilessly killed St. Ursula, the daughter of the king of the Britons, and her 11,000 virgins.[3] Attila then entered Thuringia. In a court held at Eisenach he decided to send a great host against the Danes, Norwegians, Frisians, Lithuanians, and Prussians, all of whom were conquered, humbled, and made subject to him.[4] After the court Attila left Eisenach

Regnante Domino version of the St. Ursula legend (*AASS* vol. 9, s.v. Oct. 21; cf. Grzesik, "European Motifs," 49–51).

[4] The names Thuringia and Eisenach were well-known in Hungary by the 13th century (see note 4, p. 167). In Eisenach the memory of Attila's raid was preserved in late medieval local tradition (Domanovszky, *Kézai Simon mester*, 59; Bleyer, "Hun-monda," 822–23). — For Lithuania in the Attila-story cf. *Chronicon Hungarico-Polonicum* (*SRH* 2: 301). — The other names appear in various geographical treatises, the *Dani* [in our text *Daci*, in the Middle Ages *Dacia* referred to Denmark] and *Frisones* for example in Guido's *Geographica* (p. 553). Sigibert of Gemblaux speaks of the northern campaign of Attila (*MGH SS* 6: 309).

Sicambriam introivit, ubi Budam fratrem suum manibus
propriis interfecit, proiici faciens corpus eius in Danubium,
eo quod ipso Ethela in partibus occidentis[a] praeliante inter
eum et fratrem eius metas stabilitas transgressus fuerat
dominando. Fecerat etiam Sicambriam suo nomine appellari. Et quamvis Hunis et caeteris suis gentibus interdictum
rex Ethela posuisset, ut urbs Ethelae vocaretur, Teutonici interdictum formidantes, eam Echulbuer[b] vocaverunt,
Hunni vero, curam parvam illud reputantes interdictum,
usque hodie eandem vocant Oubudam sicut prius[1]. His
itaque sic[c] peractis V. annis continue in Sicambria requievit
speculatoribus suis in mundi quatuor partes distributis.
Speculatorum siquidem prima societas ordinatim de Sicambria, in quantum unius clamor ad alium audiri potuisset, Coloniae, Germaniae civitate die ac nocte stare consueverat, altera usque Litvam tertia in Don fluvii litore,
quarta vero Iadrae, civitate Dalmatiae stationes faciebat,
quorum voce et clamore, quid Ethela ageret, seu quali
exercitationi deditus esset, mundi partes quatuor potuissent experiri[2].

14. Incidentia. Pannoniae, Panfiliae, Macedoniae, Dalmatiae et Frigiae civitates, quae crebris spoliis et obsidionibus

---

[a] occiduis *K, H, E*

[b] Echulburc *E*

[c] sic *H, E add., K om.*

---

[1] The town of Attila (Óbuda) is mentioned for the first time in
Hungary by the Anonymus, chs. 1, 47, 49, 50 (*Ecilburgu, Elciburgu*).
In his *Chronica Slavorum* of 1189, Arnold of Lübeck identifies Óbuda
with the city of Attila (*in urbem Adtile dictam, MGH SSrG* 14: 130),

and went to Sicambria, where he murdered his brother
Buda with his own hands and had his body thrown in the
Danube. Attila's reason was that while he was away fighting
in the West his brother had overstepped the boundaries of
authority he had established between the two of them and
had had Sicambria renamed after himself. Although Attila
issued an order to his Huns and his other followers that
the city was to be referred to as the City of Attila, and the
Germans out of fear respected the order and called the city
Etzelburg, the Huns paid scant heed to it and continued to
call it Óbuda, as they still do to this day.[1] For five whole
years Attila remained in Sicambria. Meanwhile he sent his
spies to the four corners of the world. The members of each
group were stationed at intervals, so that day or night one
spy's cry could be heard by the next. One line stretched
from Sicambria as far as the city of Cologne in Germany,
another to Lithuania, the third to the banks of the Don,
and the fourth to the city of Zadar in Dalmatia. As they
called and shouted to each other the four quarters of the
globe could learn what Attila was doing or what campaigns
he was contemplating.[2]

14.   Further details. The citizens of Pannonia, Pamphylia,
Macedonia, Dalmatia, and Phrygia, who had been ex-

as does pseudo-Ansbertus in the *Historia de expeditione Friderici*
("*Czilnburg*": *MGH SSrG NS* 5: 53). Archeological excavations at
Hódmezővásárhely-Szikáncs and Mezőberény suggest the real, his-
toric centre of the Huns in Hungary was to the east of the river Tisza.

[2] Knowledge of a Persian communication system based on criers,
recorded in Diodorus Siculus 19.17, may have been transmitted
through the Alexander romances (Aschoff, *Geschichte*, 1: 62–70).

per Hunos erant fatigatae, natali solo derelicto in Apuliam per mare Adriaticum, de Ethela licentia impetrata transierunt, [SRH, 157] Blackis, qui ipsorum fuere pastores et coloni, remanentibus sponte in Pannonia[1].

15. Repausato autem rege Ethela Sicambriae V. annis defectum tertiae partis sui exercitus, que remanserat Catalaunis, resarcire procuravit, curiaque solemni celebrata egressus est de Pannonia per Styriam, Carinthiam et Dalmatiam pertransiens, apud urbem Salonam mari Adriatico et Spaletum se coniunxit, ubi ambas urbes dirui fecit et cremari. Egressus tandem circa mare Traguram, Sebenicum, Scardonam, Iadram, Nonam, Senam, Polam, Parentiam, Campistyriam[a], Triestinam[b] civitatem ac cetera multa oppida occupans in montanis[2], pervenit tandem Aquilegiam, cuius magnitudine circumspecta stupefactus, se confusum reputabat, si dictam civitatem inexpugnatam reliquisset, pro eo maxime, quia quamplures Longobardi de Pannonia, qui Hunorum dominium et Ethelae con-

---

[a] Campstiriam *H*, Capostiriam *E*

[b] Terestinam *H*

---

[1] Cf. *SRH* 1, ch. 14, 263. — For the provinces see note 3, p. 33; again, a borrowing from the *Exordia Scythica*. — This route is once again based on Simon's supposed itinerary via Barletta, Naples, Monteleone, Messina and other places (Szűcs, above, p. II, and Maps 1 and 2). — The *Blacki* (i.e. *Vlachi* 'Vlachs') probably refers to the Romanians, cf. the Anonymus, ch. 9: *Blachi ac pastores Romanorum*. The first Hungarian royal charters referring to them are from 1205/9 and 1224. According to a charter of 1250, Romanians as well as Saxons, Székely,

hausted by repeated raids and sieges from the Huns, having received permission from Attila quit their native soil and crossed the Adriatic Sea to Apulia; the Vlachs, however, who had been their shepherds and husbandmen, elected to remain behind in Pannonia.[1]

15.   King Attila rested for five years in Sicambria and saw to it that the loss of the third part of his army which had remained in Catalonia was made good. Then after holding his formal court he marched from Pannonia through Styria, Carinthia, and Dalmatia till he reached the Adriatic by the cities of Solin and Split, both of which he ordered to be destroyed and burnt. Finally he left, and seized the towns on the sea—Trogir, Šibenik, Skradin, Zadar, Nin, Senj, Pula, Poreč, Koper, and Trieste—and many others in the mountains,[2] until finally he reached Aquileia. Attila was awed by the size and extent of the city, and felt that he would have met his match if he failed to capture it. He was particularly incensed because it was said that many of the Lombards from Pannonia who had scorned to live under the yoke of

and Pecheneg fought in the army of the *ispán* of Sibiu (Szeben) in 1210. From the 13th century their numbers significantly increased in the South-Carpathian region. Virtually everywhere in the Balkans they were referred to as *pastores* because their lifestyle involved seasonal movement of livestock; see Fine, *Early Medieval Balkans*, 68, 205, 216, 308).

[2] Cf. *SRH* 1, ch. 15, 269–70. This itinerary is based on a reconstruction of the author's travels on a diplomatic mission along the coast by sea to Venice in autumn 1269 (see Szűcs, "*Társadalomelmélet*," 864–65, and Map 1).

tempserant, confugisse in ipsam ferebantur. Quos quidem a civibus per nuncios repetens, et dum tradere recusarent, expugnare caepit civitatem machinarum diversis instrumentis. Quam dum capere nullatenus potuisset, obsedit eam anno uno et dimidio. Accidit ergo die uno, ut eandem circuiret civitatem multis fitonicis eius lateri adhaerentibus, in quibus iuxta suae opinionem fidei spem maximam apponebat, et videns ciconiam de mari evolantem et in pinnaculo unius palatii, in quo habebat nidum suum, resedisse, acceptoque in rostro pullo suo, in maris arundines visibiliter deportavit. Reversa tandem et alios pullos suos simul cum nido transtulisse perhibetur. Quo viso rex Ethela suis militibus ad se convocatis ait: "Cernite ergo socii, quod ciconia ista futurorum fatorum sentit indicia urbemque per nos diruendam, ad fugam ne cum civibus pereat, se communit. Estote ergo die crastina in praelio fortiores, videbitis civitatem ruituram". Tunc edicto [SRH, 158] proclamato, machinarum omni genere adhibito, cum non potuisset machinis expugnare, ingenio Sciticorum tandem usus, ex decies centenis millibus sellam unam de quolibet postulavit, et facta congerie ex sellis iuxta murum, iussit incendi sellas ipsas, quarum flamma ac ardore murus se dissolvens, corruisse in terram cum turribus perhibetur. Quo viso omnes cives urbe derelicta in insulam maris fugierunt. Eandem etenim insulam intraverant aeterno permansuri, sed in ipsa paucis annis demorantibus tandem propter metum regis Ethelae in paludes Realt, ubi nunc

Attila and his Huns had taken refuge in the city. Attila sent
messengers to the citizens demanding that these people
be handed over. When they refused he attempted to storm
the city using various kinds of engines of war. However, he
was unable to take it by any means, so he began a siege
which was to last a year and a half. Then one day the king
happened to be walking the circuit of the city with a
number of soothsayers by his side (people in whom he
placed great trust, according to his beliefs), when he noticed a stork come flying in from the sea. It landed on the
tower of one of the palaces where it had its nest, and they
could clearly see it pick up one of its chick in its bill and
carry it off to the reedbeds by the sea. At length, it seems,
the bird returned, collected the rest of its young, and
carried them away as well, nest and all. Seeing this Attila
called his troops together and said: "Well, men, you can see
that this stork knows full well what fate has in store. It can
tell the city is to about to perish at our hands, and not
wishing to die with the rest of the inhabitants, it is taking
refuge in flight. So on the morrow be the more resolute in
battle—you are going to witness the fall of the city." Attila
then issued a general order and brought up siege-engines
of every kind. But when he failed this time as well he
resorted to a trick of the Scythians: he commanded that
each of his million men bring a saddle and had the saddles
piled up against the wall. Then he ordered the heap to be
set on fire. As the flames leapt up, the heat was so intense
that the walls crumbled and came crashing down, towers
and all. At the sight of this the townspeople fled, abandon-
ing their city for an island in the sea. They thought to
remain there from then on, but being still afraid of King

morantur, intraverunt. Unde etiam eadem insula usque hodie Venetica lingua Vecca Venesia nominatur[1].

16.　Veneti siquidem sunt Troiani, ut canit cronica Venetorum[a,2]. Post excidium enim Troiae Aquilegiae permanserunt, quam et fundasse referuntur. Quidam autem Venetos de Sabaria fuisse opinantur. Sabaria vero habitata fuerat Longobardis, in qua erat generalis schola orbis terrae nationi, poetarum musis et dogmatibus philosophicis elucenter illustrata idolorumque erroribus diversis mancipata[3]. Quam quidem Archelaus rex primitus devastavit. Sed postea per Hunos de Pannonia expelluntur nuncque litora fluvii Tycini habitare dinoscuntur, qui et dicuntur Papienses[4]. [SRH, 159]

---

[a] veterorum *K*, veterum *E mentionem fecit in adnotationibus*

---

[1] For the siege, cf. *Getica*, chs. 40, 41, 42; *Pantheon* 17.187; Paul the Deacon *Historia Romana* 14.9. These, however, refer the prophecy and the setting the saddles on fire to the battle of Catalaunum, not the siege of Aquileia (A.D. 452). Simon also differs in saying the siege lasted one and a half years (historically 3 months, in Paul the Deacon 3 years). The motif of setting fire to the saddles also appears in Diodorus 2.13.2 — For the Lombards cf. *Pantheon* 23.192. — On *Vecca Venesia*, 'ancient Venice' in the Venetian dialect, see Szűcs, above, p. LXIII. Even Emperor Constantine Porphyrogenitus assumed that Venice was indirectly founded by Attila the Hun (*De administrando imperio* 28, p. 119). For the flight of the inhabitants, cf. *Pantheon* 17.187.

[2] Cf. *SRH* 1, ch. 16, 272. — The Venetian chronicles known to Simon may have been the unidentified source of the chronicle (written in French) of Martino da Canale (1267–75), *Les estoires de Venise* (Eckhardt, "Pannoniai hún történet," 480–91; Ozoeze Collodo, "Attila").

[3] The association of the Roman town Sabaria with a fictitious celebrated school may be connected with an actual school at the oldest Benedic-

Attila, after a few years they moved to the swamps at Rialto. There they live to this day, and because of this the island is still known as Vecca Venesia in the Venetian dialect.[1]

16. The chronicles of the Venetians[2] boast that the people of Venice are Trojans, and that after the fall of Troy they settled in Aquileia, which indeed they are supposed to have founded. On the other hand, some maintain that the Venetians are from Sabaria. Sabaria, however, was settled by the Lombards; there was a general school there for the people of the world, celebrated for the muses of poetry and the teachings of the philosophers, not to mention their dedication to false idols of every kind.[3] The first person to plunder the city was King Archelaus. Later, however, they were expelled from Pannonia by the Huns, and now they dwell on the banks of the river Ticino. They are also known as the Pavians.[4]

tine monastery of Hungary, Pannonhalma (Mons Pannoniae, Martinsberg), near to which there was a well called Sabaria (see the Anonymus, ch. 50); the law school at Pavia may also have influenced Simon. The notion of a *generalis schola* (or *studium generale*)—*generalis* in the sense 'visited or attended by persons from many places'—may have been known to Simon from his student days (see Cobban, *Medieval University*, 23–26; Tóth, "Ókor").

[4] The king's name is probably taken from Jordanes (*Romana* sect. 225, p. 29, 14, sect. 258, p. 33, 26, where *Archelaus Cappadocum rex* is mentioned) or Orosius *Historia contra paganos* 7.18, where it appears in a different context. For the Sabarian-Pavian connection the author may have been influenced by Sulpicius Severus' Life of St. Martin (ch. 2): *Igitur Martinus Sabaria, Pannoniarum oppido oriundus fuit, sed intra Italiam Ticini altus est*. The Lombards arrived in Pannonia around 526 and left it for North Italy in 568, where they chose Ticinium (Pavia) as their capital.

17. Postquam autem rex Ethela Aquilegiam expugnavit inde venit in Forum Iulii, ubi civitate Concordia occupata in marchiam intravit Lonbardiae[a], in qua Tervisium, Brixiam, Paduam, Cremonam, Veronam, Mantuam, Pergamum, Mediolanum, Ferrariam aliasque plures urbes Italiae suo dominio subiugavit[1]. Post haec Ravennam adproprians[b], Arrianorum archipraesul, qui in dicta civitate contra sedem apostolicam fecerat elevari XII. cardinales suam sectam imitantes, thesaurum habens copiosum, civibus ignorantibus Hunos in urbem occulte intromisit, catholicos, qui erant in ea potiores, per ipsos fecit trucidari, promittens Ethelae, quod si suae sectae adhaeserit fueritque Christianos persecutus, absque fatiga suae gentis et expensis Romanam urbem, totam Italiam et Affricam eius imperio subiugaret. Cumque Ethela annuisset, plus amore dominii, quam sectae memoratae, cognito Romani periculo, quod exinde poterat Christicolis suscitari, Romanum antistitem ad Ethelam transmiserunt petentes, ut exiret de finibus Lombardorum, propter quod ei et censum persolverent, et gentem darent quando vellet. Apostolico itaque ad Ethelam cum crucibus et clero Romano properante, convenerunt in campo ante Ravennam locuturi. Dumque in equis uterque mutuo loquerentur, graveque[a]

[a] Longobardiae *H*, Lombardiae *E*
[b] adproperans *H*, approprians *E*
[c] congrueque *H*

17. After storming Aquileia, King Attila marched from there to Friuli, where he seized the city of Concordia Sagittaria and entered the march of Lombardy, bringing under his power Treviso, Brescia, Padua, Cremona, Verona, Mantua, Bergamo, Milan, Ferrara, and many cities of Italy.[1] He then advanced on Ravenna. Here the archbishop of the Arians had had twelve adherents of his sect elevated as cardinals in opposition to the papal see. He also had a vast store of treasure. Without the knowledge of his fellow citizens he secretly allowed the Huns into the city and had them massacre the Catholics, who formed the better element of the population. In return, he promised Attila that if the king were to become a member of his sect and persecute the Christians he would be able to add the city of Rome, the whole of Italy, and Africa to his empire without any expense or struggle on the part of his people. Attila agreed, more out of lust for conquest than attachment to this sect. When the people of Rome learnt of the danger threatening Christians in consequence of this, they sent the pope of Rome to Attila to beg him to depart from Lombardy, and offering in return to pay him tribute and supply him with troops whenever he wished. So surrounded by Roman clergy and crosses the pope hastened to Attila. They met on a field in front of Ravenna to hold their talks and began parleying with each other from on

[1] Cf. *SRH* 1, ch. 17, 273–75. Attila's attack on Italy in 452 was a simple plundering campaign; the unhealthy Po valley was no more suitable than Gaul for large-scale light cavalry operations (Sinor, "Historical Attila"). Regarding the itinerary, cf. Paul the Deacon *Historia Romana* 14.11 and Martin of Troppau (*MGH SS* 22: 418).

viderentur[a] regi admittere, quae Romani postulabant, inter
colloquia contigit Ethelam sursum aspicere superque[b]
caput suum in aere hominem pendere, gladium tenentem
versatilem, qui caput eius auferre minabatur. Unde quidem
corde perterritus, universas petitiones [SRH, 160] annuit
Romanorum et sic Apostolicus cum gaudio Romam rediit
et rex Ravennam est ingressus. In qua quidem archiprae-
sulem Arrianum cum omnibus sequacibus et complicibus
captivari faciens extorsit ab eo LX. marcarum millia auri,
quos postea fecit omnes iugulari[1]. In his etiam diebus, dum
Ethela Ravennae moraretur, Zoard capitaneus, princeps
militiae regis cum Hunorum exercitu intrat in Apuliam et
Calabriam, ubi Reginam civitatem et Cathonam, in qua
Catho natus habitavit, demolitur et deinde Terra Laboris
demolita usque Montem Cassinum exercitus vastat, inde

[a] videretur *E*

[b] servareque *K*

---

[1] For a somewhat different account of Attila's sojourn in Ravenna see
Agnellus, *Liber pontificalis*, 265–391. — The name Africa, and at the
end of the chapter Egypt and Assyria, was probably taken from the
Alexander romances. — The pope at the time of the Hunnish invasion
was St. Leo I "the Great" (440–61), cf. *Getica*, ch. 42, and Paul the
Deacon *Historia Romana* 14.12. Leo met Attila at the river Mincio in
452 and persuaded him to withdraw. The description of the apparition
does not correspond verbatim with these sources or any other medieval
world chronicles, cf. also Martin of Troppau (Martinus Polonus),

horseback. The king at first showed no inclination to accede what the Romans were asking. But in the midst of their discussions he chanced to glance upwards and beheld a human being hovering in mid-air just above him, swinging a sword and threatening to take off his head at any moment. Attila received such a shock that he assented to the petitions of the Romans lock, stock, and barrel. So the pope returned joyfully to Rome while the king retired to Ravenna. There he had the Arian archbishop seized along with his followers and adherents, and after extorting 60,000 marks of gold from them, he had the lot of them killed.[1] At this time, too, while Attila was in Ravenna, his captain Zovárd, the head of the king's knights, entered Apulia and Calabria with an army of Huns. His army levelled the cities of Reggio and Catona (where Cato was born), then destroyed Terra di Lavoro, and went pillaging as far as Monte Cassino before finally returning victori-

Chronica (*MGH SS* 22: 418) and Sigibert of Gembloux, *Chronographia* (*MGH SS* 6: 309–10). The motif of an invincible king forced to retreat before prayer was introduced into literature by Josephus *Antiquitates Iudeorum* 9.8, describing Alexander the Great's entry into Jerusalem, and adopted by Paul the Deacon for Attila and the pope. — For the massacre of the Arians a parallel could be found in the Jewish Alexander-legend in the Talmud, where after a peace with the Jews Alexander let the Samaritans be killed by their Jewish enemies (Fóti, "Attila legenda").

tandem cum victoria Ravennam est reversus[1]. His itaque sic peractis de Italia rex Ethela rediit in Pannoniam. Dum, ergo per occidentem, orientem, aquilonem ac meridiem longe lateque imperando extendisset suum posse, vertebat in animo transfretare, ut Aegyptios, Assirios subiugaret et Africam.

18. Tunc interea Bractanorum regis filiam Micolt nomine sibi adducunt ad amandum, supra[a] formam humanam pulchriorem, quam quidem adamasse intime[b] perhibetur, quod excessit modum in habendo et[c] eadem enim nocte, cum ipsam carnaliter cognovisset, plus excesserat more solito in potando [SRH, 161] et usu coitus pro velle[d] consummato, ex eius naribus supine dormienti sanguis est egressus, qui locum liberum non habens exeundi, in meatum gutturis introivit, ubi coagulando praepediens anhelitum, metum orbis suffocavit. Micolt vero de somno excitata dum suum dominum crebris motibus excitasset, nec se movere potuisset, corpus cernens frigidatum et privatum calore naturali eiulando cubicularios regios ad se evocans, suum dominum exclamavit introisse universe

[a] supra *S*, suam *K*, *H*, *E*

[b] intime *H*, interim *K*, in tantum *E*

[c] et *H*, *E om.*

[d] puellae *H*

[1] Zovárd's name also appears in the Anonymus, ch. 7, 147–48, and a Hungarian chieftain of the same name was indeed fighting in Northern Italy in 924 (Liudprand, *Antapodosis* 3. 2: *Salardus praedux*), but this is mere coincidence. — On Cato and Cathona (Catona, now part of Reggio di Calabria), see Szűcs, above p. CI, and Map 2. — Terra di Lavoro (*Terra Laboris*) proves once more Simon's knowledge of Italian

ously to Ravenna.[1] After these events King Attila returned from Italy to Pannonia. Already his empire stretched far and wide, by east and west, north and south. He now began making plans to cross the seas and subdue the Egyptians, the Assyrians, and Africa.

18. In the meantime, a daughter of the King of the Bactrians called Micolt was brought for Attila's bed. This girl was more than humanly beautiful, and they say that the king was so deeply smitten that he longed to possess her beyond anything else. The very first night he went to bed with her he drank and copulated in excess of even his normal bounds, and when his will and his lust was satisfied he fell asleep on his back. As he lay there a flow of blood started in his nostrils. Denied free egress the blood run back into his throat. There it coagulated and cut off his breathing; and so the Terror of the World suffocated. Roused from sleep, Micolt shook her lord repeatedly but failed to stir him. She felt the coldness of the body and realised that the natural heat had left it. She let out a shriek and called in the king's chamberlains, wailing that her lord had gone the way of all flesh. With terrible cries and shouts the guards summoned all the watch to the doors of the

language and geography. This detailed knowledge of Italian geography could be connected to the author's travels. Between 1269 and 1271 five Hungarian delegations visited the Anjou court in Sicily. Using the local royal registers (*I Registri della cancellaria Angioina*, vols. 5, 6, 7) Szűcs reconstructed the routes followed in 1270–71 by the Hungarian envoys (one of whom was most likely Simon of Kéza). They landed at Barletta and travelled via Naples as far as Messina, where they joined King Charles and accompanied him as far as about San Germano (Szűcs, "*Társadalomelmélet*," 850–55); see Maps 1 and 2.

viam carnis. Qui quidem terribiliter exclamantes ad palatii hostia universos vigiles fecerunt cursitare[1]. Sepelieruntque eum in loco superius memorato cum Wela[a] et aliis capitaneis[2].

19. Divulgato ergo eius obitu obstupuit orbis terrae, et utrum plangerent inimici eius, vel gauderent, haesitabant, multitudinem filiorum formidantes, qui quasi populus vix poterat[b] numerari. Unum etenim ex filiis post ipsum credebant regnaturum, sed Ditrici astutia Veronensis ac principum Alamanniae, quibus rex Ethela in collo residebat imperando, in partitas diversas Hunorum communitas est divisa, ita quidem, ut quidam Chabam regis Ethelae filium ex Grecorum imperatoris filia, scilicet Honorii genitum[3],

[a] Vela *H*

[b] poterant *H*

---

[1] Cf. *SRH* 1, ch. 18, 275–76. Micolt, a fictitious name, but of Biblical inspiration, David's first wife being called Micol (Eckhardt, "Micolt"), though Löfstedt connects it with the Old French/Anglo-Norman name "Maelgut" ("Attila," 67–68). In Jordanes' version the girl is called "Ildico" (*Getica* 49.254). The description may owe something to the picture of Roxane in the Alexander tradition; cf. *Exordia Scythica*, 321.

[2] That Attila is also said to have been buried at Keveaszó suggests that this Roman monument played an important role in the Hungarian Hunnish legends. Simon does not allude to a tradition which Jordanes mentions (*Getica* 49.258) and which later became widespread, that the king was put into a threefold coffin of iron, gold, and silver and entombed secretly at night. Another embellishment, that he was buried in the bed of the river Tisza, first appears in the 15th-century continuation of John of Utino's world chronicle, without mention of the river's name (Bóna, *Hunnenreich*, 203–6; Ecsedy, "Oriental Background"; Veszprémy, "Martin von Troppau," 983).

palace, and they came running in all directions.¹ Attila was buried in the same place as Vela and the other captains.²

19.   The news of Attila's death stunned the world, and his enemies were torn between joy and lament. They stood in fear of his multitude of sons, who were beyond number and almost constituted a nation in themselves. They felt sure that one of these sons would reign after him, but Dietrich of Bern and the princes of Germany, who had smarted under Attila's yoke, contrived to divide the community of Huns into different factions, so that some wished to place Csaba on the throne, Attila's son by the daughter of the Greek emperor Honorius,³ while others

³ Cf. *SRH* 1, ch. 19, 276–78. Csaba's name and fate is often mentioned in Hungarian chronicles, e.g. the Anonymus, ch. 45, perhaps based on a 9th-century Hungarian chieftain who inspired legends that were passed on by oral tradition. However, Simon is the first to suggest a relationship between Csaba and the Székely. The Székely may have picked up the legend of Csaba during their movements in Hungary. The Székely of County Bihar, for example, may have been in contact with the settlers of Békéscsaba (Southeast Hungary), a place named after a chieftain Csaba (Györffy, *Krónikáink*, 231). His stay in Greece might have been a memory passed on by nomadic tribes like the Pechenegs or Cumans, who were employed on a number of occasions by Byzantine emperors and were occasionally settled in their territory. — For the multitude of sons cf. Jordanes *Getica* 49.254, who reports that Attila married Ildico *post innumerabiles uxores*. — The marriage of Attila to "the daughter of Honorius" (rather than Honoria) is unique to this work. Jordanes (*Getica*, ch. 42) and Paul the Deacon (*Historia Romana* 14.13) correctly record that Honoria was the sister of Valentinian and daughter of Galla Placidia and Valentinian's co-emperor Constantine; and indeed, Attila tried to arrange a marriage with Honoria, but was rejected.

alii vero Aladarium ex Cremildi Germaniae principissa[1] procreatum praeficere in regem post Ethelam nitebantur. Quia vero pars sanior Chabae adhaerebat, extera autem natio Aladario, eapropter uterque inceperunt imperare. Tunc Ditrici astutia, quae favebat[a] Aladario, praelium inter ambos suscitatur. In primo ergo praelio Aladarius superatur; in secundo autem, quod Sicambriae [SRH, 162] per XV. dies continue committitur, exercitus Chabae sic devincitur et prostratur, quod perpauci filii Ethelae Hunique remanerent. Istud enim est praelium, quod Huni praelium Crumhelt usque adhuc nominantes vocaverunt. In quo quidem praelio tantus sanguis Germanicus est effusus, quod si Teutonici ob dedecus non celarent et vellent pure reserare, per plures dies in Danubio aqua bibi[b] non poterat, nec per homines, nec per pecus, quoniam[c] de Sicambria usque urbem Potentiae sanguine inundavit[2].

20. Fugiit igitur Chaba cum XV. millibus Hunnorum in Graeciam ad Honorium, et quamvis retinere voluisset et Graeciae incolam efficere, non permansit rediens in Scitiam

[a] fovebat *K*

[b] aqua bibi in Danubio *H*

[c] quam *K, E*

---

[1] Aladár (Aladarius) is Simon's invention. Jordanes mentions a certain Ardaricus, king of the Gepids (*Getica* 50.263). Aladár as a personal name in Hungary is documented from 1202, in the form Olodar (Fehértói, *Személynévtár*, 258). In Píðrik's Saga, the son of Krimhild is called Aldrian (Williams, *Etzel*, 259). — Krimhild is Attila's second wife in the *Nibelungenlied*.

favoured as Attila's successor Aladár, his son by the German princess Krimhild.[1] The adherents of Csaba represented the sounder element, but Aladár had the backing of a nation of foreigners. The result was that both candidates began to rule. Hereupon Dietrich, who supported Aladár, used his wiles to drive the two to open warfare. Aladár fared the worst in the first contest. But in the second battle, at Sicambria, which lasted for fifteen days on end, Csaba's army received such a crushing defeat that very few of the Huns or the sons of Attila survived; this battle the Huns still refer to by the name of the battle of Krimhild to this day. But an enormous amount of German blood was also shed in this battle; indeed, though the Germans are ashamed to admit the truth openly, the river Danube from Sicambria as far as the city of Potentia was swollen with blood, and for several days neither men nor animals could drink the water.[2]

20. Csaba, however, escaped, and with 15,000 Huns fled to Honorius in Greece. The emperor was willing to keep him on and to let him reside in Greece, but Csaba declined to stay and returned to his father's people and his relations

[2] The expression *pars sanior* ("the sounder element") derives from canon law (*Wörterbuch zur deutschen Rechtsgeschichte*, s.v. "Mehrheitsprinzip"), and also occurs in Hungarian royal privileges, e.g. those issued in 1238 and in 1273 (*RA* no. 647, 2428). — The battle of Krimhild in the *Nibelungenlied* is Krimhild's revenge. Simon must have known the description of the battle of the river Nedao in Jordanes' *Getica* (ch. 49), where the Huns were forced to withdraw to the north-west Balkans, but imitates only one phrase: *"pene populus fuit."*

ad patris nationem ac cognatos. Qui dum Scitiam introisset, mox incepit suadere, quod penitus redirent in Pannoniam ultionem de Germanicis accepturi[1].

21.   Remanserant quoque de Hunnis virorum tria millia
ex praelio Crimildino erepti per fugae interfugium, qui
timentes occidentis nationes in campo Chigle[2] usque Arpad permanserunt, qui se ibi non Hunnos, sed Zaculos
vocaverunt. Isti etenim Zaculi Hunorum sunt residui, qui
dum Hungaros in Pannoniam iterato cognoverunt re-
measse, redeuntibus in Rutheniae finibus occurrerunt, in-
simulque Pannonia conquestata partem in ea sunt adepti,
non tamen in plano Pannoniae, sed cum Blackis in montibus confinii sortem habuerunt, unde Blackis commixti
[SRH, 163] literis ipsorum uti perhibentur[3]. Isti quippe[a]

[a] quidem *H*

---

[1] Cf. *SRH* 1, ch. 20, 278. The Anonymus mentions only Csaba's
journey to Greece (ch. 45). According to the *Getica* (chs. 50–52) a son
of Attila, Irnik (Ernach), settled on the borders of Scythia Minor. The
story probably commemorated the division of the people into two
branches in Hungarian prehistory. It is impossible to establish with
certainty whether these Hungarians were the same as the "Turks" who
according to Byzantine sources lived along the river Vardar in Greece
between the 9th and 14th centuries. In any case Honorius died in 423,
and Attila's sons clashed in 454. For the motif of several battles one after
another, cf. Jordanes *Getica* 48.248–49 (Vinitharius is defeated only in
the third battle, and dies from an arrow, which recalls Dietrich's fate).

[2] Cf. *SRH* 1, ch. 21, 278–79. Csiglamező (*csigla* (?)'fenced area' and
mező 'meadow'): a settlement in the Trans-Danubian region, mentioned in royal charters. Some suggest that the name includes the sense
"beyond the fortified borderland," referring to the status of the Székely
as border guards.

in Scythia. When he arrived in Scythia, he immediately set about urging the whole people to return all the way to Pannonia in order to wreak vengeance on the Germans.[1]

21.   Another group of the Huns survived, three thousand men who saved their lives by fleeing from the battle of Krimhild. Out of fear of the Western nations they remained on the field of Csigla[2] until Árpád's time, referring to themselves not as Huns but as Székely. These Székely are in fact remnants of the Huns, and when they found out that the Hungarians were returning to Pannonia, they came to meet them on the borders of Ruthenia, and then joined with them in the conquest of Pannonia and acquired part of the country. However, this was not in the plains of Pannonia but in the mountains, which they shared with the Vlachs, mingling with them, it is said, and adopting their alphabet.[3] The Székely believed that Csaba perished in

[3] The Székely were held to be the people of Attila by the Anonymus as well (ch. 50), but their origins are still debated. Their language preserved no ancient, non-Hungarian features and is already Magyar in the earliest sources. The historical fact is that the Székely are not indigenous to Transylvania, but were relocated from Western parts of Hungary in the 12th century. From the 12th century they became known as a special population, enjoying privileged status as free warriors (Györffy, "Ursprung"). On the border region of Transylvania, Romanians and Székely lived side-by-side from the 12th century. Simon may have seen runic script—which he believes to be of Vlach/ Romanian origin—on medieval Székely monuments, several of which survive. The inscriptions are probably written in an ancient Hungarian runic alphabet, in which oriental Turkish runes were adapted to the Hungarian language—an indication of the ethnic diversity of the Hungarians of the 9th–10th centuries (Györffy-Harmatta, "Rovás-írásunk").

Zaculi in Graecia perisse Chabam putaverunt, unde vulgus adhuc loquitur in communi: "Tunc redire debeas, dicunt recedenti, quando Chaba de Graecia revertetur"[1].

22.   Iste igitur Chaba filius Ethelae est legitimus ex filia Honorii imperatoris Graecorum genitus, cui Edemen et Ed filii sui sunt vocati[2]. Edemen autem, cum Hungari in Pannoniam secundario sunt reversi, cum maxima familia patris sui et matris introivit, nam mater eius de Corosminis orta erat. Ed[a] vero in Scitia remansit apud patrem. Ex isto enim Chaba generatio Abae est egressa. Cum igitur Chaba adiens in Scithiam nobilitate genitricis in communi se iactaret, Hunorum nobilitas ipsum contemnebat, asserentes eum non verum esse[b] alumnum regni Scitiae, sed quasi missitalium exterae nationis, propter quod ex Scitia uxorem non accepit, sed traduxit de gente Corosmina[3].

23.   Postquam autem filii Ethelae in praelio Crunhelt cum gente Scitica fere quasi deperissent, Pannonia extitit X. annis sine rege, Sclavis tantummodo, Graecis, Teutonicis,

[a] Eed *K*

[b] esse verum *H*

---

[1] This saying survives in modern Székely tradition, but not with the negative connotation, i.e. that the return of a (disliked) person is not really looked forward to (since Csaba never returned).

[2] The Anonymus (chs. 9–10) implies that the aristocratic Aba clan, the family of Samuel of Aba, king of Hungary 1040–44, were of Cuman—more plausibly, Kabar—origin. There was a count palatine Csaba from the Aba clan in the time of St. Stephen (not to be confused

Greece; the common people have preserved a saying among themselves which they address to a person departing: "May you return when Csaba returns from Greece!"[1]

22. Csaba was Attila's legitimate son by the daughter of the Greek emperor Honorius. Csaba in turn had two sons, Edemen and Ed.[2] Edemen entered Pannonia with his father's and mother's great entourage (his mother being a Chorasminian) when the Hungarians came back for the second time, whereas Ed remained in Scythia with his father. Csaba is the ancestor of the clan of Aba. When Csaba came to Scythia and boasted in the community of his mother's high birth, the Hunnish nobility treated him with scorn, saying that he was little better than a half-breed from a foreign nation, and not a true scion of the Scythian realm. For this reason he did not take a wife from Scythia, but brought one from the Chorasminians.[3]

23. So almost all Attila's sons and the Scythians perished in the battle of Krimhild, and for ten years afterwards there was no king in Pannonia. The only people left there were immigrants—Slavs, Greeks, Germans, Moravians, and

with chieftain Csaba who lived in the 9th century). At the end of the 13th century the Aba kindred acquired a possession called the Field of Csaba; this may have been known to Simon.

[3] Cf. *SRH* 1, ch. 22, 280. Ed and Edemen (or Edumen) were mentioned by the Anonymus as well, perhaps invented as mythical ancestors from 1 Sam. 6:11–12, "the Lord blessed Obed-Edom and all who lived with him" (Györffy, *Krónikáink*, 208, 232). — Chorasminian means here Muslim, referring to the "Káliz" people, cf. Simon ch. 6 and note 5, p. 19 above. — On the alleged disapproval of Csaba's marriage by the "Hun nobility," see Szűcs, above pp. LXVII–LXIX.

Messianis et Vlachis[a] advenis remanentibus in eadem[1], qui
vivente Ethela populari servitio sibi serviebant. Surrexit
tandem Zvataplug[b] filius Morot, princeps quidam in Polonia, qui Bracta subiugando Bulgaris Messianisque imperabat, incipiens similiter in Pannonia[c] post Hunnorum
exterminium dominari[2]. Hunc quidem Hungari de fluvio
Hung variis muneribus allectum et nunciis explorantes,
considerata militia illius immunita, ipsum Zvataplug irrup-
tione subita [SRH, 164] prope fluvium Racus, iuxta Ban-
hida, in quodam oppido, cuius interrupta adhuc eminent,
cum tota militia peremerunt, et sic Pannoniae populis, qui
superius sunt notati, inceperunt dominari[3]. Tradunt quidam, quod Hungari Morot, non Zvataplug in secundo
eorum reditu in Pannonia reperissent principantem. Hoc

[a] Ulahis *H, E*

[b] Zvatapolug *H*

[c] Pannonias *H*

---

[1] Cf. *SRH* ch. 23, 280–82. When listing the peoples of Hungary, the
Anonymus (ch. 9) names Slavs, Bulgarians, and Vlachs; the others are
Simon's addition. The meaning of *Messianis* is debated; ch. 32 suggests
the author meant the Moravians.

[2] The Moravian prince Svatopluk (870–94) in fact died before the
Hungarians arrived in the Carpathian basin. Regino's chronicle, one of
the author's sources (ad ann. 895, p. 143), mentions Svatopluk
("Zuendibolch") together with the invading Hungarians, but it was
Regino's practice to subsume the events of several years under one
entry. — Svatopluk's imaginary realm—embracing the entire East
Central Europe—is pure fiction. There is no reason to connect him
with Poland, though the variant reading *Svatopolug* may imply a pun
with *Polak* 'Pole.' On Svatopluk and the Moravians see Wolfram,
Geburt Mitteleuropas, 359–68, and Sós, *Slawische Bevölkerung*. — The

Vlachs[1]—who had been base-born servants of Attila when the king was alive. Finally Svatopluk, the son of Marót, a prince in Poland, who had subdued Bactra and ruled as emperor of the Bulgars and the Moravians, proceeded to make himself lord of Pannonia once the Huns had been eliminated.[2] However, the Hungarians on the river Ung lured Svatopluk away with a variety of presents; they then sent messengers to appraise the situation. After sizing up Svatopluk's ill-equipped host, they suddenly fell upon him by the river Rákos near Bánhida, slaughtering him and all his men in a certain town whose ruins are still visible. As a result the Hungarians succeeded as overlords of the above-mentioned peoples of Pannonia.[3] Another tradition recounts that it was not Svatopluk but his father Marót whom the Hungarians found ruling in Pannonia on their

imaginary country of Bracta may perhaps have something to do with Bactria in the histories of Alexander, or may be a pun on the word *bractari* ('inebriate, delude') which appears in the former Hungarian Chronicle version in the present context (*SRH* 1: 281, 2: 30).

[3] The sentence "With a variety of presents . . . " much abbreviates the account in the Anonymus, ch. 14, where the motif of buying the land with symbolic presents suggests that some details of this account of the conquest are borrowed from earlier Hungarian legends. The Anonymus has the Hungarians travel via the Carpathian mountains to the river Ung, which accords with his derivation of the name "Hungarian" from the name of the river (today Uż or Uh), cf. below ch. 25. — Bánhida is now part of the city of Tatabánya, with a bridge (Hung. *híd*) over the creek formerly called the Rákos. The medieval main road between Buda and the west crossed the Rákos at Bánhida. The ruins, which Simon takes to be the site of a battle, were probably near present-day Környe, an ancient Roman fortification which may have been called Vincentia.

idcirco esse habetur, quia Morot pater eius nomine maior erat, sed confectus senio repausabat in castro, quod Bezprem nominatur. Audito infortunio, quod filio acciderat, morte subita ob dolorem finivit vitam suam. Filius vero in dominando novus erat.[1]

EXPLICIT LIBER PRIMUS DE[a] INTROITU

INCIPIT SECUNDUS LIBER DE REDITU

24. [D]igestis igitur Hunorum natalibus, praeliis felicibus et sinistris, quotiensque sua loca immutaverint, nunc videndum est, quo tempore redierint in Pannoniam iterato et qui fuerint redeuntium capitanei quantusque numerus armatorum, praesenti opusculo apponere dignum duxi[2].

25. Imperante igitur Ottone Svevo in Germania et Italia, in Francia Lodowico rege[b] Lotarii filio, et Graeciam Antonino Duro filio Theodori gubernante, D-oCCC-o LXXII-o anno ab incarnatione Iesu Christi Hunni sive Hungari denuo ingressi in Pannoniam [SRH, 165] trans-

---

[a] primo *H add.*
[b] regis *K*

---

[1] By "another tradition" the author is referring to the Anonymus; the latter's name for this prince is "Ménmarót," from the Hungarian *marót* 'Moravian.' — Veszprém is a city north of Lake Balaton and the Bakony mountains. It was one of the earliest centres of the Árpád dynasty, the

second entry. The basis for this story seems to be that Marót was the better known name, but being old and weak he was resting in his castle called Veszprém, and when he heard of the disaster which had overwhelmed his son, he was so grief-stricken that he forthwith ended his life. The son, however, was new to the throne.[1]

END OF THE FIRST BOOK, ABOUT THE ENTRY

BEGINNING OF THE SECOND BOOK, ABOUT THE RETURN

24. Thus far we have been discussing the origins of the Huns, their victories and defeats, and their various migrations. Let us now turn to the time when they returned again to Pannonia. This account will include a list of the captains who led the return and the number of warriors under them, information which I thought worthy of inclusion.[2]

25. It was the year 872 of our Lord's incarnation, and in Germany and Italy Otto of Swabia was emperor, Louis, son of Lothar, was on the throne of France, and Antoninus Durus, the son of Theodore, was governor of Greece, when the Huns, or Hungarians, entered Pannonia once again.

probable seat of the first bishopric of Hungary, and later associated with the queens of Hungary who were customarily crowned by the bishops of Veszprém. The Anonymus claims that it had formerly been occupied by the Romans.

[2] Cf. *SRH* 1, ch. 25, 283. On Simon's notion of the arrival of the Hungarians as a return, see Szűcs, above p. LIV.

ierunt, per regna Bessorum, Alborum Comanorum et civitatem Kyo[1], et deinde in fluvio Hung vocato, ubi castrum fundavere, resederunt. A quo quidem fluvio Hungari a gentibus occidentis sunt vocati. Cumque et alia VI. castra[2] post hunc fundavissent, aliquandiu in illis partibus permansere.

26. Tandemque Zvatapolug[a] interempto quemadmodum superius est narratum, in VII exercitus sunt divisi,[3] ita quidem, ut unus exercitus sine centurionibus decurionibusque unum haberet capitaneum, cui tanquam duci deberent unanimiter intendere ac parere[4]. Habebat enim unus exercitus XXX. millia virorum armatorum exceptis decurionibus ac praefectis. Egressi ergo vexillis erectis cum

[a] Zvataplug *H, E*

---

[1] Cf. *SRH* 1, ch. 26, 284–86. In spite of the apparent chronological exactitude—following the style of chancellery documents—the characters are fictitious: Otto may be Otto duke of Swabia (973–82) and Bavaria (976–82), or Odo of Paris (West Frankish king, 888–98); Louis, may be Louis II (Frankish emperor 850–75), while Antoninus Durus, presumably intended as a reference to a Byzantine emperor, is entirely fictitious. The year 872 is obscure; the number 72 may derive from the traditional historical chronology–72 years separate 445 (supposed death of Attila, instead of 453) and 373 (assumed exodus of the Huns from Scythia)—but the date is in fact not too far from 895–96, the historical date of the Hungarian conquest. While in ch. 7 Simon misdates the Hun's departure from Scythia in order to strengthen "historical claims," the difference here of 20 years is not explicable by any historical construct. — Simon follows the Anonymus and the earlier Hungarian chronicles for the route of the Hungarian migration (Pechenegs, White Cumans, Kiev). The Old Russian Annals record

They passed through the realms of the Pechenegs and the White Cumans and by the city of Kiev,[1] and finally settled on the river Ung, where they built a fortress. The name the Western peoples give them, the Hungarians, derives from this river. After this they proceeded to build six other castles[2] and remained in that region for some time.

26. After finally disposing of Svatopluk, as recounted above, they divided into seven hosts,[3] each having besides centurions or decurions a single commander to whom unanimous obedience was due, as its leader (a host contained 30,000 warriors, not counting decurions and higher ranks).[4] Thereupon they raised their banners and moved

that the migrating Hungarians passed the city of Kiev in 898 (*PSRL*, 1; *PLV*), but we do not know whether these annals were known to medieval Hungarian historians.

[2] Like the Anonymus, Simon derives the name of the Hungarians from the river Ung. The total of seven castles may allude to the German name for Transylvania, Siebenbürgen (which in fact derived from a local river, the Szeben or Zibin; see Binder, "Siebenbürgen").

[3] Cf. *SRH* 1, ch. 27, 286–87; ch. 54, 304. The seven conquering Hungarian tribes are explicitly commemorated in Anonymus's word *Hetumoger* (modern Hung. *hét* 'seven,' *magyar* 'Hungarian'); Constantine Porphyrogenitus also notes that "the Turks were seven clans . . ." (*De administrando imperio* 38.171.

[4] People governed directly by the king, such as the Székely, other privileged military groups, and servile elements on royal estates, who also had the responsibility of collecting taxes, had officers known as "*centuriones*," who were assisted by "*decuriones*" in charge of a tenth of a century; see the law of Ladislas I (*DRMH* I: 18), and cf. Göckenjan, "Stammesstruktur"; Györffy, *Wirtschaft*, 93–101).

uxoribus, liberis et armentis Danubium in Pest et in portu
Zub transierunt, ubi castrum quoddam circa Danubium, in
quo erant milites Zvataplug recollecti, qui fuere erepti per
fugam, quando dominus ipsorum interierat, expugnarunt.
In quo quidem affinem Morot nimis vetulum cum aliis
perimentes, usque hodie fabulose Morot ipsum fuisse asseverant[1].

27.　　Ex istis ergo capitaneis Arpad, filius Almi, filii Elad,
filii Vger de genere Turul rebus ditior erat et potentior
gente[2]. Hic igitur Arpad cum gente sua Ruthenorum Alpes
prior perforavit, et in fluvio Ung primus fixit sua castra,
eo quod eius prosapia ista prae caeteris Scitiae tribubus
praerogativa investitur dignitate, ut exercitum praecedit
in eundo, retrograditur redeuntem[3]. [SRH, 166] Et cum
transmeato Danubio Pannoniam introissent, ipse Arpad in

---

[1] Both Pest and Szob (at the confluence of the river Ipoly and the
Danube) have been important crossing points since the Middle Ages.
The name of the settlement opposite Szob, Marót (today Pilismarót),
the remains of Roman watchtowers along the Danube, and local folklore may have influenced the author's choice of setting for this episode.

[2] Cf. *SRH* 1, ch. 28, 287. Árpád was founder of the dynasty which ruled
Hungary till 1301. In the Anonymus, Árpád is the son of Álmos, the
son of Ügyek, who was from the kindred of Magóg. Constantine
Porphyrogenitus also mentions Árpád and Álmos: " . . . there is a
voivode . . . called Almoutzis, and he has a son called Arpad" (38.173).
The Anonymus, on the other hand, omits Előd in the genealogy of

out, taking with them their wives, children, and livestock. They crossed the Danube at Pest at the riverport of Szob, after seizing a nearby fortress occupied by soldiers of Svatopluk who had escaped after the death of their lord and regathered there. Among the occupants killed was a very ancient relative of Marót—this gave rise to a story they repeat to this day, that this person was Marót himself.[1]

27. Among these captains Árpád the son of Álmos son of Előd son of Ügyek, of the Turul kindred, was richer in possessions and enjoyed a more powerful following.[2] Árpád and his clan were the first to forge their way through the Ruthenian Alps and to pitch camp by the river Ung, as his family enjoyed the prerogative among the Scythian tribes of advancing at the head of the host when it marched forward, and at the rear when it returned.[3] They then crossed the Danube and entered Pannonia, Árpád setting

Árpád (ch. 6), and connects him with the chieftain Szabolcs. — The *de genere Turul* formula ("of the Turul kindred") refers here to the similarity of the royal dynasty and a noble kindred, cf. also Simon, ch. 10. The reference to the *turul*, Attila's totem, seems to imply that Simon also accepted the genealogical connection between Árpád and Attila, which the Anonymus makes specifically.

[3] Nomadic tribes like the 9th-century Hungarians would have placed their inferior troops up front; in referring to this position as a prerogative Simon is thinking in chivalric terms. He would have found comparable descriptions in the Alexander romances and in the narrative parts of contemporary royal charters (cf. Rodericus de Rada *Historia* 8.9, p. 271, and for a general overview of knightly warfare, see Verbruggen, *Art of Warfare*).

loco illo fixit tabernacula, ubi modo Albensis[a] civitas est fundata. Illeque locus primus descensus existit Arpad ducis[1].

28. Alterius vero exercitus capitaneus Zobole vocabatur, qui in eo loco fixit sua castra, ubi modo Chakwara[b] iacet desolata. Ab isto Zobole generatio Chak esse habet[2].

29. Tertii quidem exercitus Iula fuit capitaneus. Hic, licet[c] cum aliis in[d] Pannoniam introisset, in partibus Erdevelu tandem habitavit[3].

30. Sed quarti capitaneus Vrs est nominatus; iste circa flumen Soio sua tabernacula fixisse perhibetur[4].

[a] Albensis *H*, Albana *K*, Alben *E*

[b] Chakvara *H*

[c] iacet *K*, *H*; *E om.*

[d] in *H om.*

---

[1] Together with Esztergom, Fehérvár (today Székesfehérvár) was the most significant city of medieval Hungary and the usual coronation and burial site of the Hungarian kings. The connection with Árpád is perhaps not entirely unfounded, as a certain "Valley of Árpád" (Árpád-völgy) in the vicinity of Székesfehérvár was referred to in 1193 (*ÁMTF* 2: 325; Deér, "Aachen," 5–31). Toponyms suggest that the true residence of Duke Árpád may have been by the Danube near modern Budapest.

up his tents at the place where later the city of Székesfehérvár was founded. This place was Duke Árpád's first
residence.[1]

28. The leader of the second host, Szabolcs, pitched camp
where the ruins of Csákvár now stand. Szabolcs is held to
be the ancestor of the Csák kindred.[2]

29. The third host was commanded by Gyula. Although
he came into Pannonia with the others, Gyula finally settled in Transylvania.[3]

30. The name of the captain of the fourth host was Örs.
Örs is said to have set up camp by the river Sajó.[4]

[2] Cf. *SRH* 1, ch. 29, 290. Szabolcs is also mentioned in the Anonymus,
chs. 6 and 50, in the same context. Szabolcs's name survived as an
ancient (and present) county of Szabolcs in Northeast Hungary, but
it has no known connection with this kindred. Csákvár, in western
Hungary, was the centre of the ancestral territory of the Csák kindred,
one of the most powerful Hungarian kindreds.

[3] Cf. *SRH* 1, ch. 30, 290. The Anonymus (ch. 6) and Simon offer
different theories about Gyula. In fact, the name was the title of a
dignitary, the warlord (Heerkönig) in the tribal age before Árpád (cf.
notes 1, p. 84 and 4, p. 102). — *Erdevelu* (modern *Erdély*) 'over the
forest' is the Hung. equivalent of Transylvania. See also note 2, p. 79.

[4] Cf. *SRH* 1, ch. 34, 292. The Anonymus refers to Örs as a Cuman
(ch. 8), not as one of the seven Hungarian chieftains. Simon correctly
locates the possessions of the Örsúr ('Lord Örs') kindred along the
river Sajó, in Eastern Hungary.

31. Quinti vero exercitus Cund[a] est dictus capitaneus. Hic circa Nyr habitavit, huius filii Cusid[b] et Cupian sunt vocati[1].

32. Lel[c] ergo exercitus sexti ductor fuerat. Iste circa Golgocha[d] primitus habitans, exinde Messianis[2] et Boemis [SRH, 167] exstirpatis, tandem in partibus Nitriae[e] saepius fertur habitasse. Ex isto Zuard oritur tribus et cognatio[3].

33. Septimi siquidem exercitus Werbulchu[f] dux est dictus. Hic in Zala, circa lacum Boloton[g] descendisse perhibetur. Pro eo enim Werbulchu[h] est vocatus, quia cum avus eius in praelio Crimildino per Teutonicos fuisset interfectus, et id ei pro certo constitisset, volens recipere vindictam super eos, plures Germanicos[i] assari fecit super veru et

---

[a] Eund *H*

[b] Eusid *H*

[c] Iel *K*

[d] Golgotha *H*

[e] Nittriae *K*

[f] Verbulchu *H*

[g] Bolotim *H*, Bolotum *E*

[h] Verbulchu *H*

[i] Germanos *H*

---

[1] Cf. *SRH* 1, ch. 31, 291. According to the Anonymus (ch. 6), Künd (*Cundu*) was the father not of Küsid but of Kursan (for whom see Wolfram, *Geburt Mitteleuropas*, 542). Künd—also in the form Kende—was in fact the title of a Hungarian dignitary, probably the sacral ruler.

31. The leader of the fifth host, Künd, settled in the Nyírség region. His sons were named Küsid and Kaplony.[1]

32. Lél was the commander of the sixth host. It is stated in many accounts that Lél first dwelt near Hlohovec and afterwards settled in the region around Nitra once the Moravians[2] and Bohemians were eliminated. He was the ancestor of the Zovárd tribe and kindred.[3]

33. The leader of the seventh army was called Vérbulcsu. He is said to have settled at Zala around Lake Balaton. The reason he was called Vérbulcsu was that, having learnt of his grandfather's death at the hands of the Germans in the battle of Krimhild, he exacted vengeance by having a number of Germans roasted on a spit [veru], and is said to

The Kaplony kindred considered Küsid as their forefather, and their monastery was in the Nyírség region (at Kaplony, today Căpleni in Romania). Györffy argued that the last sacred ruler died ca. 905, and that this opened the path for the Árpád clan to attain pre-eminence.

[2] Cf. *SRH* 1, chs. 32, 291–92. Hlohovec and Nitra are mentioned in the Anonymus (ch. 33, 37) as centres of the Slavs under Bohemian sovereignty, which were invaded by the Hungarian captains Zovárd (Szovárd), Kadocsa, and Huba. In medieval Hungary Nitra was the centre of County Nyitra and the seat of a bishopric; cf. *LMas* 6: 1201–2.

[3] Lél (traditionally spelt Lehel in Hungarian) is a descriptive name, from *lélegzet* or *lehelet*, Hungarian for respiration and breath. In the Anonymus (ch. 6) Lél is mentioned as a military leader, and his father Tas is named as one of the seven conquering chieftains, while Zovárd is stated to be a relative of chieftain Álmos. The village of Lél—now a field-name—in Northwest Hungary was a possession of the Szovárd kindred. The ancestral lands of the Zovárd kindred were in Counties Komárom and Esztergom.

tanta crudelitate in eos dicitur[a] exarsisse, quod quorumdam quoque sanguinem bibit sicut vinum[1]. Isti quidem capitanei loca descensumque, ut superius est dictum, sibi elegerunt, similiter et generationes aliae ubi eis placuit eligentes.

34. Cum autem resedissent Pannonia occupata, tandem Moraviam et Boemiam bonis omnibus spoliarunt Waratizlao eorum duce in praelio interfecto[2].

35. Post haec vero Carinthiam hostiliter adeuntes, ultra castrum Leopah Meraniae[b] dux Gotfridus nomine duxque Eburhardus cum Aquilegiensi patriarcha ipsis occurrentes atrociter insimul pugnaverunt. Et quamvis ex Hungaris plures corruissent in praelio memorato, utrique[c] duces occiduntur patriarcha per fugam liberato. Abinde spoliata Carinthia, Styria et Carniola[d], cum maxima praeda in Pannoniam revertuntur[3].

[a] crudelitate dicitur *H*

[b] Meraniae *E*, Ineraniae *K*, Vieraniae *H*

[c] uterque *K*

[d] Carniolia *H, E*

[1] Cf. *SRH* 1, ch. 33, 292. The Anonymus refers to Vérbulcsu simply as Bulcsu (ch. 39). The first element is Hung. *vér* 'blood,' but Simon also plays on Latin *veru* 'skewer.' Making him a grandson of a participant in the battle of Krimhild confirms the chronology at the beginning of ch. 25. Constantine Porphyrogenitus also mentions a Bulcsu (Boultzous) who was baptised by the emperor around the year 948 and awarded the title *patricius* (ch. 40). — Zala is a county bordering on Lake Balaton, and the lands of the Vérbulcsu kindred were indeed in this region (*KMTL*, 132–33).

have behaved with such savagery to them that he drank the blood of certain captives as though it were wine.[1] So these captains chose the above-mentioned places to settle, and the other kindreds settled wherever they liked.

34.   After occupying and settling Pannonia, they subsequently raided Moravia and Bohemia, pillaging everything and slaying Duke Vratislav in battle.[2]

35.   Next they mounted an expedition against Carinthia. There they were met by Duke Geoffrey of Merania and Duke Eberhard and the patriarch of Aquileia beyond the castle of Ljubljana. A bloody battle ensued. The Hungarians lost many of their men in this fight, but the two dukes were also killed, and the patriarch only escaped by flight. Thereupon they ravaged Carinthia, Styria, and Carniola, and returned to Pannonia with vast quantities of booty.[3]

[2] Cf. *SRH* 1, ch. 54, 304. Vratislav was a Bohemian duke who died in 921 fighting against the Hungarians (*Handbuch*, 214). Some, however, have taken Simon's allusion to refer to another figure, a certain Brazlawo mentioned as the last Frankish *dux Pannoniae* in the *Annales Fuldenses* (ad ann. 884, 892, 896).

[3] Cf. *SRH* 1, ch. 55, 304. The castle of Ljubljana is mentioned in records from the middle of the 13th century. — The text in *SRH* runs: *dux Meranie Gothfridus nominatus et dux Carinthie Eberhardus, necnon Gregorius Aquilegie patriarcha*. But there was no duke of Andechs-Merania by the name of *Gottfridus*; indeed, there were no dukes of Meran before the middle of the 12th century. Eberhard may be based on Duke Bernhard of Spanheim (1202–56), while the *Gregorius* of the *SRH* may refer to Patriarch Gregory of Montelongo (1251–69).

36. Conradus vero imperator, ut audivit lacerationem [SRH, 168] gentis suae, exiens de Italia intravit Augustam Sveviae civitatem, ut exinde in Hungariam introiret Hungaros invasurus. Sed interea Romae bellum generatur intestinum et caesar Romam redit[1].

37. Tunc Hungari exeuntes intrant in Bulgariam, ex qua armenta et captivos extrahunt infinitos, redeuntes tandem cum victoria in Pannoniam.

38. Tempore iterum alio per Forum Iulii intrant Lombardiam, ubi Luitardum Wercellenae civitatis episcopum, imperatoris Caruli consiliarum fidissimum[2] occidentes, ex ipsius ecclesia thesaurum maximum rapuerunt, totaque pene[a] Lombardia demolita cum maxima praeda in Pannoniam revertuntur.

39. Post haec Saxoniam, Turingiam, Sveviam, Reno circa Maguntiam transpassato, orientalem Franciam et Burgundiam demoliti ecclesias etiam plures destruxerunt. Et cum Renum in Constantia in reditu pertransissent et cum maximo onere venissent in Bavariam, circa castrum Abah

[a] bene *K*

---

[1] Cf. *SRH* 1, ch. 56, 305. In fact Conrad (911–18) was king of the Germans. However, his trip to Rome is an assumption on Simon's part; Simon's source, the Hungarian chronicles, reads simply: *inter Romanos bellum generatum est intestinum, propter quod ipsum retrocedere oportebat.* Later German legends tell of a king Conrad who fought the Hungarians (Wisniewski, "*Pestis patriae*," 355). A century later Conrad II did invade Hungary.

36.   When Emperor Conrad heard of the savage defeat inflicted on his people, he marched from Italy to Augsburg, a city in Swabia, in order to invade Hungary and strike the Hungarians from there. In the meantime, however, civil war broke out in Rome, and the emperor returned there.[1]

37.   Then the Hungarians marched out into Bulgaria, from where they took untold numbers of cattle and prisoners before returning in triumph to Pannonia.

38.   In a further campaign they invaded Lombardy via Friuli. They murdered Liutward, the bishop of Vercelli and Emperor Charles' most faithful counsellor,[2] and stole vast treasures from his church. Then after devastating nearly all of Lombardy they returned to Pannonia with an enormous amount of plunder.

39.   They next raided Saxony, Thuringia, Swabia, and, after crossing the Rhine at Mainz, eastern France and Burgundy, destroying many churches into the bargain. On their return they crossed the Rhine at Constance and were passing into Bavaria heavy-laden when a German army

---

[2] Cf. *SRH* 1, ch. 57–58, 305–6. The Bulgarian raid is mentioned by the Anonymus (chs. 41, 45). The incursions into Italy in 899–900 are based on Regino's account (ad ann. 901) and the Anonymus (ch. 53). But the word *consiliarius* "counsellor" only occurs in Regino's text and not in the Anonymus, another indication that Simon or one of his sources had used Regino's work directly. — Liutward was bishop of Vercelli from 879/880 till 887, and the chancellor and close associate of Emperor Charles III (i.e. the Frankish king Charles the Fat, d. 888). His murder by the Hungarians took place in 899 (Fasoli, *Incursioni*, 98–99).

Alamannicus exercitus ipsos invadit ex abrupto[1]. Quibus viriliter resistentibus, praelio confecto Teutonici sagittis devincuntur. Ubi [SRH, 169] capitur Hertnidus de Svaurchunbrac[a] imperatoris mariscalcus[2], id est militiae suae princeps et alii quamplures nobiles cum eodem, et licet inaestimabilem pecuniam pro redemptione eorum tradidissent, ante Ratisponam in signum positi, sagittis crudelissime, civibus in muro stantibus et admirantibus, perforantur[3]. Et sic tandem cum victoria et praeda maxima ad propria revertuntur.

40. Transactis igitur paucis temporibus Lel et Bulchu per communitatem Hungarorum in Teutoniam destinantur et cum Augustam pervenissent ultra fluvium Lyh, in prato fixere sua castra, civitatem diuturnis et nocturnis bellis molestantes. Cumque subitis saltibus capere non valerent, obstinati nolentes recedere de suburbio, Vrricus episcopus cum civibus, ad caesarem missis nunciis, animant eum, ut succurrat civitati, quia Hungari obsidentes eos, licet sint

[a] Svaurchumburc *H*, Svarchumburc *E*

---

[1] Cf. *SRH* 1, ch. 59, 306–7. For these campaigns cf. Regino for the years 902–12, and the Anonymus, ch. 54. The battle at Abbach perhaps occurred in 913. Abbach was a famous castle, a few km. West of Regensburg; the 15th-century humanist Aventinus reports the emperor Henry II was born here. Aventinus is also our only other source for Abbach as a target of Hungarian raids (*Annales Boiorum* 5.21).

[2] Hertnid von Schwarzenburg (also -berg, -bruck) is another unidentified character; but Hertnid was a common name in the kindred of the Wildonier in Styria, who, although referred to as "of Riegersburg," had

suddenly fell upon them near the castle of Abbach.[1] They fought back stoutly and in the event the Germans were finally overwhelmed by the Hungarians' arrows. In the battle Hertnid of Schwarzenburg, the Emperor's marshal[2] (that is, the head of his army), was taken prisoner, and numerous other nobles as well. Although an incalculable amount of money was paid for their ransom, they were set in front of the walls of Regensburg as targets and shot to death with arrows in the cruellest manner while the citizens stood and watched in appal from the walls.[3] After this the victorious Hungarians returned home with vast plunder.

40. Not long after the community of Hungarians sent Lél and Bulcsu to the land of the Germans. Arriving at Augsburg beyond the river Lech they pitched camp in the meadows and mounted attacks upon the city day and night. Though they were unable to take the city by rapid assaults, they stubbornly refused to retire from the outlying parts of the town. Hereupon Bishop Ulric and his fellow-citizens sent messengers to the emperor urging him to come to the aid of the city: though the Hungarians besieging

a possession called Schwarzenegg, whence perhaps "Schwarzenburg" (Frizberg, "Wildon"; Posch, "Riegersburg"). — The word *mariscalcus* ("marshal") was known in Hungarian Latinity as well; a charter of 1255 reads: *marschalcus regis Ungarorum in Styria* (*Steirisches Urkundenbuch*, vol. 3, no. 163).

[3] While the whole episode is fictitious, the Hungarians during their 9th-century raids might often have approached Regensburg; late medieval local legends like the Dollinger-Saga tell of duels between local heroes and pagan challengers (Kunstmann, "Craco").

plurimi, non se custodiunt, qui facillime poterunt debellari. Egressus itaque imperator de Ulmensi curia, veniens celeriter et absconse, explorato processu et exercitu Hungarorum, in hora tertia, cum plueret, irruit super eos et unum exercitum viciniorem civitati festinanter debellavit. Quo viso Lel et Bulchu fugae remedium quaeritantes in navem se colligunt submittentes se per Danubium, ut fugiant in Hungariam. Qui quidem in transitu Ratisponae captivati caesari transmittuntur. Quos caesar iudicio suspendii condemnando Ratisponae fecit occidi in patibulo[1]. Quidam vero ipsos aliter damnatos fabulose asseverant, quod caesari praesentati unus illorum cum tuba in caput ipsum caesarem occidisset feriendo[2]. Quae sane fabula verosimili adversatur et credens huiusmodi levitate mentis denotatur. Nam personae criminosae ligatis manibus conspectui principum praesentantur. Verum quidem est, et libri continent[a] cronicarum[3], ut blasphemati audacter caesari muriose sunt locuti asserentes,quod si ipsos occidi fecerit, de gente sua de caetero nullus captus vivere poterit,

[a] liber continet *H*

---

[1] Cf. *SRH* 1, ch. 60, 307–8. Simon, unlike the Anonymus, records the massive defeat the Hungarians suffered at Lechfeld near Augsburg on 10 August 955. — Bishop Ulric (d. 973) is the first recorded saint to be formally canonised (in 993) by a pope in Rome. — In the sources of this campaign Ulm is mentioned only by Simon, perhaps because he had visited the region. — That the Hungarian chieftains were hanged in Regensburg on 15 August is confirmed in other historical sources, including the Anonymus, ch. 55.

[2] The tale of Lél's horn is rooted in Hungarian oral tradition. The Anonymus was not familiar with the version of the legend recorded by

them were very numerous, they had not mounted any watch and could easily be crushed. The emperor thereupon set out from his court at Ulm, reaching the city after a swift and secret march. He sized up the Hungarian army and observed their movements. Then he fell upon them at the third hour during a rainstorm, swiftly overwhelming the army which was nearer the city. When they saw what had happened, Lél and Bulcsu sought remedy in flight. They boarded a boat and set off down the Danube, hoping to make Hungary. However, they were intercepted as they passed Regensburg and sent captive to the emperor. The emperor condemned them to be hanged, and they were executed on the gallows at Regensburg.[1] Some authors give a different version of their fate, telling a fanciful story of how when they were brought before the emperor one of them struck the emperor on the head with his trumpet and killed him.[2] Of course this is quite implausible, and anyone believing such a tale would be making an exhibition of his credulity. After all, felons are normally brought before princes with their hands bound. The truth, as recorded in the chronicles,[3] is that they foolishly uttered shameless blasphemies before the emperor and said that if they were put to death, in future no German captives would be

Simon and only remarks that Lél blew his horn. The motif of the use of a horn in imminent danger recalls the legends of Roland and of Solomon and Markolf, while oriental parallels of the Hungarian legend were recorded by William of Rubruck (ch. 9).

[3] Simon's critique of folk tradition by reference to judicial procedure is noteworthy. It is, however, unclear which are the truthful chronicles he refers to; the Illuminated Chronicle (*SRH* 1: 307–9) has a more elaborate but similarly fanciful version.

sed vel in perpetuam tradetur servitutem, aut nullo iudicio praecedente occidetur. Quod et factum est. Quia ut Hungari audierunt,ut caesar sic ipsos occidisset, omnes [SRH, 170] captivos Teutonicos, tam mulieres quam parvulos usque ad XX. millia iugularunt.

41. Alius vero exercitus, qui distabat ab Augusta, impetum caesaris ut praesensit[a] super socios, in unam sylvam se collegit, et ut eius exercitum dispersum recognovit, persecutus est maiorem aciem gentis suae, quae tendebat versus Renum. Quam[b] in campo coniungens cursitando, se insimul adunavit sicut apes: quam[c] sagittis vulnerando nec descendere, nec recedere permiserunt, qui se tandem velut mortuos in manus dederunt Hungarorum. Quos quidem ut ceperunt, omnibus caput detruncarunt pro exequiis sociorum. Fuerant autem numero milites et scutiferi quasi[d] octo millia, quorum capita sunt truncata. Abinde egressi postmodum Danubii fluvium in Ulma transierunt, et ad Vultense caenobium cum venissent, thesaurum magnum exinde rapuerunt, et post haec tota Svevia demolita Renum Vuormaciae transierunt, ibique duos duces, scillicet Loteringiae et Sveviae cum maximo exercitu contra eos venientes invenerunt. Quibus devictis et fugatis tandem Franciam intraverunt, ubi Christianis et cenobitis persecutio valida facta est per eosdem. Exinde autem egressi usque fluvium

[a] persensit *H, E*

[b] Quem *K*

[c] quos *K*

[d] quidem *K*

allowed to live but would either be condemned to servitude forever or put to death without trial. So indeed it was done; for when the Hungarians heard that the emperor had executed them in this manner, they strangled all their German prisoners, 20,000 persons in all, even the women and children.

41. However, when the other army, which was some distance from Augsburg, got news of the emperor's attack on their comrades they gathered in a forest, and as soon as they ascertained that the enemy force had split up they trailed the main body, which was making for the Rhine. Moving swiftly, the Hungarians caught up with the enemy in open country, gathering round suddenly like a swarm of bees, and harried them with arrows so that they could neither dig in nor retreat. In the end the Germans, who were almost dead, gave themselves up. Once they were in their hands the Hungarians beheaded every man in retribution for their slaughtered comrades; the number of the warriors and their squires who were beheaded came to 8,000. The Hungarians then departed, crossed the Danube at Ulm, and reached the monastery of Fulda, which they plundered of a great deal of its treasure. They laid waste the whole of Swabia, then crossed the Rhine at Worms. Here they came upon two dukes, from Lorraine and Swabia, advancing against them with a very large army. However, they succeeded in defeating and routing them, and finally entered France, where they began a savage persecution of the Christians and the monks. From there they advanced

Rodani Ragusium[a] venientes[1], duas civitates, scilicet Segu-
sam et Taurinam spoliarunt, per Alpes Italiae sibi viam
praeparando. Et cum planum vidissent [SRH, 171] Lonbardiae, concitatis cursibus spolia multa rapuerunt et sic
tandem ad propria revertuntur. Postquam vero Lel et Bulchu, ut superius est narratum, interissent, exercitus siluit,
non intrans ulterius in Germaniam. Nam Francia et Germania unanimiter concordantes simul in unum adunati
venientibus Hungaris deberent resistere usque vitam.
Propterea Hungari in Alamanniam usque tempora regis
Stephani semper ire dubitabant, ne gens occidentis eos
invaderet simul adunata[2].

42.   Postquam autem Italiae provincias aliquas spoliassent
V. annis fuere sine motu. Tandem in Bulgariam adeuntes
usque Idropolim pervenerunt, dumque exercitum super se
venientem non vident, usque Constantinopolim venientes
descenderunt prope murum. Tunc Graecus unus magnus
sicut gigans emittitur, qui duos Hungaros cum eo luctari

---

[a] Ragusium *H, E om.*

---

[1] Cf. *SRH* 1, ch. 61, 308–10. The killing of German captives is the work
of the author's imagination, but even the Anonymus inserted a fictitious episode of revenge (ch. 55). This episode is followed by a series
of historical events. For Fulda, Worms, and the Gallic and Italian
campaigns cf. Regino *Chronicon* 155, 159, 168, ad ann. 915, 932, 954
(Fasoli, *Incursioni*, 195). However, according to Szűcs, their itinerary
is a reflection of Simon of Kéza's journey as Hungarian ambassador to
Lyons via northern Italy some time before 1269/70 ("Társadalomelmélet," 866–67). — *cursitando* ("moving swiftly") is from a verb not
otherwise recorded in Hungarian Latinity before the 14th century; the

to [Bourgoin][1] on the river Rhone and plundered two cities, Susa and Turin, thus opening a way through the Italian Alps. When they set eyes on the plain of Lombardy, they made rapid raids and captured a great deal of plunder. Finally they returned home. However, after the deaths of Lél and Bulcsu recorded above, the army rested and would not go into Germany again. For France and Germany had agreed among themselves that they must join forces and resist the incursions of the Hungarians to the death. Thereafter up to the time of King Stephen the Hungarians were always hesitant to enter Germany, for they feared that the Westerners would unite against them and attack them.[2]

42. After raiding some provinces in Italy, the Hungarians did not move for five years. Finally they marched to Bulgaria, advancing as far as Adrianopolis. When they saw that no army was marching against them, they continued as far as Constantinople and camped by the walls. Hereupon a Greek was sent out, a man as big as a giant, who shouted a challenge for two Hungarians to come and wrestle him.

meaning, 'to move, to ride, to attack *more piratico*,' originated in the Dalmatian area and became connected with *huszár, cursor* 'light cavalryman' (see *Lexicon Latinitatis Medii Aevi Jugoslaviae*, vol. 1, 329–30). — *Ragusium* is a corruption of the Latin name of Bourgoin, Bergusium—which Szűcs ("Társadalomelmélet," 577) mistakenly identified as Racconigi in Italy—and an archetypal error in the Latin; the 18th-century copyists either reproduced the erroneous reading or were unable to make sense of it and omitted it.

[2] After 955 the Hungarians did in fact cease their marauding campaigns against Western Europe. In ch. 8 Simon notes the reign of Géza, Stephen's father, as a historical turning point in Hungarian-German relations.

postulabat, vociferans in hunc modum, ut si ambos Hungaros in terram[a] non prostraret, extunc Graecia censualis[b] Hungaris subiaceret. Cumque idem Graecus exercitui esset plurimum infestissimus, quidam Hungarus Botond dictus Graeco opponitur ad luctandum, areaque praeparata arrepto dolabro, quem ferre consueverat, super portam urbis, quae aerea erat, praecucurrit tantamque fissuram in ea fecisse dicitur cum dolabro uno ictu, ut Graeci propter monstram ipsam portam resarcire noluerunt. Quo quidem facto ad aream luctandi[c] inermis aggreditur et ad spectaculum Hungari in equis, Graeci ad muri propugnacula convenerunt. Cumque Graecus exisset de urbe iturus ad aream, vidit Botond solum stantem paratum ad luctandum, exclamavit, quare alium Hungarum[d] non adiungeret sibi in auxilium. Tunc Botond aggresso ipso sic eum comprehendisse perhibetur, ut praeteriit parva hora in luctando, quod Graecus prostratur, non valens resurgere ullo modo. Quo viso Graecorum imperator et alii Graecorum proceres, imperatrix etiam cum suis dispotinis de muro egredientes ad sua palatia perrexerunt, pro summa verecundia, quod acciderat, reputantes. Et licet Graecus sic allisus superviveret cum fracto brachio, occasio tamen sibi fuit ipsa lucta mortis suae. Obtento itaque Hungari certaminis bravio pro censu postulando ad Graecos nuncios destinant, quibus imperator subridendo nullum verbum dicitur respondisse.

[a] terra *K*

[b] censualiter *H*

[c] luctandus *K*

[d] Hungarorum *H*

The terms he offered were that if he could not throw both Hungarians to the ground, then Greece would submit to the Hungarians and pay tribute. As this Greek endlessly harassed the army, a Hungarian called Botond was chosen to wrestle him. The ring had already been prepared when Botond seized the battle-axe he used to carry, ran up to the metal gate of the city, and, according to the story, with one blow of his axe opened such a rent in the gate that the Greeks never after attempted to mend this marvel. After this Botond walked unarmed to the wrestling ring. The two sides gathered to watch, the Hungarians on their horses and the Greeks on the battlements. The Greek emerged from the city and started for the ring. When he saw Botond waiting alone for him, he asked in surprise why he hadn't brought another Hungarian to fight beside him. Hereupon, the story goes, the Greek made a lunge, but Botond grabbed hold of him, a struggle ensued, and in no time the Greek was flat on the ground, quite unable to get up again. At the sight of this the Greek emperor and the leading persons, together with the empress and her ladies, left the walls and retired to their palaces in deep shame for what had taken place. Although the defeated Greek survived with only a broken arm, the wrestling match led to his death. Having won the competition, the Hungarians sent messengers to the Greeks demanding the tribute as their prize; however, the emperor, it seems, answered them with a smile and nothing more. So after taking counsel the Hungarians left Constantinople with their leader Tak-

Tunc Hungari cum Tocsun[1] eorum duce consilio inito
egressi de loco[SRH, 172] illo, totam Graeciam et Bulgariam spoliantes, ex ipsis aurum, gemmas, lapides pre-
tiosos[a], captivos sine numero et armenta infinita rapiunt,
redeuntes tandem cum gaudio in Pannoniam. Istud enim
existit ultimum spolium, quod fecere Hungari sub ritu
paganismo constituti[2]. Communitas itaque Hungarorum
cum suis capitaneis seu ducibus, quos pro tempore praeficere usa erat, usque tempora ducis Geichae hinc inde huic
mundo spolia et pericula dinoscitur intulisse.

43.   Anno vero dominicae incarnationis nongentesimo
sexagesimo septimo Geicha dux divino praemonitus ora-
culo genuit sanctum regem Stephanum[3], Mihal vero, frater[b] Geichae genuit Wazul[c] et Zar Ladislaum[4]. At rex Stephanus plures quidem filios genuit[d], sed super omnes

[a] pretiosas *K*

[b] eius *H add.*

[c] Vazul *H*

[d] genuit filios *H*

---

[1] Cf. *SRH* 1, ch. 62, 310–11. Though the Anonymus gives a different
account of the episode at Constantinople (ch. 42), he also uses the word
dolabrum ("battle-axe") for Botond's weapon. The story is commonly
associated with the Hungarian attack on Byzantium in 958. Breaking
the city gates symbolically means the capture of the city; Boleslaw the
Brave made a cut in the Golden Gate of Kiev with the same symbolic
intention (*Chronica principum Poloniae*, ch. 9, p. 440). Constantinople
also had a Golden Gate (situated at the south end of the land walls,
today part of the Yedikule or 'Seven Towers') which the Anonymus
notes as well, but Simon, expressing his doubts, diminishes it to

sony,[1] and proceeded to lay waste the whole of Greece and Bulgaria, seizing gold, jewels, and precious stones as well as captives and livestock beyond count before finally returning in joy to Pannonia. This, however, was the last raid the Hungarians undertook while living as pagans.[2] Thus it can be seen that the Hungarian community under their captains or leaders chosen for the occasion plundered and threatened our world in various places up to the time of Duke Géza.

43.   In the year of our Lord's incarnation 967 Duke Géza begot the holy king Stephen, after receiving a prophecy of premonition from God.[3] Géza's brother Michael, however, begot Vazul and Ladislas the Bald.[4] King Stephen in turn begot a number of sons, among whom one stands out,

---

"metal." — The root of the name Botond is perhaps a Turkic verb meaning 'to beat, defend.' However, as the word *bot* ('rod, stick') was also used in Hungarian for mace, a favourite weapon of the Pechenegs, the legend itself could be of nomadic, Pecheneg origin (Tóth, "Botond").

[2] For Taksony, cf. note 1, p. 29 — The Hungarians led several raids into South and East Europe, but these are poorly documented. For the Hungarians' raids against Bulgaria, cf. Györffy, "Streifzüge". Their last raid in Southern Europe in fact ended in defeat at Arcadiopolis (Lüle Burgas) in 970.

[3] Cf. *SRH* 1, ch. 63, 311–12. The date 967 is uncertain. The legends of St. Stephen recount the prophetic vision of his mother bearing a son who would christianise his people (*SRH* 2: 379, 404). See Györffy, *Stephen*, 78–81.

[4] Wazul: probably a Hungarian(?) version of Basil/ Vasilij (Váczy, "Vazul"). *Zar Ladislaus* ("Ladislas the Bald"): from old Hung. *szár* 'bald.' Stephen's two cousins will become important later in the story.

unum genuit Emricum nomine, Deo et hominibus ho-
norabilem[1]. Sanctus namque rex Stephanus coronatus[2] et
tandem duce Cuppan[a] interfecto[3], Iula avunculo suo cum
uxore et duobus filiis de Septem Castris in Hungariam
adducto, et adiuncto Septem Castra Pannoniae[4], post haec
cum Kean Bulgarorum duce et Sclavorum praeliatus est[5].
Quo devicto de ipsius thesauro Beatae[b] Virginis ecclesiam
de Alba ditare[c] non omisit, quam fundasse perhibetur[6].

44. Postquam autem magnificavit Dominus misericor-
diam suam cum beato rege Stephano subiecitque eius dominio multarum gentium nationes, statuit pompis huius
saeculi deposito regni diademate renunciare Deique solius
servitio, exterioribus curis expeditus, deditus esse, coronam vero regni Emrico duci, suo filio[d] se daturum di-

[a] Euppan *H*

[b] beatissimae *H*

[c] ditare *E*, dicare *K, H*

[d] filio suo *H*

---

[1] There is no clear evidence that Stephen had other sons than Emeric
(on whom see note 1, p. 104); cf. Vajay, "Grossfürst Geysa."

[2] At the end of the year 1000 or the beginning of 1001.

[3] Stephen defeated Koppány—in all likelihood his uncle and an adher-
ent of paganism—in 997; see also notes 2–3, pp. 162–3.

[4] We are well informed about this Gyula (not the same as the legendary
one mentioned in ch. 29, nor with Stephen's grandfather on his
mother's side, though all may have received their name from the ancient
title of a dignitary of the tribal age), see *Annales Altahenses* ad ann. 1003
and the Anonymus, ch. 27. He seems to have been the last of the major

Emeric, an honourable man before God and men.[1] After St. Stephen was crowned[2] and chief Koppány was finally put to death,[3] the King brought his uncle Gyula with his wife and two sons from Transylvania to Hungary and annexed Transylvania to Pannonia.[4] He then made war on Kean, the leader of the Bulgars and Slavs.[5] After defeating Kean, King Stephen made a gift from Kean's treasures to the church of the Virgin Mary at Székesfehérvár, a church which he is held to have founded.[6]

44.   After God had showered his mercy upon St. Stephen and brought numerous nations and peoples under his rule, the King decided to set aside his crown, renounce the trappings of this world and, free from other cares, devote himself to God's service alone. He intended that the crown of the kingdom should pass to his son Duke Emeric.

leaders resisting Stephen's monarchy, probably an Orthodox Christian, but he submitted to the king without major bloodshed. — In the Middle Ages the name Transylvania applied to the region between the Southern and Eastern Carpathians and the Meszes mountains (Munţii Mezeşului, Romania).

[5] Stephen made war against Bulgaria in the 1110s in alliance with Emperor Basil II (976–1025). The Anonymus cites the name Kean in his account of the Hungarian conquest (ch. 11). According to other sources he was a leader of an emerging Bulgarian-Slavic principality in southern Transylvania (*KMTL*, 338; Mályusz-Kristó, *Commentarii*, 1:254–55).

[6] The church is mentioned in the legends of St. Stephen (*SRH* 2: 385, 396, 417). A chasuble (*casula*), the later Hungarian coronation mantle, was donated to this church by Gisela and Stephen in 1031. Székesfehérvár became a ceremonial centre of the Árpád dynasty at an early date, as proved by the fact that King Peter was enthroned there in 1045 by Emperor Henry III (Deér, "Aachen").

sposuit. Erat enim beatus rex Stephanus literatus, naturali quoque ingenio caelitus eruditus; similiter et Emricus.
Cum itaque sanctissimus pater curam ministrationis[a] gubernandi filio sanctissimo committere intenderet, dux ipse morte est praeventus[1]. [SRH, 173] Flevit ergo eum
pater eius insolabiliter totaque Hungaria, et prae nimio
dolore ac tristitia incurrit aegritudinem, pedum enim dolore urgebatur. Nam maxime eapropter, ut de suo sanguine
dignus nullus esset regni corona sublimari et qui ipso
mortuo gentem tam novellam in fide catholica posset conservare. Interea vero viribus corporis caepit repente de-
stitui et gravatum langore[b] se sentiens, misit nuncios festinanter, qui Wazul[c] filium sui patruelis de carcere Nitriae educerent[d], quem ipse post eum regem faceret super
Hungaros. Quo audito Kysla regina, habito consilio infi-
delium, misit comitem Sebus, qui regis nuncium prae-
veniens, Wazul[e] oculos effoderet auresque eius plumbi
infusione obturaret fugeretque abinde in Boemiam[2]. Quem

[a] ministrationis et gubernandi *Madzsar coniecit ("Hún krónika," p. 87)*

[b] languore *H, E*

[c] Vazul *H*

[d] educerent *H*, educeret *K*

[e] Vazul *H*

---

[1] Cf. *SRH* 1, ch. 69, 318–21. Prince Emeric (Hung. Imre), named after
his uncle Emperor Henry II, was Stephen's designated heir but died in
a hunting accident on 2 September 1031; he was canonised together
with his father in 1083.

Stephen was literate and endowed by heaven with natural intelligence, and so was Emeric. However, although the most holy King intended to entrust the ministration and care of government to his most holy son, untimely death snatched the Duke away.[1] The father wept unconsolably, and all Hungary with him. In his grief and suffering his health declined, and pain in his legs caused him suffering. But his greatest grief was that he felt that none of his family was worthy to bear the crown nor capable of keeping the newly converted people within the Catholic faith once he himself had passed away. In the meantime his bodily strength rapidly began to wane. Feeling his powers slipping away, he sent messengers in haste to have his uncle's son Vazul brought from prison in Nitra, in order to make him king of the Hungarians after himself. However, as soon as Queen Gisela got wind of this she hatched a plot with a group of traitors, and sent the *ispán* Sebus ahead of the messenger. Sebus had Vazul's eyes put out and molten lead poured into his ears; he then fled to Bohemia.[2] When Vazul

[2] For the phrase "feelings his powers slipping away . . . ," cf. the legends of St. Stephen (*SRH* 2: 399, 430). — Like Simon, most of the chronicles—quite groundlessly—blame Gisela for the Vazul's mutilation (an action designed to render a potential heir ineligible to rule), partly in order to defend the reputation of the holy king, and partly in response to anti-German sentiment at the court (see Bak, "Queens as scapegoats," 225–27). — The switch from "messengers" to "messenger" goes back to the original. The faulty construction *misit nuncios...qui educeret* was due to careless adoption from the earlier chronicle which read: *misit . . . nuncium, scilicet Budam filium Egiruth, . . . ut . . . educeret*—a clear sign of Simon copying his source in a hasty way. — Sebus (Sebös) is mentioned in the *Annales Altahenses* ad ann. 1039: *Sebes marchio*.

cum tandem regis nuncius ad regem adduxisset, amare flevit super casu, qui acciderat. Convocatis igitur ad se Andrea, Bela et Luenta[a], filiis Zarladislai consuluit eis, ut in Boemiam fugerent festinanter[1].

45.   Sanctus[b] autem rex Stephanus XLVI. anno sui regni[c] in die Assumptionis Beatae[d] Virginis migravit ad Dominum[2]. Sepultus est Albae in ecclesia Beatae[e] Virginis gloriosae. Confestim igitur Hungarorum[f] *citara in luctum est conversa,* et omnis populus regni planxit tam sanctissimum regem ululatu magno. Iuvenes eorum ac virgines scalidis induti vestibus per triennium choreas non duxerunt[3]. Regina vero Kysla consilio iniquorum Petrum Venetum filium sororis suae, cuius pater dux fuerat Venetorum regem fecit super Hungaros, ut pro libitu posset motus suae voluntatis perficere, regnumque Hungariae amissa libertate Teutonicis subderetur[4].

[a] Leventa *H*, Lewenta *E*

[b] Beatus *H, E*

[c] regiminis *H, E*

[d] Beatissimae *H*

[e] Beatissimae *H*

[f] Hungariae *H*

---

[1] Andrew, Béla, and Levente were in fact the sons of Vazul, but the Hungarian chroniclers wanted to disguise the embarrassing fact that their kings were the descendants of the brutally blinded Vazul (see the Genealogy).

was at length brought back by the King's messenger, the King wept bitterly at his fate. He therefore called together Andrew, Béla, and Levente, the sons of Ladislas the Bald, and counselled them with all speed to seek refuge in Bohemia.[1]

45. St. Stephen went to our Lord on the Feast of the Assumption in the 46th year of his reign,[2] and was buried in the church of the Glorious Virgin in Székesfehérvár. Forthwith "the harp" of the Hungarians "was turned to grief," and the whole populace of the kingdom mourned and wailed aloud for their most holy king. The young men and girls dressed in mourning and performed no dances for three years.[3] Meanwhile Queen Gisela and her council of traitors installed her sister's son Peter the Venetian, whose father had been Duke of the Venetians, as king over the Hungarians, in order to be free to pursue her desires at will and to reduce the country to bondage under the Germans.[4]

[2] Cf. *SRH* 1, ch. 70, 321–23. King Stephen died on 15 August 1038; thus, his 46 years reign is an exaggeration.

[3] Cf. Job 30:31. The description of the mourning ceremonies is based on the earlier Hungarian chronicle (*SRH* 1: 322), and repeated with additional Biblical echoes in the Legend of St. Ladislas, ch. 7 (*SRH* 2: 522). Gallus Anonymus (38.2) describes the mourning for Boleslaw I in similar terms.

[4] Peter, king of Hungary 1038–41 and 1044–46, was in fact the son of St. Stephen's sister and Otto Orseolo, the doge of Venice. According to some scholars, Peter lived till 1059 (Vajay, "Grossfürst Geysa").

46. Postquam autem Petrus regnare incepisset, omnem mansuetudinem regiae abiecit maiestatis et furore Teutonico desaeviens regni nobiles contemnebat cum Alamannis et Latinis[1], bona terrae *superbo oculo et insatiabili corde* devorando[2]. Munitiones autem, castra et omnes regni dignitates ab Hungaris [SRH, 174] auferens tradebat Teutonicis et Latinis. Erat quoque idem lascivus ultra modum, cuius satellites turpitudinem intemperatae libidinis operantes, uxores filiasque Hungarorum, ubicunque Petrus rex ambulabat, violenter opprimebant. Nullus etiam eo tempore de uxoris filiaeque castitate certus erat propter insultus aulicorum Petri regis. Videntes igitur principes et nobiles regni mala gentis suae, quae fiebant contra legem, communicato consilio rogaverunt regem, ut suis iniungeret a tam detestabili opere desistere sine mora. Rex vero elationis faustu inflatus ac furore, malitiam, quam in corde gerebat occultando, cum toto veneno effudit in publicum ita dicens: „Si aliquamdiu sanus ero, omnes iudices spectabiles, centuriones, principes et potestates statuam Teutonicos et Latinos terramque Hungariae regni hospitibus adimplens in dominium tradam Teutonicis". Hoc

---

[1] Cf. *SRH* 1, ch. 71, 323–24. The expression *furor Teutonicus* ("Teutonic fury") was common in the Middle Ages (Dümmler, "Furor,"); a similar phrase appears in a Hungarian royal charter from 1245: *in eadem Theuthonicalis furie tempestate* (*RA* no. 809, Mályusz-Kristó, *Commentarii*, 1: 282). — The term *Latini* ("Latins") normally meant in medieval Hungary Romance-speaking, mostly Lombard, French, and Walloon

46. As soon as he began to rule, Peter threw aside every trace of the forbearance befitting a monarch's majesty, and in consort with Germans and Latins raged with Teutonic fury,[1] treating the nobles of the kingdom with contempt and devouring the wealth of the land "with a proud eye and an insatiable heart."[2] Fortifications, castles, and every office in the kingdom was taken away from the Hungarians and given to Germans or Latins. In addition, Peter was extremely debauched, and his hangers-on behaved with shameful and unbridled lust, violently assaulting the wives and daughters of the Hungarians wherever the king travelled. No one at the time could feel sure of the chastity of his wife or daughter in the face of the importunity of Peter's courtiers. On seeing the wrongs suffered by their people in contravention of the law of the realm, the princes and nobles of the kingdom took counsel and went to the king, begging him to order his followers to cease at once from their vile behaviour. But the king, swollen with pride and rage, poured forth publicly all the malice and venom which he had been hiding in his heart, with the words: "As long as I have the strength to do so, I shall replace every judge of the realm, every centurion, every magnate and officer with a German or a Latin; I shall fill the country with foreigners, and I shall deliver it in thrall

settlers in the older urban centres of Hungary. Here it refers to the Italians in Peter's entourage. See Amman, "Die französische Südostwanderung."

[2] Ps. 100:5.

itaque fuit discordiae seminarium inter Petrum regem et Hungaros[1].

47.   Anno ergo regni Petri tertio principes et nobiles regni Hungariae episcoporum consilio in unum convenerunt contra Petrum quaerentes solicite, si aliquem de regali genere possent reperire, qui esset idoneus regnum gubernare eosque a Petri tyrannide potenter liberare. Cumque in regno talem invenire potuissent ullo[a] modo, ex semetipsis quendam comitem nomine Aba, sororium sancti regis Stephani super se regem praefecerunt[2]. Aba vero rex congregato exercitu Hungarorum processit contra Petrum pugnaturus. Cernens autem Petrus Hungarorum adiutorio se privatum, fugiit ad Henricum caesarem in Bavariam, petiturus auxilium sibi dari. Petro itaque de regno effugato illi tyranni, quorum consilio afflicti erant Hungari, sunt detenti. Ex quibus unum in frusta conciderunt, oculos

[a] *pro* nullo modo

---

[1] For "every judge" the Latin has *iudices spectabiles*; *spectabilis* in Gratian refers to a class of judges, but here it is a borrowing from the earlier Hungarian chronicles. — For *cum toto veneno effudit* ("poured forth all the venom") cf. Prov.23:32 *et sicut regulus venena diffundet* (playing on the double meaning of *regulus* 'a petty king'; 'a kind of serpent'). — The biblical *principes et potestates* here refers to high dignitaries ("every magnate and officer"); however, it is not used elsewhere in this sense in Hungarian Latinity, though a parallel appears in Agnellus, *Liber pontificalis*, 200.

to the Germans!" This, then, was the breeding ground of discord between King Peter and the Hungarians.[1]

47. In the third year of Peter's reign on the advice of the bishops, the princes and nobles of the realm of Hungary in great concern came together against Peter to consider whether a suitable candidate could not be found among the royal kin to seize the throne and to free them from Peter's tyranny. No such person having been found anywhere in the kingdom, they elevated from among themselves an *ispán* called Aba, who was King Stephen's brother-in-law, as king over them.[2] King Aba then gathered an army of Hungarians and marched out to settle with Peter on the battlefield. Seeing that he could expect no help from the Hungarians, Peter fled to Emperor Henry in Bavaria to seek his support. With Peter out of the kingdom, his bullying henchmen whose counsel had brought suffering on the Hungarians were rounded up. One was hacked to

[2] Cf. *SRH* 1, ch. 72, 324–26. Samuel Aba was king of Hungary 1041–44. The Aba kindred, the only noble clan Simon connects with a Hun ancestor (see ch. 22 and Szűcs, above p. LXIX), was related to King Stephen and was to play an important role in Hungarian history. They receive significant attention in the work of the Anonymus as well (ch. 32), who explains Aba's name as signifying "piety." — According to some recent views, Bishop Gerard and the Hungarian prelates supported Aba as a protector of canonical communal life, and their sympathies towards Peter are an invention of the later chroniclers. The latter include Manegold of Lautenbach, who describes him as *Petrum oppressorem, legum paternarum corruptorem* (*MGH Libelli de lite* 1: 364). — The phrase *in unum convenerunt* has biblical parallels, e.g. Josh. 11:5 etc.

duorum filiorum eiusdem eruentes; alios vero in manganis[a] ferreis confregerunt, quosdam lapidibus obruentes[1]. Sebus vero, qui Wazul oculos eruerat, pedibus confractis ac manibus in rota peremerunt. Aba vero in[b] regem consecrato, ea quae Petrus statuerat, in irritum revocans Hungarorum scita iussit observare.

48. Tertio autem anno Abae[c] regis descendit Petrus rex cum Henrico caesare ducens maximum exercitum contra Abam. [SRH, 175] Quod Aba dum scivisset, nuncios mittens ad caesarem probavit, si cum eo pacem posset ordinare vel minime. Cui caesar in respondendo se ostendit inimicum, intellectoque, ut intenderet restituere Petrum Hungaris, iratus invasit Austriam et usque in fluvium Tremse spoliavit et post haec est reversus[2]. Tandem quoque, misso exercitu in Carinthiam pro spolio faciendo, cum inde redirent onerosi, Gottfridus Austriae marchio circa Petoviam insultum faciens super eos, eorum spolia fertur abstulisse[3]. Tunc enim Austria non duces, sed habebat marchiones[4]. Cumque eo tempore Coloniae degeret im-

---

[a] manganidis *K*

[b] in *E add.*

[c] Aba *H, E*

---

[1] Henry III was emperor 1039–56. — For these engines cf. *Annales Altahenses*, ad ann. 1041. The *manganum* or mangonel was a frequent instrument of torture and execution, cf. Rahewin *Gesta Friderici* 4.47 (*FvS* 17); Veszprémy, "Követő."

pieces, and his two sons had their eyes put out; others were broken on iron engines or stoned to death.[1] Sebus, the man responsible for putting out Vazul's eyes, was put to death on the wheel after having his arms and legs broken. Aba was then consecrated as king and revoked all of Peter's decrees, ordering that the laws of the Hungarians were to be observed.

48.   However, in the third year of Aba's reign King Peter marched against him in company with the Emperor Henry at the head of a huge army. On learning the news Aba sent envoys to the Emperor to see if there was any possibility of coming to a settlement. However, the Emperor's hostility was obvious from his response; it was now clear to Aba that the Emperor had every intention of placing Peter back on the throne of Hungary. The King's angry reaction was to invade Austria, plundering the country as far as the river Traisen before returning home.[2] Subsequently he sent another army on a plundering expedition into Carinthia, but as they were returning laden with booty it seems that Geoffrey, the margrave of Austria[3]—in those days Austria had margraves, not dukes—surprised them near Pitten and robbed them of their plunder.[4] At the time the Emperor

[2] Cf. *SRH* 1, ch. 73–75, 326–29. For "coming to a settlement," cf. *Annales Altahenses*, ad ann. 1042–43, here borrowed via the Hungarian chronicles.

[3] Geoffrey (d. 1050), son of Arnold II, was count of Wels-Lambach and margrave of Carinthia (*Annales Altahenses*, ad ann. 1042).

[4] Emperor Frederick I first bestowed the title of Duke of Austria in 1156, on Henry II. — *Petovia* is either Pitten in Lower Austria (*Österreich im Hochmittelalter*, 201), or Ptuj (Pettau) on the river Drava in Styria, the centre of Hungarian occupation under King Béla IV.

perator, audito, quod Hungari lacerassent Teutonicos sine causa, cum principibus Alamanniae consilium iniit, qualiter ab Hungaris illatam sibi iniuriam iniuria simili propulsaret. Movit itaque expeditionem ingentem et consilio ducis Ratizlai Boemorum ex aquilonali parte Danubii venit ad Hungariae confinia[1]. Legati vero Abae regis et Hungarorum promittebant caesari, ut in omnibus satisfacerent, nisi quia Petrum in regem non susciperent, quod caesar summopere perficere affectabat. Obligatus enim erat ei iuramento, ut ipsum in regnum Hungariae iterato collocaret. Cum autem Hungari Petrum non admitterent, missis muneribus dataque fide, quod captivos Teutonicorum libere permitterent remeare, caesar consilio inductus ducis Loteringiae et plus allectus muneribus, rediit Bizantiam, Burgundiae civitatem[2].

49. Ex hinc ergo rex Aba securitate accepta caepit esse insolens et saeviebat superbe in Hungaros, nobiles contemnens, sicut[a] et iusiurandum pro nihilo reputabat violare. Hungari vero nolentes id ei sustinere, conspiraverunt, ut eum morti traderent et occiderent. Sed quidam prodidit consilium, ex quibus, quos capere potuit, sine iudicii examine interfecit, quod ei extitit in summum maxime detri-

[a] sed K

[1] Břetislav I was duke of Bohemia 1034–55. — To repay injury by injury was a legal principal of the medieval concept of the just war (Russell, *Just War*, 132–33)

[2] The Annales Altahenses (*MGH SS* 20: 799, 801) mention two dukes of Lower Lorraine, Gozzilo I (d. 1044) and his son Geoffrey II

was at Cologne, but when he heard that the Hungarians had made an unprovoked attack on the Germans he took counsel with the German princes to retaliate against the Hungarians and repay injury with injury. He assembled a great army and, following the advice of Duke Břetislav of Bohemia, advanced along the northern course of the Danube to the borders of Hungary.[1] Envoys sent by King Aba and the Hungarians promised the Emperor that they would offer satisfaction on all points short of accepting Peter back as king. However, this was the Emperor's foremost intention, since he had given an oath to Peter to restore him to the throne of Hungary. The Hungarians still refused to accept Peter, but sent gifts and guaranteed that their German prisoners-of-war would be given free passage home. The Emperor took fresh advice from the Duke of Lorraine, and after receiving further gifts he returned to the city of Besançon in Burgundy.[2]

49.   But now that his position was secure, King Aba began to grow haughty, and bullied the Hungarians arrogantly, treating the nobles with scorn and likewise showing no scruples about breaking his oath. Unwilling to endure this treatment from him, the Hungarians formed a conspiracy to murder the King and do away with him. However someone betrayed the plot, and those of the conspirators that Aba could catch were put to death without trial—an action which proved a fatal blunder. He summoned fifty

(1065–70). Simon's *Consilio inductus ducis Loteringiae* ("took advice from the duke of L.") is a misreading of the Hungarian chronicle source: *contra insultus Gothfridi ducis Lotoringorum filii ducis Gozzilonis* 'against the assaults of Geoffrey duke of the Lorraine, son of Duke Gozzilo' (*SRH* 1: 328).

mentum. Nam viros quinquaginta consiliandi [SRH, 176] causa in unam domum evocavit, quibus in eadem inclusis, crimen non confessos, nec convictos legibus, caput fecit detruncari. Unde Beatus Gerardus, Chenadiensis episcopus canonica severitate regem corripiens praedixit sibi periculum imminere[1].

50. Tunc quidam ex Hungaris fugientes ad caesarem locuti sunt contra Abam dicentes, quod pro nihilo iuramentum reputaret violare, nobilesque, qui eum regem fecerant, contemnebat. Quibus dixit imperator: "Oportet ergo, ut captivos reddat, damna emendando." Caesar igitur Hungarorum animatus consilio, cum exercitu Norico et Boemico Austriam introivit dissimulans se in Hungariam intraturum, sed simulans cum Aba concordare. Tunc nuncii Aba regis repetebant incessanter a caesare Hungaros, qui ad caesarem fugerant, conquerentes ac dicentes praedones et latrones ipsos esse, guerreque inter caesarem ac Hungaros praecipuos incentores[a], ideoque huiusmodi iniquitatis artifices in manus Abae regis tradi oportere. Quod facturum se caesar promisit ullo[b] modo. Concitato igitur

[a] intentores *K*

[b] *pro* nullo

---

[1] Cf. *SRH* 1, ch. 75, 329–30. The reference to Aba's oath-breaking was taken by contemporary Bavarian commentators (*Annales Altahenses Maiores*, Berno abbot of Reichenau, etc.) to mean the breaking of his oath to the Emperor, by his Hungarian opponents to mean the breaking of his coronation oath. — For "someone betrayed . . ." the original source is *Annales Altahenses*, ad ann. 1044. — For the phrase *crimen non confessos* ("they had not confessed to any crime") cf. *Cod. Iust.* 1.3.10 and Benedicti *Capitularium* 2, no. 115, *PL* 97: 763. This legal

men to one house on the pretext of asking their counsel, then locked them in and had them all beheaded, although they had not confessed to any crime or been legally convicted. Thereupon St. Gerard, the bishop of Csanád, used the authority of the church to chastise the King roundly, predicting the danger in store for him.[1]

50. Next, some Hungarians fled to the Emperor and denounced Aba, saying that the King had no scruples about breaking his oaths and scorned the nobles who had put him on the throne. The Emperor replied with the words, "Then he will have to return the prisoners in order to make good the damage." On the advice of the Hungarians the Emperor advanced into Austria with a force of soldiers from Noricum and Bohemia, ostensibly to discuss terms with Aba and hiding his plan to march into Hungary. Envoys from King Aba repeatedly asked the Emperor to deliver up the Hungarians who had fled to him, describing them as brigands and robbers and protesting that they were the prime fomenters of the conflict between the Emperor and the Hungarians and as such should be handed over to the King for their wicked plotting. The Emperor refused to do so on any account. Speeding his advance he crossed the

explanation is Simon's addition to the original text (Gerics, "Auslegung," 341). — The life of St. Gerard (b. Venice c. 980, canonised in 1083) is told in his two Legends (*SRH* 2: 471–506), which Simon knew. Gerard was tutor to Prince Emeric and author of the theological work *Deliberatio supra hymnum trium puerorum* (*CCCM* 49) and homilies. Gerard's admonition is recorded in ch. 13 of his *Legenda Maior*; for the problem of which king was the object of condemnation, cf. note 2, p. 111. — Csanád was an episcopal see in the Middle Ages, by the river Maros; today it is Cenad in Romania, but its name survives in the bishopric of Szeged-Csanád. Gerard was its first bishop.

cursu invasit fines Hungariae intrans per Supronium et, cum vellet in Bobut pertransire, non poterat propter aquas. Hungari ergo, qui erant cum caesare et Petro rege, duxerunt caesaris exercitum sursum iuxta flumen Rebche et utraque flumina tota nocte equitando orto sole facili vado transierunt. Occurrit autem ei rex Aba in Menfeu[a] cum multitudine armatorum nimis praesummens de victoria, quare[b] Bavari quidam nunciaverant ei caesarem cum paucis introisse. Et[c] ut dicitur, Aba rex victoriam habuisset, nisi quia Hungari quidam amicitiam Petro reservantes super terram sua vexilla proiecissent et fugissent. Commisso igitur praelio diu et acriter, tandem caesar divino fretus adminiculo victoriam est adeptus[1]. Aba vero rex fugiit versus Tizam et in villa quadam in scrobe veteri[2] ab Hungaris, quibus regnans nocuerat, iugulatur et iuxta quandam ecclesiam sepelitur. Post aliquot autem annos, cum esset effossum corpus eius de sepulchro, sudarium ac ipsius vestimenta[d] invenerunt incorrupta et loca vulnerum [SRH, 177] resanata sepelieruntque tandem corpus eius in proprio monasterio[3]. Ex Teutonicis etenim in illo praelio sine nu-

[a] Menfeo *H*

[b] quod *H*, quia *E*

[c] et *E*, ei *K, H*

[d] vestimenta ipsius *H*

---

[1] Cf. *SRH* 1, ch. 76, 330–33. The Latin for "prime fomentors" is corrupt; the *Annales Altahenses* read *incentores* 'ones who set the tune or begin to sing' instead of *K*'s unparalleled *intentores*; the original reading may have been *incensores* 'inciters, instigators.' — The marshy area around Sopron and Babót formed part of the Hungarian border defence system (see Map 3, also note 2, pp. 128–9). — Ménfő is near Győr. — The battle was fought on 5 July 1044.

Hungarian frontier at Sopron, but was unable to cross to Babót because of the water. The Hungarians in the company of the Emperor and King Peter conducted the imperial forces up the river Répce, and after riding all night they crossed both rivers at sunrise by a shallow ford. King Aba met them with a large force at Ménfő, very confident of victory, because some Bavarians had told him that the Emperor had brought few troops with him to Hungary. Indeed, it is said that the victory would have gone to King Aba but for the fact that some of the Hungarians, who had remained loyal to Peter, threw their banners to the ground and fled. The battle was long and hard, but relying on God's help the Emperor finally won the day.[1] Aba fled in the direction of the river Tisza, but in a particular town he was seized by the Hungarians who had suffered under his rule and strangled in an old storeroom,[2] his body being buried by a certain church. However, some years later, when his body was disinterred, his shroud and his garments were found to be uncorrupted and marks of his wounds had healed, and his body was finally laid to rest in his own monastery.[3] The Germans lost more men than they could

[2] What *scrobis* (lit. 'ditch') means here is unclear. Traditionally Hungarian historians translated it as "storeroom"; elsewhere it refers to a deep pit with sharp stakes in it, used for trapping animals.

[3] 14th-century chronicles refer to the monastery of Sármonostor, near the town of Gyöngyös, though historians have surmised that Simon supposed it to be the basilica in Debrő (today Feldebrő), in the same county. — Simon's account of Aba's escape differs from that in the *Annales Altahenses* ad ann. 1044, where Aba was captured and sentenced to death by common verdict of the Hungarians and Germans (*communi iudicio nostrorum et suorum capitalem subit penam*).

mero ceciderunt. Unde idem locus, ubi praelium est commissum, eorum lingua usque hodie Florum Paiur est vocatus et Weznemut[a] nostra lingua[1].

51. Caesar vero obtenta victoria descendit Albam civitatem ubi Petro restituit regnum, et sic tandem est reversus
Ratisponam[2].

52. Rege ergo Petro et Hungaris, qui eum in regnum
reduxerant, vires et potentiam resummentibus, caeperunt
esse insolentes. Qua de causa omnes Hungari solicite intendebant, qualiter ammoto Petro filios Zarladislai redu-
cere potuissent. Dum autem ista ita fierent, Andreas, Bela
et Luenta[b] de Boemia in Poloniam transeuntes a Misca
Polonorum duce amicabiliter sunt recepti; ubi Bela Po-
moramiae ducem duello devincens, filia Miskae sibi datur
in uxorem[3]. Quod Andreas et Luenta[c] aegre ferentes, ne
ipsius nomine viverent in Polonia, in Rutheniam transierunt. Et dum ibi a duce Lodomeriae[4] propter Petrum
regem suscepti non fuissent, ad terram vadunt deinde Co-

[a] Veznemut *H*

[b] Lewenta *E*

[c] Lewenta *E*

---

[1] The name "Vésznémet," from *veszett német*, in German *verlorene Bayern*, i.e. "perished Germans," no doubt rests on a local tradition.

[2] Cf. *SRH* 1, ch. 77, 333. Also cf. *Annales Altahenses* ad ann. 1044.

[3] Cf. *SRH* 1, ch. 78–79, 334–35. Mieszko II, son of Bolesław the Brave, was duke of Poland 1025–34. Béla's wife was indeed a Polish princess.

count in this battle, so that to this day the battlefield is called "Verlorene Bayern" in their language, or "Vészné-met" in our tongue.[1]

51. After his victory the Emperor proceeded to Székes-fehérvár, where he restored Peter to the throne, before returning to Regensburg.[2]

52. But Peter and the faction of Hungarians who restored him were no sooner back in power than they began to grow insolent. So the Hungarians as a whole made anxious plans to depose Peter and invite back the sons of Ladislas the Bald. While this was transpiring, Andrew, Béla, and Levente had moved from Bohemia to Poland. There they received a warm reception from Mieszko, the Duke of Poland, and Béla, after defeating the Duke of Pomerania in single com-bat, was given Mieszko's daughter in marriage.[3] Andrew and Levente, however, took this badly; they felt that they would be living in Poland under their brother's shadow, and moved to Ruthenia. There the Duke of Lodomeria[4] refused to receive them out of regard for King Peter, so they next went to the land of the Cumans. The Cumans at

His single combat with the Pomeranian, however, is folklore, but was taken as historical by later historians such as Długosz, who was familiar with the Hungarian chronicles and interpreted it similarly to the Hungarian Botond-story. The *Annales Altahenses* ad ann. 1046 mention a certain Zemuzil from Pomerania but make no mention of a duel.

[4] Lodomeria, i.e. Vladimir on the river Bug, was a Russian principality, which was united with Galicia (Halič) from 1199 and became integrated into the royal title of Hungarian kings (*"rex Gallicie et Lodomerie"*) in 1206. Cumans may have been living in this area in Simon's time but hardly in the 11th century.

manorum. Qui cum eos perimere cogitarent, credentes ipsos exploratores regni sui, tandem per captivum Hungarum recogniti optime deinceps pertractantur.

53.   Interea vero Petrus rex Hungaros priori gravamine caepit molestare. Tunc in Chenad omnes in unum convenerunt consilioque habito communiter pro filiis Zarladislai transmittunt, ut ad regnum remearent. Qui cum in Pest advenissent, absconse sicut poterant, statim in curia Petri regis una nocte in equis velocibus per nuncios trium fratrum proclamatur, quod omnes Teutonici et Latini ubicunque inventi perimantur et resumatur ritus paganismus. Mane ergo facto sciscitatus Petrus facti causam pro certo recognovit ipsos esse in Hungaria. Et licet immenso dolore tactus esset, se laetum demonstrabat. Tunc clam mittens suos nuncios, ut Albam occuparent, revelato consilio Hungari per [SRH, 178] omnia loca incipiunt rebellare occidentes uno tempore Teutonicos, et Latinos, mulieribus quoque, infantibus et sacerdotibus, qui per Petrum fuerant praepositi, plebani et abbates, non parcentes[1]. Et cum in Albam nequisset introire, arrepta fuga ivit versus Musun, ubi exercitus venisse contra eum perhibetur, indeque, declinans equitavit festinanter versus Albam. Cives etenim demandaverant, quod rediret et civitatem sibi darent. Cum

---

[1] Cf. *SRH* 1, ch. 81–85, 336–43. This is an abridged and rather confused version of the story in the Hungarian chronicles, which tells of a pagan uprising led by a certain Vata in support of the brothers but later

first thought they had come to spy on their country and intended to kill them, but a Hungarian prisoner recognised who they were, and thereafter they were treated with the greatest consideration.

53.   Meanwhile King Peter had begun to oppress the Hungarians as harshly as before. So a general gathering took place in Csanád, where they took counsel and sent a message in common calling for Ladislas the Bald's sons to return to Hungary. The three brothers came as secretly as they could, and as soon as they arrived in Pest they sent messengers at night to ride swiftly, enter Peter's court, and issue a proclamation that any Germans or Latins found anywhere were to be put to death and paganism restored. So when Peter woke in the morning and demanded to know what was going on he discovered that the brothers were back in Hungary. Peter was deeply unhappy but put on a cheerful front. He sent messengers in secret to Székesfehérvár to secure the town. However his ploy came out in the open and the Hungarians everywhere rose in revolt, slaughtering Germans and Latins together and sparing neither women, infants, nor priests—provosts; parish priests or abbots appointed by Peter.[1] Unable to enter Székesfehérvár, Peter fled in the direction of Moson. There it was rumoured that an army was marching against him so he turned aside from Moson and rode back in haste to Székesfehérvár, the citizens having sent word that he should

suppressed by them. In fact only two of the brothers, Andrew and Levente, arrived at first, Béla returned later.

vero in quandam villam circa Albam pervenisset, subito exercitus ipsum circumdedit, ubi captivatus oculi eruuntur, licetque superviveret, in maerore animi finiens vitam suam Quinqueecclesiis subterratur, quam fundasse perhibetur[1].

54.   Tunc tres fratres Albensem ingressi civitatem, ab omnibus episcopis, nobilibus omnique populo cum summa laude sunt suscepti, et Andreas aevo potior in regni solium sublimatur[2].

55.   Quidam autem istos fratres ex duce Wazul[a] progenitos asseverant ex quadam virgine de genere Tatun, non de vero thoro oriundos, et pro tali missitalia illos de Tatun nobilitatem invenisse[3]. Frivolum pro certo est et pessime enarratum. Absque hoc namque nobiles sunt et de Scitia oriundi, quia[b] isti sunt filii Zarladislai.

56.   Gerardus ergo episcopus de Chanad in istis casibus in Pest, per Hungaros de monte submissus in biga, [mar-

[a] Vazul *H*

[b] quare *H*

---

[1] Moson (Germ. Miesenburg, Wieselburg), a well-known frontier castle at the junction of the Lajta and the Little Danube which controlled the main road through Austria, is mentioned already in the Nibelungenlied (*ze Misenburc der rîchen*—*ÁMTF* 4: 160). — The "village near Székesfehérvár" is named as *Zamur* in the 14th-century chroniclers (*SRH* 1: 343), perhaps modern Zámoly. — The bishopric of Pécs was founded by King Stephen I ca. 1009, and its first medieval cathedral was built by King Peter in the 1040s (Tóth, "Cathedrale").

return and that they would surrender the town to him. But when he reached a village near Székesfehérvár he was suddenly surrounded by the army; he was taken prisoner and his eyes were put out. He survived this, but ended his life sick at heart. He is buried at Pécs, in his own foundation, as it is held.[1]

54. The three brothers then entered Székesfehérvár, where they were received with paeans of praise by the whole populace, bishops, nobles and people alike, and Andrew, as the oldest of the three, ascended the throne.[2]

55. It is sometimes claimed that the brothers were the sons of Duke Vazul by a girl from the Tátony clan and not his sons by true wedlock, and that the Tátony family derive their noble status from this connection.[3] This tradition is certainly baseless and a quite mischievous invention. The fact is that, being from Scythia, the family were of noble origin in any case, irrespective of the fact that the brothers were the sons of Ladislas the Bald.

56. During these revolts Bishop Gerard of Csanád won the crown of martyrdom in Pest when he was pushed off

---

[2] Cf. *SRH* 1, ch. 86, 343. King Andrew reigned 1046–60.

[3] Cf. *SRH* 1, ch. 87, 344. The princes' descent from Vazul is in fact the correct tradition; see note 159 and Genealogy. — The words *non de vero thoro* imply *concubinatus*, an accepted form of marriage in 11th-century Hungary (Gerics, "Quaedam puella"). — There was a village called Tátony in County Somogy (Mályusz-Kristó, *Commentarii*, 1: 322–23).

tyrio]ᵃ coronatur, qui monachus prius fuerat de Rosacensi abbatia, quae est de territorio Aquilegiae. Deinde Pannoniam ingressus in Beel fuit diutius eremita[1].

57. Cum igitur Andreas diadema regni suscepisset, cum Noricis, Boemis et Polonis guerram dicitur tenuisse, quos superans debellando tribus annis fecisse dicitur censuales. Propter quod [SRH, 179] Henricus imperator descendens usque Bodoct, V. mensibus Albam obsedit civitatem, ubi tandem sic viribus et potentia dicitur defecisse, ut ipsius Teutonici et Latini in suis tentoriis noctis tempore se vivos sepelirent. Nam Hungari in obscuris in eorum castra descendentes, eos crudeliter sagittis enecabant. Tandem vero caesar ille ductus penuria a rege Andrea et Hungaris veniam caepit postulare, quod omnia onera dimitteret in Hungaria praeter equos faceretque iusiurandum, ut deinceps nec ipse, nec ipsius successores contra regnum Hungariae hostili manu in Hungariam introirent, nec etiam de Bodoct moveret interea suos pedes, donec Sophiam suam filiam Salomoni regi de Alamannia ductam traderet in uxorem, quam primitus filio regis Franciae cum maximo dederat sacramento. Rex vero habito consilio misericorditer eidem

---

ᵃ martyrio *H, E, lacuna in K*

---

[1] Cf. *SRH* 1, ch. 83, 340–41. Gerard's martyrdom took place on 24 Sept 1046 in Buda, at a hill today named after him; the reference to Pest is again a sign of the author's hasty abridgement of the chronicle versions. For the details cf. the *Legenda Maior* of St. Gerard (ch. 15, *SRH* 2: 502). — Gerard was formerly a monk of San Giorgio in Venice; the Bene-

the hill in a cart by Hungarians. He had earlier been a monk in the abbey of Rosazzo in the territory of Aquileia, and later, after coming to Pannonia, spent considerable time as a hermit at Bakonybél.[1]

57. After assuming the crown, we are told that Andrew went to war with the Austrians, Czechs, and Poles, all of whom he defeated and forced to pay tribute for three years. In response, Emperor Henry advanced to Bodajk and spent five months besieging Székesfehérvár. But eventually it seems his strength and his forces were so weakened that his German and Latin soldiers were burying themselves alive in their tents at night—because the Hungarians would descend on the camp in the darkness and despatch them mercilessly with their arrows. In the end the Emperor was so short of supplies that he craved pardon from Andrew and the Hungarians, offering to leave all his baggage apart from the horses in Hungary and to take an oath that in future neither he nor his successors would enter with forces hostile to the kingdom of Hungary; in the meantime, he insisted, he would not stir from Bodajk until his daughter Sophie, who he had previously promised on the solemnest of oaths to the son of the King of France, had been brought from Germany and given in marriage to King Solomon. After taking counsel, it is said, the King took pity

dictine monastery of Rosazzo in Northern Italy, near Udine and Görz, was a later foundation, and became the *Hauskloster* of the Spanheim dynasty (Baum, "Die Gründung," 623–26). — Bakonybél in the Bakony mountains was a Benedictine monastery founded by St. Stephen.

dicitur indulsisse[1]. Qui amoto suo castro primum descensum in monte Barsunus fecisse comprobatur. Quia vero fame ac siti defecerant, in eodem loco ex parte regis potus et cibus in maxima copia fuit ministratus. Indeque crapulati quamplurimi, cum caesaris vigiles incautis obtutibus Hungaros vidissent hinc inde equitantes, in pactis fraudem interesse crediderunt, quod exercitui declarantes dixerunt, ut ad persequendos eos advenissent[a]. Et quamvis plures, in feretris habentes purpurea lectisternia, aegritudine fatigati ducerentur, dimissis feretris et lectis purpureis equos ascenderunt, orto sole villam Urs coniungentes. Et cum castellanus, qui in porta erat, cognovisset, quod gens armata per asperas et inmeabiles indagines dimissa via regia pertransiret, cum suis se armavit[2]. Dumque transeuntem turmam a longe aspiciens tueretur, aegroti, qui dimissis feretris et lectisterniis in monte Barsunus in equis equitaverant, allocatis curribus[b] per indagines transiebant.

[a] ad persequendum eos advenisset *K, H, E*

[b] allocati curribus *coniecit* Madzsar *("Hún krónika," p. 87)*

---

[1] Cf. *SRH* 1, ch. 90, 347–51. The emperor attacked Hungary in 1051 (thus not near the beginning of Andrew's reign) and advanced as far as Székesfehérvár before being repelled. He may well have had Slavic contingents, as the Czechs and Poles were at that time dependent on the empire. Bodajk, mentioned by the Anonymus as well (ch. 50), was on a strategic main road westwards from Székesfehérvár. — Sophie is called Judith in German sources. Her engagement took place in 1058. Solomon reigned 1063–74. The son of the king of France, if anyone, would have to be Philip, son of Henry I, born in 1053; it is more likely, though, that this detail was made up by the Hungarian chroniclers.

[2] Örs is today Mezőörs, between Székesfehérvár and Győr. The author felt in the name Örs the sense of Hung. *őr* 'guard.' Of course, a real

on him and agreed to indulge him.[1] It is established that the Emperor then struck camp, making his first stop at Mount Bársonyos, where, exhausted by hunger and thirst, they were supplied with liberal quantities of food and drink on the king's orders. Thereupon many of them overindulged, and the imperial watchmen, seeing the Hungarians riding back and forth, supposed on the basis of careless observation that the truce had been treacherously breached and spread a report among the army that the Hungarians had come to attack them. Many of the soldiers were so weak and sick that they were being transported on litters furnished with purple bedding, but they abandoned their litters and purple beds, took to their horses, and by sunrise reached the village of Örs. The castellan in charge at the checkpoint was told that there was a body of men in arms struggling through the impenetrable lines of obstacles off the main highway, so he and his soldiers put on their arms.[2] He could see the troop passing in the distance; meanwhile the sick, who had given up their cots and bedding and had ridden over Mt. Bársonyos on horseback, had now acquired carriages and were making their way through the roadblocks on these. But when their squires looked back

checkpoint (*porta*) may well have existed there on the main road. Like *porta*, *indagines* is a term referring to the border guard system, which had wastes (Hung. *gyepü*) and obstacles or roadblocks permitting access only where there was a *porta* (Göckenjan, *Hilfsvölker*, 5–22). — *Castellanus* became the name for the royal or seigneurial officer in charge of a castle in the 13th century (first recorded in 1262: *LexMA* 2: 63). Earlier he was called "*comes curialis*," and acted as virtual deputy of the count (cf. *DRMH* 1: 142). — *Gens armata* ("a body of men") is an Italianism, *gente d'arme* 'soldier, warrior.' In our text it frequently occurs in the simple form *gens*.

Quorum scutiferi, ut retro viderunt aciem castellani, derelictis curribus et dominis super[a] currus, sicut melius potuerunt, abfugerunt. Tunc rustici venientes currus aufe-
rendo dominos in curru occiderunt, cadavera in aquas abi-
actantes. In quibus [SRH, 180] quidem aegrotis quidam
milites, aliqui comites, nonnulli fuere marchiones. Unde
usque hodie in transitu ipso equorum ferramenta, gladii et
plura his similia aquis exsiccatis solent inveniri. Mons vero
Barsunus propter lectisternia sic relicta, quae fuere purpurea, de terricolis extitit nominatus[1].

58. Post mortem itaque sancti regis Stephani transacti
sunt anni undecim, menses quatuor usque ad annum primum imperii Andreae regis. Interea vero Petrus rex primo
et secundo regnavit annis V. et dimidio. Aba vero regnavit
annis tribus[2]. Andreas autem confectus senio anno imperii
sui duodecimo filium suum Salomonem adhuc puerulum
cum consensu fratris sui Belae et filiorum eiusdem, scilicet
Geichae et Ladislai, regem constituit. Ipse autem obiit anno
regni sui decimo quinto et in Tyhon monasterio proprio
cum David suo filio sepelitur[3].

[a] servarunt *K*.

---

[1] Bársonyos is a settlement and mountain Northeast of Székesfehérvár.
Simon here reports a folk etymology: *bársonyos* is Hungarian for
'velvety, made of velvet,' though in fact the word seems to have referred
to flowers or the soil (Kiss, *Földrajzi nevek*, 1: 171). As a place name
Bársonyos occurs in a royal charter of 1281 (*RA* no. 3094, p. 272)

and saw the castellan's soldiers lined up for battle, they abandoned the carriages and their masters in them and fled as fast as they could. Some peasants then came up, seized the carriages, murdered the occupants, and threw their bodies into the waters. The invalids included a number of knights, counts, and even margraves, and to this day horse-bits, swords, and various other pieces of equipment turn up at the river crossing when the water is low. The name Bársonyos was given to the mountain by the local inhabitants after the velvet bedding that was abandoned there.[1]

58.   Eleven years and four months intervened between the death of King Stephen and the first year of King Andrew's reign. The first and second reigns of King Peter occupied five and a half years of this period, while Aba's reign accounted for a further three.[2] In the twelfth year of his reign, Andrew, now advanced in years, obtained the agreement of his brother Béla and Béla's sons Géza and Ladislas and appointed his young son Solomon as his successor. Andrew passed away in the fifteenth year of his reign and lies buried in his private monastery at Tihany, together with his son David.[3]

[2] Cf. *SRH* 1, ch. 92–93, 353–57. For the kings mentioned see the Genealogy.

[3] The monastery of Tihany was founded by King Andrew in 1055 in honour of the Blessed Virgin Mary and St. Anianus, bishop of Orléans (who saved his city from the Hunnish army by his prayers). The foundation deed of Tihany is the earliest authentic charter to survive in its original form in Hungary, and preserves the earliest written Hungarian words as place names. Andrew's gravestone still survives in the crypt. David, who died after 1091, also made donations to the abbey.

59. Post hunc regnavit Benyn Bela[1]. Quo regnante Hungari fidem derelinquunt et baptismum, anno in fide oberrantes, ut nec pagani, nec catholici viderentur. Postea tamen motu proprio fidei adhaeserunt. Iste enim omnia fora die sabbathi esse voluit pro vendendo ac emendo, bizantiosque currere fecit per districtum regni sui, qui denariis argenteis multum parvis[a] scilicet XL. cambii debuit. Unde usque hodie denarii XL. numero aurum appellantur; non quod sint aurei, sed quia denarii XL. argentei valebant bizantium unum[2]. Regnavit autem duobus annis et in tertio migravit ex hoc saeculo in suoque monasterio dicto Sceugzard sepelitur. Hic enim calvus erat et colore brunus, propter quod suum monasterium diminutive, sicuti erat ipse corpore dispositus, sic vocari iussit[3].

60. Tandem vero inter Salomonem, Ladizlaum et Geicham gravis discordia suscitatur, alumni patriae inter se dividuntur. Quidam enim Salomoni, aliqui Ladizlao et Geiche adhaeserunt. Rex autem Salomon caesarem, suum socerum contra Ladislaum et Geicham per Nitriam[b] cum exercitu maximo introducit. Qui [SRH, 181] Waciam[c]

---

[a] per ius *K, H*

[b] Nittriam *K*

[c] Vaciam *H, E*

---

[1] Cf. *SRH* 1, ch. 94–95, 358–60. The meaning of Béla's nickname "Benyn" is disputed (*pugil* 'boxer,' *benignus* 'kind,' *albus* 'white'?). Simon clearly refers to a pagan rebellion led by a certain John son of Vata which broke out at a meeting called by King Béla and which was swiftly put down. That heathen practices survived at least into the later 12th century is suggested by several laws and synodial decrees under Ladislas I and even later (*DRMH* I: 57–58, 121–22).

59. Andrew was succeeded by Benin Béla.[1] In his reign the Hungarians abandoned the faith and baptism, and for a year they wavered in their convictions, seeming to be neither Catholics nor pagans, but finally of their own accord they returned to the faith. The king decreed that all markets for buying and selling should be held on Saturdays and put bezants into circulation throughout his realm—the exchange being set at 40 little silver pennies to one bezant, so that to this day 40 pennies are referred to as a gold piece, not because they are made of gold, but because 40 silver pennies are worth one bezant.[2] Béla reigned for two years and in the third departed this world. He is buried in his monastery known as Szekszárd—he was bald and of brown complexion, so he had his monastery given this diminutive name which reflected his own physical features.[3]

60. However, Solomon, Ladislas, and Géza ended up in serious dispute, whereat the loyalties of the inhabitants of the kingdom were divided, some adhering to Solomon, some to Ladislas and Géza. Against Ladislas and Géza King Solomon invited his father-in-law the Emperor to enter the kingdom at Nitra at the head of a substantial army. The

[2] It is more likely that it was Béla's son, Géza, who introduced Saturday markets and coined the heavier coin, the so-called bezant (*bizantius*), but these reforms may have been attributed later to Béla as ancestor of the later kings of the house of Árpád (Györffy, *Krónikáink*, 186).

[3] Szekszárd is a town 65 km south of Budapest. The etymology of Szekszárd, as if from old Hung. *szeg* 'brown' and *szár* 'bald,' with the diminutive suffix -*d*, is not entirely convincing; the meaning seems rather to be "dark brown" or "yellowish brown" (Kiss, *Földrajzi nevek*, 2: 547). The monastery was founded by Béla in honour of the Holy Saviour in 1061. Archeological excavations have not found the king's grave.

perveniens Ladislai exercitu speculato finxit se infirmum, per Posonium in Austriam est reversus, dimisso de Boemis et Noricis sufficienti auxilio Salomoni. Tunc caesare retrogresso praelium in Munorod inter ipsos est commissum. Et quid ultra? Salomon devincitur, prostrantur Teutonici et Boemi. Et dum se suosque devictos cognovisset, fugam iniit, Danubium in Scigetfeu pertransiens, inde tandem in[a] Musunium se collegit. In praelio autem Munorodino non solum Teutonici et[b] Boemi ceciderunt sed etiam maior pars de militia regni periit[1].

61. Salomon ergo metuens fratres suos, cum tota familia in Styriam introivit, ubi in Agmund monasterio familia sua derelicta in Musunium est reversus volens colligere exercitum iterato. Sed cum de die in diem deficeret, illorumque processus reciperet felicia incrementa, confusus rediit ad caesarem adiutorium petiturus. Et licet pro militia solidanda affluentem pecuniam tradidisset, Teutonici ob timorem Hungarorum recipere noluerunt. Unde spe omni destitutus rediit in Agmund ad reginam, cum qua dies aliquos cohabitans in veste monachali deinde Albam venit. Et cum Ladislaus frater eius in porticu ecclesiae Beatae[c] Virginis manibus propriis pauperibus elemosinam ero-

[a] in K om.

[b] aut K

[c] Beatissimae H

---

[1] Cf. *SRH* 1, chs. 121 and 127–28, pp. 388–91 and 398–400. Simon compresses the extensive coverage in the 14th-century chronicles of the bitter conflicts between the crowned king Solomon and the princes

Emperor advanced as far as Vác, but after assessing Ladislas's army he returned via Bratislava to Austria on the
pretext of illness, leaving behind sufficient Czech and
Austrian troops to support Solomon. After the Emperor's
departure the two sides joined battle at Mogyoród. The
result, in brief, was that Solomon was defeated and the
German and Bohemian troops massacred. Once he realised
that he and his forces had lost the day, the king fled the
field, crossing the Danube at Szigetfő before rallying finally at Moson. The Germans and Bohemians, however,
were not the only casualties at the battle of Mogyoród;
most of the military strength of the realm also perished
there.[1]

61.   In fear of his brothers Solomon moved his household
to Styria and left them in the monastery at Admont before
returning to Moson to reassemble his army. But his forces
were growing weaker day by day whereas with reinforce-
ments his brothers' prospects were growing increasingly
favourable, so in frustration Solomon returned to the emperor to ask for his help. Even though he had ample money
to pay for troops, the Germans were too frightened of the
Hungarians to accept it. The king was now completely at
a loss, and after returning to his queen at Admont he spent
a few days with her before returning to Székesfehérvár in
monk's habit. There, the story goes, his brother Ladislas
was distributing alms to the poor with his own hands on
the porch of the church of the Blessed Virgin, and Solomon

Géza and Ladislas (Bollók, "Ladislas"). — Mogyoród is a settlement
some 20 kms. Northeast of Budapest. The battle was fought on 14
March 1074.

garet, ipse ibi inter eos dicitur accepisse[1]. Quem mox cognovit Ladislaus, ut inspexit. Reversus autem Ladislaus a distributione elemosinae inquiri fecit diligenter, non quod ei nocuisset, sed ille malum praesummens ab eodem, secessit inde versus mare Adriaticum, ubi in civitate vocata Pola usque mortem in summa paupertate in penuria finiens vitam suam, in qua et iacet tumulatus, nunquam rediens ad uxorem usque mortem[2]. Regina vero Sophia uxor eius in maxima castitate perseverans, nunciis frequentibus maritum visitabat mittens ei expensam, ut habere poterat, invitando nihilominus, quod eam videre dignaretur usque mortem. Qui quamvis in corde habuisset, ob nimiam egestatem tactus [SRH, 182] verecundia ire recusavit. Quem cum de medio sublatum cognovisset, licet multi principes de Germania sibi copulari matrimonialiter voluissent, spretis omnibus, quae habebat saecularia faciens venumdari, egenis est largita. Ipsa vero monialis effecta arctissimam vitam deducendo migravit ad Dominum et in praefato monasterio tumulata, sicut sancta veneratur[3].

[1] Cf. *SRH* 1, chs. 126 and 136, 397 and 410–11. Simon was evidently familiar with a version of the traditions preserved in Henry of Mügeln's *Rhymed Chronicles* (*SRH* 2, ch. 47, 191–92) and as an addition to the *Chronicle of Dubnic* (*SRH* 1, p. 411, text note), which say that Ladislas wanted to capture Solomon but he was afraid of the wrath of the people, or else he feared him and searched for him but Solomon was nowhere to be found.

was among the recipients.[1] When Ladislas looked closely he realised who it was. After the distribution was over Ladislas made careful inquiries. He intended Solomon no harm, but Solomon assumed he did, and quit Székesfehérvár, making for the Adriatic. There he passed the rest of his days in complete poverty in a city named Pula; he died in destitution and was buried there, never having returned to his wife.[2] But his wife Queen Sophie remained completely chaste and sent frequent messengers to her husband with whatever money she could spare for his livelihood, asking him to agree to see her before he died. In his heart Solomon wished to, but he was so ashamed of his poverty that he refused to go. After she learnt of his death, although many princes in Germany sought her hand, she spurned all suitors, sold her wordly possessions, and gave the money to the poor. She then joined a convent and led a life of great strictness, and when she departed to the Lord she was buried in the aforementioned monastery and was venerated as a saint.[3]

[2] This folk tradition might be rooted in historical facts, as Solomon was related to the margraves of Istria (Rokay, *Salamon*, 1–40). The lid of his tomb was found in Pula.

[3] Simon is most likely confusing her with the pious daughter of King Béla II, who indeed retreated to the monastery of Admont. A letter she sent from Admont to her brother, Géza II—in which she refers to him as king of the Huns—has survived (1146). In fact Solomon's widow Sophie/Judith soon married the Piast ruler Władysław I Herman (1079–1102).

62. Post Salomonem vero autem regnavit Geicha annis tribus et mortuus est. Waciae[a], quam fundasse dicitur, tumulatur[1].

63. Post Geicham vero regnavit Ladislaus XXX. annis et tribus mensibus. In Warod[b] requiescit. Istius igitur temporibus in VII. Castris, in monte, qui Kyrioleis dicitur, Bessi Hungaris infestissimi spoliata Hungaria fugientes coniunguntur et per eundem Ladislaum regem ac Hungaros taliter superantur, ut nec unus ex ipsis fertur remansisse[2].

64. Ladislao autem migrato regnavit post eum filius Geichae regis, Kalomannus annis X. et octo, cuius corpus iacet Albae. Hic quidem praesul erat et exinde translatus in regem coronatur. Qunwes enim Kalman est vocatus, quoniam[c] libros habebat, in quibus ut episcopus legebat suas horas[3]. Iste quoque in regnum Dalmatiae misso exer-

a Vaciae *H, E*

b Varad *H*

c quam *K*

---

[1] Cf. *SRH* 1, ch. 130, 403. Géza I reigned 1074–77. The bishopric of Vác was founded by King Stephen I at the end of his reign, but Géza perhaps have had a part in building the cathedral or made generous donations to it.

[2] Cf. *SRH* 1, ch. 102–3, p. 366–69. Ladislas reigned 1077–95, so the 30 years and 3 months is evidently a miscopy. He was first buried in the monastery he founded in Somogyvár (South of Lake Balaton); later his body was transferred to Várad (today Oradea, in Romania), to where King Ladislas had moved the bishopric from nearby Bihar (Biharia). Thereafter he was honoured as the founder of the bishopric, and Várad became the centre of his very popular cult. — The Pechenegs (whom the Hungarian sources often refer to as Cumans) attacked Transylvania several times in these decades, and Ladislas fought together with his

62. Géza became king after Solomon, but died after a reign of three years. He is buried at Vác, the church he is said to have founded.[1]

63. Ladislas succeeded Géza and reigned for thirty years and three months; he is buried in Oradea. The Pechenegs, arch-enemies of the Hungarians, raided Hungary during his reign. As the Pechenegs fled back, King Ladislas and the Hungarians caught up with them at a mountain called Chiraleş in Transylvania, and inflicted such a crushing defeat that not a one of them is said to have survived.[2]

64. After Ladislas' death the throne passed to Géza's son Coloman. He reigned for eighteen years and is buried at Székesfehérvár. Coloman had been a bishop before rising to being crowned king. He was known as "Könyves Kálmán" because of the books he owned, from which he used to read his hours when he was bishop.[3] He also sent

brother Géza and King Solomon against them (Stanescu, "La crise du Bas-Danube byzantin"; Göckenjan, *Hilfsvölker*, 97). It was during one of these battles that the episode from the heroic St. Ladislas-cycle most commonly depicted in medieval Hungarian churches took place, when the king rescued a girl from a nomad horseman (see Kovács, "Customs as Symbols"; Marosi, "Heilige Ladislaus." — Chiraleş (Germ. Kyrieleis, Hung. Kerlés) is a mountain and settlement in Transylvania, in County Doboka. The name is of Slavic origin, *krles*, deriving ultimately from "Kyrie eleison" (*ÁMTF* 2.75; Kiss, *Földrajzi nevek*, 1: 721).

[3] Cf. *SRH* 1, ch. 152, 432–33. King Coloman (Hung. Kálmán) reigned 1095–1116. His nickname *könyves* 'learned' derives from *könyv* 'book.' Initially Coloman was to have become a priest or even a bishop, perhaps of Oradea. Evidence of the high level of cultural life in his court is Hartvic's Legend of St. Stephen (*SRH* 2: 377–400), various legal texts, and the original (non-extant) version of the Hungarian chronicle. Judging by a letter of Pope Urban II (1096) Coloman was educated in theology and canon law (*Diplomata*, 317–18).

citu occidi fecit regem Petrum, qui Hungaris in montibus, qui Gozd dicuntur[a], occurrens est devictus in montibus memoratis et occisus. Unde iidem montes usque hodie in Hungarico Patur Gozdia nominantur. Sedes enim huius regis et solium in Tenen erat civitate[1]. Hoc ergo facto et regno Dalmatiae [SRH, 183] conquastato galeas, naves et territas cum Venetis solidavit, mittens cum eis exercitum Hungarorum in Apuliam, ubi Monopolim et Brundusium civitates occuparunt civibus quibusdam fidem Venetis observantibus. Cumque easdem civitates ad tenendum Venetis reliquissent, concitatis cursibus planum Apuliae in quibusdam locis devastantes, tribus mensibus in ea permansere. Tandemque ad naves redeuntes per mare in Dalmatiam revertuntur capitaneo Hungaro et regis Hungariae banerio ibidem cum Venetis derelictis. Quas quidem civitates Guillelmus iunior rex Siciliae per auxilium Pisanorum cum magnis sumptibus postmodum vix rehabuit[2].

[a] dicitur *K, H*

---

[1] The conquest of Croatia, initiated by Ladislas I in 1091, was completed by Coloman in 1097. Peter Snačić (Svačić) ruled as the last independent Croatian king 1091–97. It is possible that King Peter had something to do with a Petrova Gora near Karlovac or another near Knin (Moseč). Anyway, Croatia as a historical-geographical term in the 11th century refers to the territory between the Kapela (medieval: Gvozd, lit. 'forested mountain') mountains and the Dalmatian litoral. For the localisation of the battle see Goldstein, "Dinastija Arpadovića," 264–66. Knin appears in this context only in Simon's account but it was in fact the last royal residence, where later the bans of Croatia resided. A hoard found in the village Lepuri near Benkovac, containing some 2000 silver coins of King Coloman and bezants, may be associated with the Hungarian campaign in the region.

[2] Our author is the only source for Coloman's Italian expedition, though it is not out of the question that such a campaign took place in

an army into the kingdom of Dalmatia and had King Peter killed. Peter encountered the Hungarians in the mountains known as Gvozd but was defeated and killed in these mountains, whence the mountains are called "Patur Gozdia" in Hungarian to this day. Peter's royal seat and throne were in the city of Knin.[1] After defeating Peter and conquering the kingdom of Dalmatia, Coloman hired galleys, sailboats, and cargo ships from the Venetians and used them to ferry a Hungarian army across to Apulia. There he secured the cities of Monopoli and Brindisi for a faction of the citizens loyal to Venice. Leaving the same cities in the control of the Venetians he made lightning raids on various parts of the plain of Apulia and remained there for three months before returning to his ships. Then, after leaving a Hungarian captain and the banner of the king of Hungary with the Venetians in Apulia, the king crossed back over the sea to Dalmatia. Later these cities were recaptured by William the Younger, King of Sicily, but only at great expense and with the help of the Pisans.[2]

the summer of 1108. Later Italian chroniclers borrowed the story from Simon, first Paolino da Venezia (*Historia satyrica*; Muratori *Rerum Italicarum Scriptores*, 4: 989), from whom Andrea Dandolo then borrowed it (*Chronica* 9.10.11; Muratori *Rerum Italicarum Scriptores* XII\1, 224). — Of the three types of ships mentioned, the *galea* ("galley") was a *navis longa*; *navis* refers to a *navis rotunda*, a sailing ship; and the *territa*—from Arabic *tarida* or *tarrada*—was a small transport ship, an oared galley used for horse transport and for landing (Pryor, *Geography*). — William the Younger could possibly be William III (reigned 1194). With the help of a fleet from Genoa and Pisa Emperor Henry VI invaded Sicily in 1194. Earlier William I, king of Sicily 1154–66, took Brindisi from the Byzantines after a famous siege in 1156. Coloman's efforts on behalf of the Byzantines are evidenced by the hypothesis that his envoys were among the signatories of the peace treaty between Byzantium and Bohemond in Sept 1108 (Makk, *Árpáds*, 15; Anna Comnena, *Alexiad*, 13.12).

65. Post Kalomannum vero regnavit Bela annis IX[a], duobus mensibus. Albae tumulatur[1].

66. Post Belam autem regnavit Geicha XX. annis. Tandem moritur et Albae sepelitur[2].

67. Post hunc regnavit Stephanus annis XI., mensibus VIIII.Quo quidem imperante Ladislaus dux sibi usurpat regnum et coronam anno medio. Albae sepelitur[3].

68. Post istum Stephanus frater suus coronam usurpat mensibus V. et diebus V. tandemque devincitur. In quo praelio plures regni nobiles occiduntur, idem vero de regno expulsus, demum venit in Zemin[a], ubi et finivit vitam suam. Albae requiescit[4].

69. Sed post hunc regnavit Bela Graecus, quem Becha et Gregor apud imperatorem Graecorum[a] diuitius tenuerunt.

[a] undecim *H*

[b] Zemiu *K*

[c] Graecorum imperatorem *H*

---

[1] Coloman was in fact succeeded by his son, Stephen II (1116–31), who was succeeded by Béla II (1131–41). — The royal chapel at Székesfehérvár, founded by St. Stephen, became the ceremonial burial place of the Hungarian kings. After Stephen, Coloman was the first king to be buried there, followed by his successors from Béla II onwards.

[2] Géza II reigned 1141–62.

65. Coloman was succeeded by Béla, who reigned for nine years and two months, and is buried at Székesfehérvár.[1]

66. Béla was succeeded by Géza, who reigned for twenty years. After his death he was buried at Székesfehérvár.[2]

67. Géza was succeeded by Stephen, who reigned for eleven years and nine months. During his reign Duke Ladislas usurped the crown and the kingdom for half a year. Stephen is buried at Székesfehérvár.[3]

68. After Stephen died, Ladislas's brother Stephen usurped the crown for five months and five days before being overthrown. In the battle many nobles of the realm were killed, even though the usurper was driven from the kingdom. He finally settled in Zemun, where he ended his days. He is buried at Székesfehérvár.[4]

69. He was succeeded by Béla the Greek, whom Becse and Gregory kept for a long time at the court of the Greek emperor. King Béla rid the country of robbers and brig-

[3] Cf. *SRH* 1, ch. 169, 461. Stephen III reigned 1162–72; Ladislas II reigned 1162–63.

[4] Cf. *SRH* 1, ch. 170, 461–62. Stephen IV was crowned in 1163, but Stephen III defeated his army on 19 June 1163 near Székesfehérvár. Stephen IV went into exile and died in Zemun (Hung. Zimony) on the Danube opposite Belgrade, where he was permitted to reside by the Byzantines, who for some time supported his claims to the throne.

Hic quidem fures et latrones persecutus est petitionibus-
que loqui traxit originem, ut Romana habet curia et imperii.
Albae iacet tumulatus[1]. [SRH, 184]

70.   Post Belam vero regnavit Emiricus filius eius[2].

71.   Sed post hunc regnavit Andreas rex potens et illustris.
Iste etiam Terram Sanctam visitavit, ubi per omnes principes Christianorum capitaneus ordinatur et exercitum
soldani Babiloniae cum Hungaris et Zaculis effugavit et ho-
nore multiplici cum gente sua per Assirios et alias nationes praevenitur indeque cum summa gloria revertitur in
Hungariam[3].

72.   Post hunc autem regnavit Bela filius eius, apud Fratres Minores Strigonii tumulatur. Istius quidem in diebus

---

[1] Cf. *SRH* 1, ch. 171, 462–63. Béla III reigned 1172–96. He lived in the
Byzantine court for a time, where he was called Alexios and treated as
a heir to the Byzantine throne. He returned to Hungary and was
crowned in January 1173 at Székesfehérvár. — Simon's hints of the
Byzantine connections of the Becse-Gergely (Gregory) kindred are
improbable; while it is not impossible that members of the kindred
accompanied Béla during his Byzantine stay (Makk, *Árpáds*, 172), the
given names in the Becse-Gergely kindred are all Hungarian, and they
had the same coat of arms as the Dorozsma kindred, so they were
apparently native Hungarians. — The measures to suppress thieves and
so on are more commonly associated with Béla IV, judging by the
observations of Rogerius, canon of Oradea, who cites the king's radical
"police actions" as one of the reasons for the Hungarian nobles'
hostility to him (*SRH* 2: 555–56, 559). — The founding of the royal
chancellery, however, and the obligatory petitioning by noblemen is
certainly to be associated with the reign of Béla III; the later practice
was revoked by Béla IV in 1267 (1267, 7–10: "Further, the cases of

ands. The practice of submitting petitions in written form, as at the Roman Curia and the imperial court, also dates from his reign. His tomb lies at Székesfehérvár.[1]

70.   Béla was succeeded by his son Emeric.[2]

71.   Emeric was succeeded by the powerful and illustrious Andrew. Andrew went to the Holy Land, where he was elected commander by all the princes of Christendom, and where with his Hungarian and Székely forces he routed an army of the Sultan of Babylon. He and his people won all kinds of honours among the Assyrians and other nations, and he returned to Hungary covered in glory.[3]

72.   He was succeeded by his son Béla, who is buried at the Minorites in Esztergom. In his reign the Mongols, or

nobles shall be expedited without petitions," *DRMH* 1: 43; cf. Mályusz-Kristó, *Commentarii*, 1: 474–75). — His tomb and King Stephen's were discovered in Székesfehérvár in 1848, when they were transported to Budapest, and today stand in the so-called Matthias Church in the Castle of Buda. His funeral insignia, now in the National Museum, are the only complete surviving set of a medieval Hungarian king.

[2] Emeric reigned 1196–1204.

[3] Cf. *SRH* 1, ch. 175, 465–66. Andrew II (reigned 1205–35) personally led an expedition to the Holy Land in the Fifth Crusade (1217–18). As to the extent of his success opinions varied at the time and the matter is still debated (see Sweeney, "Hungary" for a positive assessment, Runciman, *History*, 2: 147–49 for a negative one). We do know that the Pope considered his return an early retreat. Simon is the only one who seems to know about the participation of the Székely. — Babylon refers to Babylon in Egypt, i.e. Cairo. The Sultan of Egypt at the time was Al-Malik I al-Adil Saifaddin, or "Saphadin" (1200–1218).

Mongli sive[a] Tartari de tribus partibus regni in Hungariam
adeunt cum quinquies centenis millibus armatorum habentes adhuc centuriones et decuriones ad milia XL. Quibus
in Soio rex praefatus contraveniens[b] a Monglis[c] devincitur
anno Domini millesimo CC.-o XLI.-o[d]. Ubi fere tota regni
militia est deleta ipso Bela coram eis ad mare fugiente. Quo
quidem de mari revertente per ducem Fridericum de Austria bello impetitur. Quem ante Civitatem Novam Hungari cum lancea in maxilla transfixum peremerunt[1].

73. Postea regnavit Stephanus rex filius eius, qui Boemiae
regem nomine Otacarum ante fluvium Rebcha contra eum
venientem cum Boemis videlicet, Australibus, Stiriensibus,
Brandburgensibus, et caeteris mixtis gentibus expulit vir-
tuose[2]. Iste etiam civitatem Budum suo dominio sub-iu-
gavit, dominumque Bulgarorum eo vivente sibi compulit
obedire[3]. Migrans tandem ex hoc saeculo et in insula vocata

[a] Mong Lisive *H, E*, Mong Lisviae *K*

[b] conveniens *H, E*

[c] Mong Lis *K, H*, Mongalis *E*

[d] ducentesimo quadragesimo *H*

---

[1] Cf. *SRH* 1, ch. 177, 467–68. Béla IV reigned 1235–70. The battle with
the Mongols took place not far from the village of Muhi on the river
Sajó on 11 April 1241. Even though only a fraction of the country's
armed forces took part in the battle, no further resistance was offered.
The king fled from the battlefield and retreated, via Austria, to the
Adriatic sea to await the end of the Mongol invasion on the island-city
of Trogir (Trau). — Frederick II "the Quarrelsome" was prince of
Austria and Styria, 1230–46. Clashes with Frederick—who had forced

Tartars, invaded the kingdom of Hungary from three directions with 500,000 armed men plus 40,000 centurions and decurions. King Béla met them at the river Sajó in the year of our Lord 1241 but was defeated. The military forces of the kingdom were almost totally annihilated at the battle and the king fled before them to the sea. On his return from the coast Duke Frederick of Austria made war on him but at the battle of Wiener Neustadt the Duke was struck through the jaw by a Hungarian lance and killed.[1]

73. His son Stephen reigned after him. When a king of Bohemia called Otakar advanced against him along the river Rábca with forces from Bohemia, Austria, Styria, Brandenburg, and a mixture of other nations, Stephen drove them out with great courage.[2] He added the city of Vidin to his dominions and exacted obedience from the lord of the Bulgars for as long as he lived.[3] He finally

the fleeing Béla to relinquish rights to him—broke out in the second half of 1242. Frederick died in the battle of the river Leitha on 5 June 1246; it is unclear by whom he was killed (Dienst, *Schlacht*, 14–16).

[2] Cf. *SRH* 1, ch. 180, 470–71. The battle between Stephen V (ruled 1270–72) and the Czech king Otakar II (ruled 1253–78) took place on 21 May 1271.

[3] Vidin was a castle of strategic importance on the Danube in Bulgaria. Its temporary occupation by Stephen took place in 1262 when he was a co-regent or "younger king". The Hungarians advanced as far as Tirnovo and fought altogether five victorious battles. The lord of the Bulgars who surrendered to Stephen in 1266 was the *despot* Jacob Sventslav. From then on the Hungarian kings used the title *Bulgariae rex*.

Beatae[a] Virginis in caenobio monialium requiescit[b] tumulatus[1]. [SRH, 185]

74.   Post hunc regnat Ladislaus tertius filius eius. Hic enim puerulus in regni solium Domino disponente coronatur. Istius ergo in diebus rex Otacarus Boemorum, qui de iure imperii plura sibi usurpaverat de facto et iniuste, unde vires resumpserat ac potentiam inauditam, in confiniis Hungariae laceraverat in diversis locis maximam portionem, pro qua ex ipso eius genitor nondum receperat dignam vindictae ultionem, eo quod praeventus esset morte insperata. Sed cum inter ista Alamanniae principes Rudolphum comitem de Habusburc in curia Francuurtensi in regem sibi praefecissent[2], ut imperii iura, quae erant occupata, deberet revocare, ipse tanquam pheudorum imperialium reintegrator in Austriam, que fuerat per Otacarum invasa et possessa, primitus introivit. Quo quidem Viennae diutius residente ac iura sua de Boemis requirente rex Boemicus contra eum tam immensum commovit exercitum ac pervalidum[c], quod propriis viribus Alamanniae princeps ei resistere dubitaret. Propter quod ergo Hun-

---

[a] Beatissimae *H*

[b] requievit *H*

[c] praevalidum *H*

---

[1] The Island of the Blessed Virgin (so called from 1265; from 1317 and still today St. Margaret's Island) was originally a royal preserve called *Insula leporum*, the Island of Rabbits. From 1252 Stephen's sister Margaret (1242–70) lived on the island in the Dominican nunnery founded by her father Béla IV and dedicated to the Blessed Virgin.

THE DEEDS OF THE HUNGARIANS

departed this world and lies at rest in a tomb in the nuns'
convent on the island known as the Island of the Blessed
Virgin.[1]

74. His son Ladislas the Third has been reigning since
then. By divine dispensation he came to the throne and was
crowned king when he was still only a boy. In his days
much of the borders of Hungary had suffered devastation
from attacks at various points by King Otakar of Bohemia,
who had usurped numerous imperial prerogatives de facto
and unjustly, and amassed unprecedented powers and
strength in the process. Because he died unexpectedly,
Ladislas's father had never had the opportunity to exact
adequate retribution from the Bohemian king. However,
in the meantime the German princes elected Count Rudolf
of Habsburg as their king at the court of Frankfurt.[2] Rudolf
was supposed to recover the imperial rights which had been
alienated. First of all he entered Austria, which had been
invaded and occupied by Otakar, with the intention of
winning back the imperial fiefs. Rudolf had been in Vienna
for some time reasserting claims over Bohemia, when the
Bohemian king advanced against him with an army so large
and strong that the German prince was reluctant to oppose

Margaret and Stephen were buried on the island (Klaniczay,
"Modelli").

[2] Cf. *SRH* 1, ch. 181, 471–72. Ladislas IV "the Cuman" reigned 1272–90
(cf. note 1, p. 2), and was crowned when he was ten years old. The
northern and western borderland of Hungary was constantly under
attack, and important strongholds were lost to King Otakar of Bohemia between 1273 and 1277. Rudolf of Habsburg was elected German
king on 1 October 1273 in Frankfurt and reigned until 1291.

gariae[a] regem magnificum, tanquam filium sanctae ecclesiae catholicae sibi postulavit humiliter in auxilium, perpe-
tua amicitia seipsum eapropter eidem obligando. Adi-
iciens insuper, ut in eo quoque sanctae ecclesiae Romanae
summum servitium exhibere videretur[1]. Ipse vero auxilio
simili quandocunque a rege Hungariae foret requisitus,
deberet subvenire. Quia vero Ladislaus Hungariae[b] rex
in corde et animo occultabat Otacari praesumptionem te-
merariam contra patrem et ipsum attentatam, eo quod
tener esset viribus corporis et aetate, petitioni principis
Alamanniae satisfacturum se disposuit. Egressus igitur de
Albensi civitate velut Martis filius, cuius quidem constel-
latio conceptionis nativitatisque[c] ei[d] deinde[e] in audacia et
caeteris virtutibus naturalibus subministrat, in virtute Altissimi et proavorum suorum, scilicet Stephani, Emirici[f]
atque Ladislai regum et sanctorum votivis praesummens
confidensque suffragiis, erecto banerio regiae maiestatis
Rudolphum in Marhec[2] coniunxit cum exercitu, qui ipsius
adventum et auxilium sicut Dei [SRH, 186] expectabat. Sed

[a] Hungari *K*

[b] Hungarorum *H, E*

[c] conceptioni nativitatique *K, E*, conceptioni nativitatisque *H*

[d] eius *K, H, E*

[e] deinde *H*, die *K, E*

[f] Emrici *H*, Emerici *E*

---

[1] Rudolf's contemporaries referred to his political programme as
Reichsgutsrevindication; see Redlich, "Anfänge," 369–70, 408. — The
reference to Ladislas as "son of the holy Catholic church" was a
propaganda ploy of the Hungarian royal chancellery; in fact the king

him with his own forces alone. So he approached the glorious king of Hungary and humbly requested him as a son of the holy Catholic church for his assistance, pledging therewith his eternal friendship, and suggesting into the bargain that in doing so he would again be seen to be showing his deep devotion to the holy church of Rome;[1] in return Rudolf would be bound to offer similar assistance to the king of Hungary at any time the latter should request it. Now King Ladislas of Hungary had continued to overlook the presumptious and high-handed liberties which Otakar had taken with his father and with himself because he was young and not fully grown, so now he agreed to grant the request of the German prince. He marched forth from Székesfehérvár with the royal banner flying like a son of Mars, whom the constellation at his conception and birth ever since endows with boldness and other natural virtues, expecting and trusting in the power of the Almighty and the saintly intercession of his forefathers, the holy kings Stephen, Emeric, and Ladislas. At Marchegg[2] his army joined forces with Rudolf who was waiting for his arrival and assistance, regarding both as heaven-sent. However, Rudolf's troops, more heavily armed and therefore slow in

had serious conflicts with the Pope and his legate, but seems to have convinced Rudolf too as this version found its way into Rudolf's report to the pope on Hungarian affairs in 1278. For the same reason Ladislas' documents so often allude to his sainted forefathers Stephen, Emeric, and Ladislas (*Regesta imperii* 6:1, no. 1005; Gerics, "Adalékok," 123).

[2] It possible that the royal banner was kept in the church in Székesfehérvár, the Hungarian "St. Denis" (Veszprémy, "Zászlóhasználat," 214–15), along with captured shields and flags, as the last sentence of this chapter suggests. For Marchegg, cf. *Annales S. Rudperti Salisburgensis* (Kusternig, *Quellen*, 52).

quoniam[a] gens Rudolphi in motu gravis erat propter arma graviora, nimisque timorata ad resistendum tam validae multitudini, ut Otacarus conducere ferebatur, pro eo contraire et moveri dubitabat. Hoc autem Ladislao rege viso et percepto, Otacaro ad praelium properanti ac parato circa castrum Stilfrid, prope fluvium Morowae[1] adpropinquat Boemicum exercitum convallando circumquaque. Quorum quidem equos et etiam semetipsos sagittis Hungari et Comani regis sic infestant vulnerando, quod Milot militiae suae princeps,[2] in quo copia exercitus praesertim confidebat, sustinere non valens Hungarorum impetum ac sagittas, cum suis fugam dedit, et post ipsum Poloni conductitii dissoluto exercitu fugierunt cum Boemis, Comanis vero inter ista praelia, onera et arnesia Boemorum regis suique exercitus sustollentibus dissipando. In isto igitur praelio rex Otacarus dispersa mente et confusa vagando in exercitu captus occiditur. Filius vero eius dux Nicolaus[3] in Hungariam deducitur captivatus cum aliis captivis baronibus, comitibus et militibus sine numero. Mortuorum autem numerum in praefato praelio potuisset aestimare sola divina sapientia. Rudolfus ergo Teutoniae rex atque Roma-

---

[a] quam *K*

---

[1] On the military significance of Stillfried (or Marchfeld), cf. *Annales Mellicenses, MGH SS* 9: 510. — The battle fought near the river Morava (March) on 26 August 1278, which became known as the battle of Dürnkrut, was the decisive conflict in the struggle between Rudolf and Otakar for mastery of the eastern provinces of the Empire. The description of the battle makes clear that Simon had access to precise contemporary information.

movement, were quite unnerved at the thought of facing a force as powerful as the one Otakar was reported to be leading, and refused to stir or to join battle. Ladislas saw the problem and the solution. Otakar was prepared and in haste to join battle. Ladislas closed on him, and at the castle of Stillfrid[1] by the river Morava surrounded the Bohemian army on all sides. The king's Hungarian and Cuman archers then proceeded to wound and harry them and their horses so mercilessly that their commander Milota,[2] in whom the rank and file placed their greatest trust, was incapable of withstanding the volleys of Hungarian arrows. He and his men fled, whereupon the contingent of Polish mercenaries broke ranks and joined the rout. In between the fighting, the Cumans managed to seize and disperse the baggage and the equipment of the Bohemian king and his army. King Otakar, found wandering over the battlefield in a state of mental distraction and confusion, was seized and put to death. His son, Duke Nicholas,[3] was taken prisoner and marched off to Hungary, along with countless other barons, counts and knights. Only the omniscience of the Almighty could estimate the number of those who fell in this battle. Rudolf, king of Germany and of the Romans, had been standing by with his followers and

---

[2] Milota Dedić, a Moravian dignitary and Styrian captain, cf. *Steirische Reimchronik* (*MGH Deutsche Chroniken* 5, line 16043, and John of Victring's *Liber certarum historiarum* (Kusternig, *Quellen*, 136, 146, 150). The Bohemians and Moravians were led by Milota. Otakar's troops from Brandenburg, Meissen, and Poland had gathered at Opawa by 5 June 1278. The battalion of Silesian and Polish auxiliaries was a reserve.

[3] Nicholas I, later Duke of Troppau (Opawa) 1278–1307, natural son of Otakar.

norum cum suis stabat inspiciendo, quae fiebant. Facta igitur hac victoria rex Germanicus Ladislao regi egit grates, quod per eum Austria et Stiria sibi fuit restituta illo die[1]. Et sic Ladislaus rex Hungariae rediit cum victoria rege Alamannico in Austria remanente. Haec est enim Ladislai regis victoria primitiva, quam divina clementia ei tribuit in aetate adolescentiae constituto. In quo quidem exercitu ipso die comes Renoldus filius Renoldi banerium regis tenuit viriliter et potenter de genere Bastech[2] oriundus, adstantes domino regi fratres eiusdem Andreas, Salomon, Ladislaus et alii regni Hungariae nobiles, sicut stellae caeli absque numero. Ut igitur in memoriam redeat regis Ladislai tam gloriosa triumphalisque victoria, in obprobrium sempiternumque dedecus Boemorum, Polonorum Morawanorumque[a] scuta et vexilla in Albensi ecclesia, sede regni ac solio in pariete suspensa in aeternum perseverant. [SRH, 187]

75. Aliud quoque miraculosum praelium Ladislaus rex adolescens habuit cum Comanis, quod praelio praecedenti

[a] Moravorumque *H, E*

---

[1] The Hungarian military help was important, as their number probably exceeded 2000 mounted warriors. Both the light cavalry (that is, the Cuman and Hungarian archers) and the heavy-armoured cavalry fought bravely in the first echelon on the Habsburg side, but that Rudolf thanked the king for "having restored" his countries to him is an overstatement. The *Steirische Reimchronik* (*MGH Deutsche Chroniken* 5, lines 16260–70) acknowledges the Hungarian knights' bravery, noting that they had learned their fighting skills in France. However, it was in fact the young Hungarian king who watched the battle from a nearby hill. With the death of Otakar the fight for the

looking on as these events unfolded. When the victory was won the German king offered King Ladislas his thanks, declaring that through his help all Austria and Styria had been restored to him that day.[1] So King Ladislas of Hungary returned victoriously while the German king remained in Austria. This, then, was the first of King Ladislas' victories accorded to him by divine mercy before he was even an adult. *Ispán* Reynold son of Reynold, of the clan of Básztély,[2] firmly and unflinchingly held the royal banner in the host that day, while his brothers Andrew, Solomon, and Ladislas, and other nobles of the realm of Hungary, countless as the stars in heaven, stood by the side of their lord the king. To enshrine the memory of King Ladislas's singularly glorious and triumphant victory and to the everlasting shame and disgrace of the Czechs, Poles, and Moravians, their shields and banners remain hanging for all time on the wall of the church at Székesfehérvár, the royal seat and throne of Hungary.

75. Another miraculous battle which King Ladislas had fought before he was grown up was against the Cumans,

---

Babemberg heritage was over, and Otakar's plan for a Central European kingdom was brought to nought.

[2] Perhaps Simon was born on the Básztély kindred's domain at Kéza and started his career in the service of the kindred; this would explain his name and his interest in the non-noble categories of society, as well as why he here gives prominence to the role of Rudolf and his brothers while saying nothing about the other leaders. The Hungarians were in fact led by the palatine Matthew of Csák and the judge-royal Stephen of Gut-Keled. Regarding the career of *ispán* Reynold Básztély, see Bolla, *Jobbágyosztály*, 67. — For "countless as the stars in heaven" cf. Jer. 33:22.

comparatur. Igitur cum Comani per regem Belam, piae
memoriae avum regis in Hungariam primo introducti,
ut arena postmodum subcrevissent[1], et ipsi regi Belae ipsos dispergere in animo pervenissent per provincias, et
nunquam id facere praesumpsisset[a], in regno emergere
laesionem[2] sperans per eosdem. Hoc ipsum dicitur rex
Stephanus pater eius bonae memoriae de ipsis cogitasse, et
propter cautelam memoratam retraxisse suum velle. Ladislaus vero rex illustris, animosus ac magnivolus perfidiam
contra eum cognoscens inter eos fabricare, taliter processit
contra ipsos bellaturus, ut in praelio ipso acriter debellati,
plurimi interempti, quidam vero ex ipsis relictis uxoribus,
pueris et rebus omnibus ad populos barbaros fugierunt.
Nonnulli etiam, qui sunt residui, regiis praeceptis in tantum sunt subiecti, quod corde tremulo vix videre audent
vultum regis[3]. In hoc ergo praelio occiditur Oliverius filius

[a] praesumpsissent *K*

---

[1] The battle at Lake Hód, near today's town of Hódmezővásárhely
(South Hungary) took place some time between 17 September and 21
October 1282 (Zsoldos, "Téténytől"). — The Cumans, Turkic nomads
of the southern Eurasian steppe fleeing before the invading Mongols,
first settled in Hungary 1239–41 under King Béla IV. They served the
king well, and Béla's son, Stephen V, married a Cuman princess. The
prelates, however, were appalled by their heathen practices and the
nobles were worried by the presence of such ferocious neighbours and
by the additional armed force they lent to the king's authority. In 1278
Philip, bishop of Fermo, was sent to Hungary as a papal legate to insist
that King Ladislas take firmer measures toward their integration. On
22 June 1279 King Ladislas swore an oath promising to settle and
baptise the Cumans and to force them to abandon their customs.

and it can be compared with the proceeding one. The Cumans had been first introduced into Hungary by King Béla, the king's grandfather of pious memory, and thereafter the Cumans had increased in number like grains of sand.[1] King Béla had had in mind to disperse them through the various provinces but had never dared to put the plan into practice, for fear of provoking them to some treasonable activity within his realm.[2] His father, King Stephen of happy memory, is said to have had similar plans for them, but to have reversed his decision out of like caution. King Ladislas was noble, spirited, and ambitious, and when he learnt that the Cumans were plotting treason against him, he set out to make war on them. There was a fierce battle, which ended in utter defeat for the Cumans. A great many were killed; others abandoned their wives, children, and all their possessions and fled to the barbarian peoples. The few who are left are so abjectly subject to the King's authority that their hearts tremble in his presence and they scarcely dare look him in the face.[3] In this battle the Cumans killed

However, their resistance forced the king to take military action against them a few years later. See Pálóczi Horváth, *Pechenegs, Cumans*.

[2] During these controversies and bloody internal struggles the Cumans usually supported the central authority but inevitably became involved in factional strife. In the year 1280 they rebelled against Ladislas but the king forced them back by military threats. The reference to "treasonable activity" and "plotting treason" probably refer to their attempts to ally themselves with their fellow-Cumans living outside Hungary, cf. the chronicles (*SRH* 1: 471). — The term *laesio maiestatis* was known in medieval Hungarian law as well; e.g. it was the charge against the palatine Finta of Aba in 1283.

[3] The eulogistic language—recalling Job 41:1, *quis enim resistere potest vultui meo*— accords with Simon's propagandistic purposes.

Pata per Cumanos de genere Aba, Andreas frater Laurentii filius comitis Nicolai de Wigman[a], Ladislaus filius comitis Ponyth de Miscouch et Demetrius filius parvi Michaelis de genere Rusd[b] perimuntur[1].

DE NOBILIBUS ADVENIS[2]

76. [C]um pura Hungaria plures tribus vel progenies non habeat quam generationes centum et octo, videndum est unde [SRH, 188] esse habent illorum progenies, qui de terra Latina vel de Alamannia, vel de aliis regionibus descenderunt. Dux namque Geicha de genere Turul, cui prae caeteris Hungaris oraculum profluisse de supernis dicitur, ut reciperet fidem catholicam et baptismum, quare manus gestabat sanguine humano maculatas, nec erat idoneus ad fidem convertere tantam gentem, licet ipse domusque eius per Sanctum Adalbertum[3] baptismi gratiam recepisset,

---

[a] Vigman *H*

[b] Kusd *H, E*

---

[1] Most of these are known figures, with the exception of Oliver son of Pata of the Aba kindred. Andrew, son of count Nicholas, was a member of the Igmánd kindred, landowners in the western counties of Komárom and Győr. Ladislas, son of *comes* Panyit, belonged to the Miskolc kindred; his father was a favourite of King Stephen V and for a time ban of Severin. Demetrius and his father Michael were landowners in the north-west; Michael was at one time *ispán* of County Nyitra.

[2] While the following chapters were earlier regarded an "appendix" (to which Simon refers at the end of ch. 6), Szűcs argued (above

Oliver the son of Pata, of the clan Aba; Andrew the brother of Lawrence and son of Count Nicholas of Igmánd, Ladislas son of Count Panyit of Miskolc, and Demetrius son of Michael the Small, of the clan of Rosd, also perished.[1]

THE NOBLES OF FOREIGN ORIGIN[2]

76. Since pure Hungary has no more tribes or families than the 108 kindreds, we need to consider what were the origins of the families of those who come from the Latin lands, from Germany, or from other regions. Though Duke Géza of the Turul kindred was renowned beyond all other Hungarians as recipient of an oracle from on high telling that he should receive the Catholic faith and baptism, yet because his hands were stained with human blood, he was not a fit person to convert so great a people to the faith. Even though he and his family received the grace of baptism at the hands of St. Adalbert,[3] word came to him

pp. LXII–LXIII) that it is in fact "Part III" of Simon's history, treating of those Hungarians who were not of *pura Hungaria*, and leading on to "Part IV," on those Hungarians who lost their liberty for shirking military service. It is the most detailed information we possess on the "immigrant" aristocracy; cf. E. Fügedi, "Ungarn als Gastland," and now also Fügedi and Bak, "Fremde Ritter."

[3] Cf. *SRH* 1, ch. 37, 294–95. It is unlikely that St. Adalbert either baptised or married Stephen, as tradition early asserted him. St. Adalbert became the patron saint of the archbishopric of Esztergom which was given his relics probably by Emperor Otto III (Bogyay, *Stephanus rex*; Veszprémy, "Der hl. Adalbert").

tamen ei de coelesti throno verbum venit, quod a tali resileret cogitatu, quia[a] haec omnia facienda Sancto Stephano ex ipso nascituro Altissimi clementia ordinarat[1]. Unde hoc audito id, quod potuit et debuit circa conversationem suae gentis secundum ordinationem Sancti Adalberti Pragensis scilicet episcopi facere non omisit. Misit itaque suos nuncios in Christianam regionem suum desiderium omnibus divulgando. Quapropter hoc audito multi comites, milites et nobiles ex terris Christianorum ad eum accesserunt, quidam enim ex eis amore Dei, ut ipsum ducem contra paganos, qui fidem non acciperent, adiuvarent, et alii[b], quod de[c] ipsis paganis et persecutionibus ipsorum[d] essent liberati. Nam gens ipsa sub paganismo constituta crudelis persecutio fuerat Christianis.

77. Tunc eo[e] tempore ad ducem Geicham venit comes Tiboldus de Fanberg, qui Grauu Tibold est vocatus, unde de eadem progenie Grauu quidam usque hodie simpliciter nominantur. Ex isto illi de Bobocha orti derivantur. Isti etenim sunt Vandeuchumlant[f,2].

[a] quare *H*, quod *E*

[b] aliis *K*

[c] quod de] quidem *H*

[d] eorum *H*

[e] ipso *H add.*

[f] Vandeuchunlat *H*, de Deuchunlant *E*

[1] For "word came . . . ," cf. the legends of St. Stephen (e.g the *Legenda Maior* of Hartvic, *SRH* 2, ch. 3, 379–80).

from the throne of heaven that he should abandon his plans to do so, as the mercy of the Most High had ordained that all these deeds had been reserved for St. Stephen, the son to be born to him.[1] When he received these tidings, Duke Géza did not neglect to do what was in his power and what was his duty to effect the conversion of his people according to the instructions of St. Adalbert, bishop of Prague. He sent his messengers to the countries of Christendom announcing to everyone his desire. On hearing this many counts, knights, and nobles came to him from Christian lands, some of them out of love of God to help the Duke against the pagans who refused to accept the faith, others so that they themselves might be rid of persecution by the pagans. For these people were still living under paganism, and there had been a cruel persecution of Christians.

77. So at that time Count Tibold of Fanberg came to Duke Géza. He was called Graf Tibold, and some members of the same family are still simply called Graf to this day. The Babócsa derive their origins from him, these persons being *von Deutschland*.[2]

---

[2] Count Tibold of Fanberg is unidentified. In the Tibold kindred two members named Tibold appear in the 13th century, one of them mentioned as ban. For a certain *Tietpaldus comes* in the service of Andrew I see Berthold of Reichenau ad ann. 1060 (*MGH SS* 5). — Mályusz identifies Fanberg as Schaumburg, a castle near Eferding by the Danube (*V. István-kori Gesta*, 82). — Babócsa on the river Drava was the ancient domain of the Tibold kindred (*predium principale*, 1232; see Karácsonyi, *Magyar nemzetségek*, 1007), with a Benedictine monastery as its cultic centre. — The author's use of German (*von Deutschland*) is noteworthy.

78. Post haec venit Hunt et Pazman, duo fratres carnales, milites coridati[1] orti de Svevia. Hi enim passagium per Hungariam cum suis militibus facientes ultra mare ire intendebant. Qui detenti [SRH, 189] per ducem Geicham, tandem sanctum regem Stephanum[a] in flumine Goron Teutonico more gladio militari accinxerunt[2].

79. Postmodum intrat de Wazurbuirc[b] comes Wecelinus[c]. Hic Cupan ducem in Simigio interfecit. Istius generatio de Iaki dicti sunt[3].

80. Postea Wolfer[d] cum Hedrico fratre suo introivit de Vildonia[e] cum XL. militibus phaleratis[4]. Huic datur mons

[a] Stephanum regem *H*

[b] Vazurburc *H*, Wasurburc *E*

[c] Vecelinus *H*

[d] Volfer *H*

[e] Viltonia *E*

---

[1] *Coridati* ?"courageous" (cf. Italian *corragioso*), or perhaps 'wearing leather armour' (cf. Italian *corazza*).

[2] Cf. *SRH* 1, ch. 41, 297. Hont and Pázmány (Pázmán) are mentioned as supporters of St. Stephen against Koppány in an interpolated version of the foundation deed of the Abbey of Pannonhalma (Mons Pannoniae, Martinsberg) from the beginning of the 13th century (*Diplomata*, no. 5, p. 39). The name Hont survives in that of County Hont, suggesting one of the brothers was county *ispán*. — The first recorded case of girding—which Simon rightly regards as a German custom—was in 1146, when King Géza I was girded before his first battle (*SRH* 1, ch. 164, 454–55; cf. Veszprémy, "Szt. István," 4).

78. The next arrivals were Hont and Pázmány, two half-brothers, courageous[1] knights of Swabian origin. These two and their retainers had been journeying through Hungary with the intention of passing over the sea when they were detained by Duke Géza, and finally they girded King Stephen with the sword of knighthood at the river Hron, after the German custom.[2]

79. The next to enter Hungary was Count Wenzilin from Wasserburg. He killed Duke Koppány in Somogy. His kindred are called the Ják.[3]

80. Next Wolfger and his brother Hedrich came to Hungary from Wildon with forty knights in armour.[4] Wolfger

[3] Cf. *SRH* 1, ch. 40, 296. 9th to 11th-century German variants of the name include Wenzil, Wezelin, and Wizelin (Gerics, "Krónikáink," 593–95). — There were several Wasserburgs in Bavaria, the most important on the river Inn. — Koppány's "duchy" was somewhere in Southwest Hungary in what would later become County Somogy. As great-great grandson of Árpád after the death of Duke Géza he demanded Géza's widow and dignity on the principle of levirate and seniorate. In punishment for his revolt his body was cut into four pieces and sent to different centres of the country. The foundation deed of the Pannonhalma abbey refers to his event, describing it as a war between Germans and Hungarians. See also the previous note. — The family was probably a collateral branch of the Aribo kindred. It is now believed that they were ancestors not so much of the Ják as the Rád kindred. The Gut-Keled kindred also considered them their ancestors.

[4] Cf. *SRH* 1, ch. 39, 296. For the *militibus phaleratis* Simon's chronicle source reads *cum trecentis dextrariis phaleratis*, which Henry of Mügeln translated as *bedackte rosz* (*SRH* 2: 136). Simon may have reduced the original number as a rationalisation or out of animosity to the kindred.

Kyscen pro descensu, in quo castrum fieri facit ligneum, tandem et coenobium monachorum, in quo post mortem sepelitur. Ex isto namque Hedrici origo esse habet[1].

81. Post hunc introivit Pot de Lebyn, qui nomine alio Ernistus est vocatus. Hic cum multis militibus adiit in Hungariam. De isto comitis Conradi de Altumburg[a] origo esse habet[2].

82. Sed postea, tempore Petri regis Kelad et Gut intrant tres fratres ex gente Svevorum procreati. De castello Stof sunt nativi[3].

83. Post istos Altman intrat de Fridbiur[b] miles corridatus ex patria Turingorum, de isto illi de Bolugi oriuntur[4]. [SRH, 190]

[a] Altunburg *H,E*

[b] Fridburg *H*, Fridburc *E*

---

[1] It is unlikely that Wolfger and Hedrich came from Wildon in Styria, as Wildon castle had not been built in 1157, and their ancestors' only possession was Hengstburg. The other Hungarian chronicles are more likely right in placing their origin in Hainburg. We know of a certain Wolfger of Erlach of the Au-Erlach kindred in the 12th century. Their arrival is best dated to the time of King Géza II. They were buried in the Benedictine monastery of Güssing, but the castle there was built only later by Béla III (Dopsch, "Die Hengstburg," 185–95).

[2] Cf. *SRH* 1, ch. 42, 297–98. Pot (palatine 1209–12) of the Győr kindred, founded Lébény, a monastery in west Hungary. The chronicles gloss Pot as a nickname "messenger" (Bote, Pote—which may explain his being also called Ernest). The ancestor of this kindred is regarded as a certain *Otho comes*, who came to Hungary in the 11th century and

was given Mt. Güssing to settle in. There he built a wooden fort, and later a monks' cloister, where he was buried after his death. The Héder descend from him.[1]

81.   The next to come was Pot of Lébény, also known as Ernest. He entered Hungary with many warriors. Count Conrad of Altenburg traces his origins from him.[2]

82.   But afterwards, in the time of King Peter, three brothers of the Keled and Gut kindred came to Hungary. They were of Swabian descent, and were born at the castle of Stauf.[3]

83.   After them, Altmann, a courageous knight from Thuringia, came from Friedburg. The Balog family descend from him.[4]

founded the clan monastery at Zselicszentjakab in 1061. — Conrad of Altenburg (Óvár or Magyaróvár on the western border) was a well-known figure in Hungarian history in the second half of the 13th century. He was *ispán* of County Borsod in 1258, then Master of the Treasury from 1260.

[3] Cf. *SRH* 1, ch. 45, 298–99. Gut and Keled are mentioned as *ispánok* in charters of 1093 and 1111. — "The castle of Stauf" could be either Burg Staufen near Freiburg in Baden, or Hohenstaufen in Württemberg, both ancient seats of the Hohenstaufens.

[4] Altmann of Friedburg cannot be identified. The Balog kindred from Hungary are named after a settlement Balog (today Veľký Blh in Slovakia), originally a river name (*ÁMTF* 2: 463). Among the narrative sources only Simon mentions this kindred. The name Altmann may have been known to Simon because Stephen son of Altmann (Olthmann) from Serke in County Gömör received a donation from King Ladislas IV (*ÁMTF* 2: 547).

84. Post haec intrant Oliverius et Ratoldus tempore regis Kalomanni de regno Apulorum. De Caserta ortum habent[1].

85. Illi vero de Sambuk de comitibus Campaniae ex Francia oriuntur[2].

86. Betse vero et Gregorii similiter de Francia generatio oritur, ex cognatione Guillelmi dicti Cornes[3].

87. Buzad autem generatio de Mesn originem trahit, nobiles de districtu Wircburg[a],[4].

[a] Vurburg *H*, Wurburg *E*

---

[1] Cf. *SRH* 1, ch. 46, 299. The reference to the Norman-Sicilian links of King Coloman, who in 1097 married Busilla, the daughter of Roger I, king of Sicily (1061–1101), is not unfounded, but the Rátót kindred was named after a certain Rathold or Ratolt, a typical Bavarian name, so their Sicilian origin is unlikely. A certain Oliver, probably from this kindred, is mentioned as the Queen's Master of the Treasury in 1262 and 1268 (*RA* no. 1288, 1289, 1577, p. 393, 482–83, cf. Tóth, "Hoholt"). —Caserta is in fact not in Apulia but in Terra di Lavoro (*Terra Laboris*, see Maps 1 and 2).

[2] Cf. *SRH* 1, ch. 49, 300. The French origin of the family (Zsámboki, Zsámbéki) is plausible in view of the frequent foreign names in the family. The first known family member is a certain *ispán* Smaragdus mentioned in a charter of 1166. During the 13th century members of the family held high offices such as voivode of Transylvania and archbishop of Kalocsa. They founded a Premonstratensian collegiate church and a castle with the French name Aymard in Zsámbék (30 km West of Budapest), the seat of the kindred.

84. Next, in the time of King Coloman, Oliver and Rathold came from the kingdom of Apulia. They originate from Caserta.[1]

85. The Zsámbék family come from France and descend from the counts of Champagne.[2]

86. The Becse-Gergely are similarly a kindred of French origin, being related to William Le Cornu.[3]

87. The Buzád kindred are nobles from the district of Wartburg and originate from Meissen.[4]

---

[3] Cf. *SRH* 1, ch. 43, 298. For this Gregory cf. Makk, *Árpáds*, 172. The Becse-Gergely (Gregory) kindred (see also above, p. 144) were most likely of Hungarian origin; the basis of the legend is probably that a member of the kindred had a French wife. William Le Cornu was a prominent member of the Sicilian Anjou court between 1266 and 1284.

[4] Cf. *SRH* 1, ch. 49, 300. The Buzád were also known as the Hahót. King Stephen III invited them to Hungary to support him in his struggle against Stephen IV. Buzád was a *Leitname* of this kindred; a ban Buzád lived in the first half of the 13th century, acting as ban of Slavonia 1226–28. The original German version of Buzád was probably Bussold or Posselt, but it could also have had a Magyar origin, from *búza* 'wheat,' cf. the name Árpád from *árpa* 'rye.' — The place-name Wartenberg (west of Freising, next to Moosburg) was preserved in the traditions of the kindred. Later chronicles changed it to Wartburg, which became well known in Hungary for its famous festivities of the *minnesänger*, sponsored by the landgrave Ludwig IV of Thuringia, husband of St. Elisabeth of Hungary. In Simon's time Thuringia belonged to the landgraviate of Meissen (Tóth, "Hoholt").

88. Hiemanni[a] siquidem generatio ex Nurimberc[b] oritur, satis sunt nobiles, cum regina Kisla intraverunt[1].

89. Sed illi, qui Rodoan et Bagath[c] nominantur, eorum generatio de Boemia ortum habet[2].

90. Similiter et illorum, qui de Lodan sunt vocati[3].

91. Comitum vero Simonis et fratris eius Michaelis generatio, qui Mertinsdorfarii nominantur, diebus regis Emirici filii Belae tertii cum regina Constantia filia regis Aragoniae[4], quae uxor fuerat regis Emirici, honestis secum militibus et familia decentissima introductis, in Hungariam pomposissime introivit. Quia cum [SRH, 191] eorum generatio cum quodam magno comite pro iustis et certis causis continue dimicaret, tandem contra ipsum comitem

[a] Hummani *H*, Hermanni *E*

[b] Nurimberk *H*, Nuremberc *E*

[c] Bakath *H*

---

[1] Cf. *SRH* 1, ch. 48, 300. The Hermány—derived from Hermann—kindred is indeed of German origin, with their ancestral domain at Hermán in West Hungary. According to their tradition, they came to Hungary with Queen Gisela, but they are first mentioned in 1226.

[2] Radvány son of Bogát, mentioned as palatine in 1067 and 1071, was probably the forefather of this kindred. Their possessions were situated mostly in Northeast Hungary. Simon may have known that Paul, son of Gopoly of the same kindred, was favoured with a privilege by Ladislas IV in 1278 (*RA* no. 2890, p. 216).

[3] The ancestors of the Ludány kindred are unknown, but the family names are customarily Slavic, which makes their Bohemian origin likely. They are mentioned from the middle of the 13th century. Their

88. The Hermány kindred originate from Nuremberg. They are of quite high nobility and came to Hungary with Queen Gisela.[1]

89. The family called Bogát-Radvány, however, originate from Bohemia.[2]

90. So do those called Ludány.[3]

91. The kindred of Count Simon and his brother Count Michael, surnamed Martinsdorf, came to Hungary in the days of King Emeric, the son of Béla III. They entered in grand style, bringing with them King Emeric's bride Constance, the daughter of the King of Aragon,[4] as well as distinguished knights and a most splendid retinue. The story goes that for certain just reasons their kindred had long been at odds with a particular great count, and that

possessions were situated in County Nyitra on the Morovian border at Ludány (today Ludany nad Nitrou in Slovakia). Peter son of Soboslo (from Sobeslav or Sobieslaw) fought in the battle against Otakar in 1278 and for his merits obtained a donation from the king in 1280 (*RA*, no. 3057, p. 262).

[4] Cf. *SRH* 1, ch. 52, 302–3. Simon and Michael of Nagymarton are frequently mentioned between 1277 and 1318. A charter of 1223 issued by Andrew II records that they came into Hungary at that time. Their father Simon the Elder is mentioned in a charter of Andrew II of 1223 and fought bravely against the Tartars in Hungary in 1241–42. The Hungarian name of Martinsdorf is Nagymarton, formerly in County Sopron (today Mattersdorf in Austria). — The Hungarian king Emeric married Constance the daughter of Alfonso II (1162–96), king of Aragon, in 1196. Their son was King Ladislas III. After her husband's death in 1205 she left the country with their son, who died shortly after. Later she married the future emperor Frederick II. She died in 1222 and was buried in Palermo.

exercitum congregans fertur dimicasse. Ubi praefatus magnus comes per Symonem, patrem scilicet comitis Symonis
et comitis Michaelis, ac Bertramum patruelem ipsorum
captivatus[a] iugulatur. Symon vero et Bertramus inimicitiam
proinde[b] contrahentes cum regina memorata primi adeunt
in Pannoniam. Quorum quidem ingenuitatem experiens
rex Emiricus laetanter excepit, latisque et amplis pheudis
in diversis Hungariae partibus noscitur investisse. Quia
vero generatio saepedicta in regno Ispaniae plura castra
possidet, unum tamen ex illis existit capitale, quod Boiot
nominatur[1], unde praefati comites et eorum praecessores[2]
primum descensum circa Nergedsceg Boiot vocaverunt.
Generatio quoque eorundem in scuto aquilam ferre solet,
quam alii milites, comites in Ispania deferre non praesum-
munt. Eapropter quidem, quod exercitum soldani de
Tunisio, qui Maioricam et Minoricam insulas per naves
intrando et classes occupaverat[c], caeteris militibus regis
Aragoniae deficientibus, eorum generatio fertur expulisse.
Unde regni[d] et communitatis militia decreto est statutum,
quod priori signo, quod fuerat totum rubeum sine aliqua
expressa figura, in aquilam mutaretur[3]. Adduxerat etiam

[a] captivus *H*

[b] perinde *H, E*

[c] occupaverant *K, H, E*

[d] regis *K, E*

---

[1] Bajót is a settlement in County Esztergom, near Nyergesújfalu, and
the castle was indeed built by the Nagymarton kindred. Their "castle
in Spain" has been identified with Biota, today Ejea (Egea) de los
Caballeros in Zaragoza, Aragón, on the basis of the phonetic similarity
(*Én Anonymus*, 315).

finally they gathered an army and took to the field against him. The count was taken prisoner and strangled on the orders of Simon, the father of Count Simon and Count Michael, and Bertram, their father's brother. The ensuing enmity was what first brought Simon and Bertram to Pannonia with the aforesaid queen. Having had proof of their noble qualities, King Emeric received them with open arms and is recorded to have granted them extensive fiefs in various parts of Hungary. This kindred possesses a number of castles in the kingdom of Spain, one of which, their chief seat, is named Boiot,[1] and it was after this place that the counts and their descendants[2] named their first settlement near Nyergesújfalu "Bajót." Moreover, this kindred bears an eagle in their coat of arms which other knights and counts in Spain would not presume to do. The story behind this is that when a fleet of ships carrying the Sultan of Tunis's army sailed to Majorca and Minorca and seized the islands, and the King of Aragon's other knights failed to help, this kindred drove them out single-handedly. In recognition of this, the kingdom and the community of knights decreed that their coat of arms, which previously had consisted of a plain red field without any figure on it, should be changed to an eagle.[3] In addition, Queen Con-

---

[2] *Praecessores* is a misreading of *successores*.

[3] This "Sultan" would be Abu Zakariyya, emir of Tunis 1227–49. King James I of Aragon reconquered Majorca and Minorca between 1229 and 1235. Most Hungarian historians contest that the kindred took part in the campaign; but the family crest they used in Hungary did picture an eagle. The name Tunis became well-known after St. Louis's unsuccessful crusade of 1270.

regina Constantia cum ea sororem comitis Symonis et Bertrami nomine Totam, tam formosam et pulcherrimam, quod eo tempore vix in mundo sibi similis haberetur. Cui quidem virgini in maritum Benedictus dux, Conradi filius, cum villa Mertinsdorf[a] pro dotibus ex parte Emirici regis et reginae Constantiae est coniunctus[1].

92. Temporibus insuper Stephani regis tertii introivit in Hungariam quidam miles Gotfridus nominatus de Mesnensi regione, a quo egreditur generatio Philippi, Ladislai et Gregorii [SRH, 192] filiorum Kelad.[2] Hic namque Gotfridus cum esset ingenuus, filius scilicet comitis Hersfeldensis in curia Francuurtensi, ubi caesar eligi debuit, seditione commota lancgravium de Turingia dicitur occidisse, et inde per fugam evadens ad regem Stephanum pervenit fugitivus, a quo etiam repetitur per suos inimicos. Cumque rex Stephanus inimicis suis ipsum non traderet, in Alamannia contra eum proscriptionis sententia promulgatur, et sic remanet invitus in Hungaria. Quem quidem

[a] Mertinsdorff *H*, Meretisndorf *E*

---

[1] For Tota and her husband, cf. *RA*, no. 198, p. 362. The name of Benedict's father was actually Korlát (Pauler, *Magyar nemzet*, 2: 49). After coming to Hungary in the escort of Queen Constance, Tota enjoyed King Andrew II's confidence even after her husband's property was confiscated by the crown; indeed, the king confirmed her lawful claim to the Bajót and Nagymarton properties (*RA*, no. 362).

stance brought with her a girl called Tota, the sister of Count Simon and Count Bertram. She was exceedingly beautiful, so fair, indeed, that scarcely any woman in the world in those days was considered her like. This girl was given in marriage to Duke Benedict, son of Conrad, and her dowry was the town of Martinsdorf, a gift from King Emeric and Queen Constance.[1]

92.   In the days of King Stephen III a knight called Geoffrey from the area of Meissen arrived in Hungary. He was the progenitor of the kindred of Philip, Ladislas, and Gregory, the sons of Keled.[2] Geoffrey, who as son of the Count of Hersfeld was of noble birth, is said to have killed the landgrave of Thuringia in a revolt which broke out at the court in Frankfurt where the imperial elections were to take place. Thereupon Geoffrey fled and escaped to King Stephen's court. His enemies demanded the fugitive's extradition, and when the King refused to hand him over a sentence of banishment was issued against him in Germany. He then had no option but to remain in Hungary.

[2] Cf. *SRH* 1, ch. 50, 301. A charter of King Béla IV from 1258 mentions the three sons of *comes* Keled (*Cletus*). One of them, Gregory, was still alive in 1290, as proven by his will. A charter of King Géza II from 1156 mentions some Geoffrey and Albert as expatriates; a charter of Stephen III from 1171 also refers to them, which would account for Simon's reference to Stephen III. However, as far as we know, it was not the Keled family but the Fraknói family from Western Hungary who claimed them as their ancestors.

postmodum adversus ducem de Bozna cum exercitu rex transmittit, quo devicto ad regem reversus cum favore de caetero pertractatur[1].

93. Myurk etiam de Chakan[a] cum Venceslao et Iacobo fratribus suis, de ducibus Moraviae habentes originem, regni Hungariae novi sunt incolae, affinitate Belae regi quarto coniunguntur[2].

94. Intraverunt quoque temporibus tam ducis Geichae[b] quam aliorum regum Boemi, Poloni, Graeci, Bessi, Armeni et fere ex omni extera natione, quae sub caelo est, qui servientes regibus vel caeteris regni dominis ex ipsis pheu-da acquirendo nobilitatem processu temporis sunt adepti. Quorum nomina comprehendere aestimavi in praesenti libro onerosa[3].

[a] Kakan *H*

[b] Geichae ducis *H*

---

[1] Hersfeld is too common a place-name to be identified in this context. — The story of the murder is confused. In 1130 Henry, a close relative of the Thuringian counts Louis II and Louis III, was murdered, but there is no evidence that Geoffrey was implicated (*MGH SS* 16: 183; Mályusz, *V. István-kori Gesta*, 65–66). There are cases of murder suspects fleeing from Germany to Hungary later, including during the reign of Andrew II. Best known are Bishop Eckbert and Margrave Henry of Istria, implicated in the murder of King Philip by Margrave Otto of Wittelsbach in Bamberg on 21 June 1208. — The campaign against Bosnia has not been identified.

[2] The name Myrk makes their Moravian origin plausible. Csákány could have been a family name, as we do not know about any kindred by this

At a later date the king sent him with an army against the Duke of Bosnia. Geoffrey returned victoriously, and he was thereafter treated with favour by the king.[1]

93. Myrk of Csákány and his brothers Wenceslas and James are newcomers to the kingdom of Hungary. They descend from the dukes of Moravia and have ties of kinship with King Béla IV.[2]

94. In the days of Duke Géza and the kings who succeeded him, people of almost every foreign nation on earth came to Hungary—Czechs, Poles, Greeks, Pechenegs, Armenians, and so on. They entered the service of the king or other lords of the realm, were granted fiefs by them, and in the course of time attained nobility. However, I decided not to overburden the present book with a full inclusion of their names.[3]

name. The Csákány from County Gömör and County Szepes (North Hungary) appear in royal charters of the period, one of whom may be identical with the persons mentioned (*RA* no. 3390, 3392, 3093, 3206, *ÁMTF* 2: 489–90).

[3] Cf. *SRH* 1, ch. 53, 303–4. Armenians are mentioned in King Ladislas' charter, 1281 (*terra Armeniorum nostrorum*: *RA* no. 3097, p. 273). While Simon seems to be emphasising that settlers came not only from the west, his appeal to brevity glosses over the fact that Orthodox Christians or Muslims had in fact no chance to rise into the aristocratic society of the "immigrant clans." — The term *pheudum* ("fief") was not often used in Hungarian Latinity (before 1300 altogether about six times, with different meanings), as this Western European institution was lacking in Hungary (*LexMA* 4: 69–70).

DE UDWORNICIS[1]

95.   Sed quoniam[a] quosdam movet[b], quid sint udvornici[c], castrenses, alii conditionarii, libertini et mancipia[2], quibus fere Hungaria est repleta, et unde esse habeant, praesenti opusculo apponere dignum duxi. Factum est, quod cum Hungari possessa Pannonia Christianos et paganos more gentium quosdam captivos occiderent resistentes, aliquos ex captivis virtuosos ad praelium deducentes secum, aliquam ipsis portionem de spoliis erogarent, quosdam vero diversis servitiis mancipando in proprietatem circa sua tabernacula solerent conservare[3]. Iidem captivi ex fructu

[a] quam *K*

[b] movet *E*, monet *K, H*

[c] udwornici *H, E*

---

[1] The Latinised term *udvornici* comes from Hung. *udvarnok*, pl. *udvarnokok*, from the Hung. *udvar* (from Slavic *dvor*) 'court.' They were peasants on settlements attached to the royal household, supplying it with agricultural products grown on their own plots. Their head and judge was the palatine. They were organised into centurionates and decurionates, and structured into differentiated privileged groups. The status of the *udvornici* of Simon's time was regulated by Palatine Matthew of Csák on 25 August 1282 (cf. Wenczel, *ÁUO* 4: no. 149, p. 243; *DRMH* 1: 1222:1).

[2] Men of the royal castles—*castrenses, civiles, cives*—were termed in Hung. *várnép*. As servants organised into centurionates and decurionates, they supplied the castles with agricultural products, and a part of them also had warrior duties. Their leaders were the "castle warriors" (*jobbagiones castri*), on whom see note 1, p. 182, below. — *Libertini*

THE *UDVARNOK*[1]

95.   On the other hand, some people have wondered who the *udvornici* are, and the men of the castles, and other dependent persons, freedmen, and servants[2] who exist in such numbers in Hungary, and where such persons originate from. I therefore thought it worth appending an explanation to the present volume. It came about that when the Hungarians took possession of Pannonia they took prisoners of war, both Christian and non-Christian. Some of these were put to death when they continued to offer resistance, according to the custom of nations; the more warlike of the remainder they took with them to fight on the battlefield, and gave them a portion of the spoils; others in turn became their property and were kept around their tents to perform various servile duties.[3] These captives

("freedmen") referred originally (in the 11th century) to liberated servants (*servi*), but from the 12th century to those servants who nevertheless remained dependants (*proprii*) of a landlord but had a farm on their lord's possession, and still later to tenant peasants (*jobagiones*) who were personally free but rendered dues. From the 13th to the 14th century they were also called *conditionarii* ("dependent persons"), emphasising their service according to set conditions.

[3] The phrase *more gentium* ("according to the custom of nations") regards the killing or incarceration of captives from a legal point of view (Cortese, *Norma giuridica* i. 64–83; cf. Szűcs, above p. LXXV). — For the phrase *ex captivis*, cf. Iust. *Institutiones* 1.5. and the *Summa* of Stephen of Tournai (d. 1203): . . . *quia melius iudicaverunt captos servare quam interficere* (Stephani D I, p. 10). — For the problem of the Christian captives see Huguccio D. I. c. 9.: . . . *ut secundum ius divinum Christianus captus ab hostibus vel econtra non efficiatur servus hostium sed remaneat liber vel servus illius cuius ante erat* (Russell, *Just War*, 120).

animalium et praeda sola habebant vitam suam, ut Comani[1]. Mox vero ut fidem receperunt et baptismum, Romana ecclesia Christo cognito duci Geichae et sancto
[SRH, 193] regi Stephano dedisse dicitur firmiter in man-
datis, ut spolia non committerent, captivos Christianos
deinceps relinquerent pristinae libertati, cum multi nobiles
inter captivos habeantur. Quia vero regnum erat amplis-
simum et gentibus vacuatum, nec etiam communitas tota
in hoc Apostolico assensum tribuebat, dispensatum est
postmodum per papam in hunc modum, quod captivi terras
colerent et ex terrae fructibus viverent, prout alii Christiani. Ideoque captivi terras non habentes propria voluntate censum dare susceperunt, qualem domini tribuerunt.

96. Processu autem temporis fide roborata potiores regni
vivere volentes otiose habentesque captivos sine numero,
non dimiserunt eos abire liberos, ut volebat Apostolicus,
sed curiae suae famulantes ordinarunt ex eisdem, quos
patrio nomine udvornicos vocaverunt. Hoc enim obse-
quium licet eo tempore de suis captivis plures regni nobiles
habuissent, Kalomanni[a] diebus, filii regis Geichae, extitit
reprobatum[2]. Voluit tantummodo huiusmodi servitia de

[a] Kolomanni *H*

---

[1] It is characteristic that Simon describes the imaginary life of the
captives of the ancient Hungarians by comparing them to the Cumans,
a pastoral and hunting people of his times.

[2] Simon implies that what might be called secular great estates had
begun to emerge in the later 11th century; there is no indication that

lived the lifestyle of Cumans,[1] subsisting off the produce
of animals or off booty. Subsequently, however, it is reported that when they had accepted the Faith and baptism,
the Roman Church gave firm instructions to Duke Géza
and the holy king Stephen (since they were now Christians) that they should abandon their life of plunder and
restore their Christian captives to their former liberty,
there being many of noble birth among the captives. However, the kingdom was vast and depopulated, and the community were by no means united in assent to the apostolic
decree. Consequently, the pope issued a new dispensation,
to the effect that the captives were to be allowed to culti-
vate the land and live off the fruits of it like other Christians. In return, the prisoners without lands of their own
accord undertook to pay tribute in such kind as the owners
demanded.

96.   As the years passed and the Faith took firmer root,
the better of the realm acquired a taste for the life of ease.
They had unlimited numbers of captives, but instead of
letting them go free, as the pope would have liked, they
created from them a class of servants attached to their
courts, known in their own language as *udvornici*. A great
number of the nobility of the realm came to have servants
in this capacity drawn from their captives; however, by the
time of Coloman, the son of King Géza, the practice was
disapproved of.[2] The king insisted that he alone, and the

King Coloman would have opposed such a development; the Hungarian kings are held to have treated the *udvornici* according to canon law,
especially those kings who were regarded as "law-givers" (Gerics,
"Krónikáink," 310).

captivis suis ipse solus obtinere, et praelatos, quibus largitus erat de captivis suis. Et ne communitas nobilium reprobationem huiusmodi grave ferret, palatino regni, qui pro utilitate nobilium praeficitur, rex suos udvornicos uti dedit. Sed quia Hungari novi Christiani grave habebant onus fidei, eo quod disuescere de spoliis eos oportebat graves labores et onera suis captivis imponebant, quod displicens praelatis, Apostolico super his sunt locuti. Audiens vero Apostolicus clamorem praelatorum, scrutata vita laudabili sancti regis Stephani, de nunciis, qui aderant, in talem vocem fertur prorupisse: "Ego, inquit, sum apostolicus, ille autem verus apostolicus[1]. Unde et ecclesias regni sui eius committo arbitrio ordinare, captivos per eundem redemptos ei tantummodo possidere." Propter quod omnes redemit, quos potuit ab Hungaris invenire, praeter illos, quos regni nobiles ecclesiis dimiserant possidere. Ex quibus quidem ordinavit servire suis castris obsequio leviori.[2]

[1] For the pope's alleged exclamation, see Hartvic's Legend of St. Stephen, ch. 9 (*SRH* 2: 414). Papal letters expected Ladislas IV to follow the example of his canonised forebears; e.g. Nicholas IV writes in 1288: . . . *tu desertis progenitorum vestigiis, fallibili collusione degenerans*. . . . (Theiner, *Monumenta*, 1: 357). In the same breath Simon here speaks on behalf of the right of royal appointment, a heated issue at this period (cf. a charter of 1282 of Pope Martin IV in Theiner, *Monumenta*, 1: 350–51). He consequently changed the Legend's wording, replacing *dispositioni* '(leaving) to his disposition' for the more radical *arbitrio* ("as he thinks best") (Gerics, "Adalékok," 127–28; idem, "Krónikáink," 311).

[2] No such detail about Stephen I has survived, but the redemption of captives and slaves is a hagiographic commonplace. Procuring liberty for bondmen—for reasons of Christian mercy—is, however, regulated

prelates to whom he had chosen to allocate prisoners, should have access to this class of servants. And so that the community of nobles should not become resentful at the prohibition, the king made over his own *udvornici* for the use of the palatine of the realm, the officer responsible for overseeing the interests of the nobility. But as new Christians the Hungarians found the Faith a heavy burden, inasmuch as it obliged them to abandon the practice of plundering, and began to impose heavy labour and burdens on their captives. This met with opposition from the prelates, who voiced their complaints to the pope. The Holy Father listened to the prelates' outcry, and having read through the details of St. Stephen's exemplary Life, according to the messengers who were present it is said he was moved to exclaim: "I may be the successor of the apostle, but this man is the apostle's true follower! I therefore entrust the churches in his realm to his hands to arrange as he thinks best,[1] and commit the captives he has ransomed to his sole possession." In consequence the king bought back from the Hungarians all the prisoners he could find, apart from those the nobles of the kingdom had already given over to the churches, and put some of them to serve on lighter duties within his castles.[2]

in the laws of King Stephen (Stephen I:18, 21, 22, II:4, 5; *DRMH* 1: 5–6, 9). Regarding the redemption of serfs in the 13th century see Keller, *Aufhebung*. The reference to "some of them" may point to a privileged layer among servile populations, who claimed that their liberties originated from St. Stephen and called themselves "freemen of the Holy King" (Bolla, *Jobbágyosztály*, 51; Györffy, *Wirtschaft*, 120); this term survived also in place names (e.g. Szentkirályszabadja).

97. Iobagiones vero castri sunt pauperes nobiles, qui ad regem venientes, terram eis tribuit de castri terris, ut pheuda castri et castrum guerrae tempore custodirent[1]. [SRH, 194]

98. Alii vero conditionarii ex eisdem captivis disponuntur, quos tandem Kalomannus rex ad tantas manieres variavit. Statutum etiam extitit per sanctum regem Stephanum, quod conditionarius, si se vellet redimere, centum bizantiis redimeret se et domum, si vero esset sine coniuge et familia, personam[a] suam XXIIII. bizantiis[b], vel servitio tantundem compensante[2]. Inviti enim Hungari captivos suos regi redimere permiserunt. Compulsi quidem sunt per sanctum regem Stephanum ac praelatos[3].

99. Ex illis captivis hic scribitur et tractatur solummodo, qui[c] ex gente Christiana fuere captivati, de illis autem,

[a] parvam *K*

[b] bizam *K*

[c] quia *K, H, E*

---

[1] Castle-warriors, *iobagiones castri*, Hung. *várjobbágy* were the upper layer of dependent warriors serving the royal and comital castles, see Bolla, *Jobbágyosztály*, 239–54. In the 13th century a good proportion of them succeeded in rising into the nobility; e.g. between 1271 and 1281 King Stephen V and Ladislas IV ennobled more than 70 castle warriors of County Vas, and altogether 84 castle warriors appear in the sources from this period (Zsoldos, *Árpádok*, 205–6).

97. Castle-warriors are persons of noble condition but small means who approached the king and were granted land from the lands belonging to a castle, on the understanding that they should guard the castle and its fiefs in time of war.[1]

98. Other dependent persons were drawn from the same stock of prisoners of war, and they were eventually divided by King Coloman into a number of categories. There is also a decree issued by King Stephen stipulating that if such a man wishes to purchase his freedom he can redeem both himself and his family for a hundred bezants, or if he has no wife or household he can redeem his person for twenty-four bezants or the equivalent in service.[2] The fact is that the Hungarians only grudgingly allowed the king to buy back their prisoners. They did so because King Stephen and the church leaders compelled them.[3]

99. The above summary refers only to captives taken from the Christian populace. He made no pronouncement

[2] A vague reference to the laws of King Stephen on liberty and liberation of slaves and bondmen, see above note 2, pp. 180–81. On the different categories of bondmen see Coloman's law, chs. 38–40, 45, 74, 80–81 (*DRMH* 1: 27–8, 30–1).

[3] In spite of the above mentioned laws of King Stephen, which regulate the manumission of bondmen, there is no evidence that the king would have expressly supported or forced such acts.

qui de populo erant barbaro, propterea[a] nihil dicit. Vult namque sedes apostolica, ut pagani Christianis sint subiecti. Unde illi captivi vheg nominantur. Hos enim unicuique Hungaro dimisit ecclesia possidere et tenere[1].

[a] propterea *H*, propria *K*, papa *E*

---

[1] Simon's source is the so-called Cuman laws of Ladislaus IV (1279): *idem dominus legatus paternaliter condescendit hoc modo: quod captivos, quos in regno et terris nostris Christianos quoquo modo retinebant, precise et absolute reddere, nec retinere tenebuntur, alios vero captivos suos, in extraneis regnis captivatos, retinebunt* (1279:8, *DRMH* 1:69). Cumans took part in ten military campaigns in Western Europe between 1246

about those from the barbarian population, for it was the wish of the Holy See that pagans should be subject to Christians. These captives were termed *uheg*; as far as the Church was concerned, any Hungarian could possess and keep such persons.[1]

and 1278, and certainly they took many captives. The *Continuatio Vindobonensis* ad ann. 1278 (*MGH SS* 9: 710; Kusternig, *Quellen*, 80) mentions a hundred thousand Christian captives. From 1282 on there are details proving that the Cumans also bought servants for money. — *Qui de populo* ("those from the (barbarian) population") is based on the *Liber extra* (X, 5, 6, 13) issued by Innocent III (Gerics, "Kró-nikáink," 310). — The development of the meaning of the term *uheg* is believed to be as follows: first, 'a foreign captive, a slave'; then specifically, 'a heathen slave'; and finally, 'a liberated bondman, a *libertus*.' Here it is used in the second meaning.

BIBLIOGRAPHY

Editions of Simon of Kéza's *The Deeds of the Hungarians* in chronological order:

Magistri Simonis de Kéza, Chronicon Hungaricum. Edited by Alexius Horányi. Vienna: Kurzbeck, 1781, 17–145. Rev. 2nd ed. Buda: Landerer, 1782.

Magistri Simonis de Kéza, de originibus et gestis Hungarorum libri duo. Edited by Josephus Podhradszky. Buda: Landerer, 1833.

"Magistri Simonis de Keza, Gesta Hunnorum et Hungarorum." Edited by Stephanus Ladislaus Endlicher, 83–130. In *Rerum Hungaricarum Monumenta Arpadiana*. Sankt-Gallen: Scheitlin and Zollikofer, 1849. Reprint, Leipzig: Hiersemann, 1931.

"Magistri Simonis de Keza, Gesta Hungarorum." Edited by Flórián Mátyás, 52–99. In *Historiae Hungariae fontes domestici*. Pars prima. *Scriptores*, vol. 2. Leipzig, 1883.

"Ex Simonis de Keza, Gestis Hungarorum." Edited by Lothar von Heinemann. In *MGH SS* 29, Hannover, 1892, 523–46 (only a partial edition).

"Simonis de Keza, Chronicon Hungaricum elegans opusculum." Edited by Henrik Marczali. In *A magyar honfoglalás kútfői* (Sources on the Hungarian conquest). Edited by Gyula Pauler and Sándor Szilágyi, 476–86. Budapest: MTA, 1900. Reprint, Budapest: Nap Kiadó, 1996 (only a partial edition).

"Simonis de Kéza, Gesta Hungarorum." Edited by Sándor Domanovszky. In *SRH*, vol. 1, 141–94.

"Chronicon Hungaricum." Edited by Ferenc Albin Gombos. In *Catalogus fontium historiae Hungaricae*. Edited by ———, vol. 3, 2132–57. Budapest: Szent István Akadémia, 1938.

"Simonis de Kéza, Gesta Hungarorum." Edited by D. Bartonková. In *Magnae Moraviae fontes historici,* vol. 1, 264–67. Prague and Brno: Státny pedagogické nakladatelství, 1966 (only a partial edition).

BIBLIOGRAPHIES ON SIMON OF KÉZA

A magyar irodalomtörténet bibliográfiája 1772-ig (Bibliography of Hungarian literary history till 1772). Edited by Béla Stoll, Imre Varga, and Sándor V. Kovács. Budapest: Akadémiai, 1972, 181–82.

Repertorium fontium historiae medii aevi. Rome: Istituto Storico Italiano per il Medio Evo, 1990, vol. 6, 608–9.

Kersken, Norbert. *Geschichtsschreibung im Europa der "nationes." Nationalgeschichtliche Gesamtdarstellungen im Mittelalter.* Cologne, Weimar, and Vienna: Böhlau, 1995, 662–70.

LITERATURE

Agnellus. *Liber pontificalis ecclesiae Ravennatis*. In *MGH SSrerLang*, Hannover, 1878, 275–391.

Amman, H. "Die französische Südostwanderung im Rahmen der mittelalterlichen französischen Wanderungen." *Südost-Forschungen* 14 (1955) 406–28.

Anonymi descriptio Europae Orientalis. Edited by Olgierd Górka. Cracow: Academia Litterarum, 1916.

Aschoff, Volker. *Geschichte der Nachrichtentechnik*. Berlin and Heidelberg: Springer, 1984.

Attila: The Man and His Image. Edited by Franz H. Bäuml and Marianna D. Birnbaum. Budapest: Corvina, 1993.

Bak, János M. "Queens as Scapegoats in Medieval Hungary." In *Queens and Queenship*. Edited by Anne Duggan, 223–33. London: Boydell & Brewer, 1997.

Balić, S. "Islam im mittelalterlichen Ungarn." *Südost-Forschungen* 23 (1964): 19–35.

Bartal, Antal. *Glossarium mediae et infimae Latinitatis regni Hungariae*. Budapest: MTA, 1901. Reprint, Hildesheim and New York: Olms, also Budapest: Állami Könyvterjesztő, 1983.

Baum, Wilhelm. "Die Gründung des Klosters Rosazzo und die Anfänge der Grafen von Görz." *Der Schlern* 61, no.10 (1987): 623–37.

Bendefy, László. "Anonymus és Kézai Simon mester Scythiája" (Description of Scythia in the chronicles of Anonymus and Simon of Kéza). *Földrajzi Közlemények* 39 (1938): 201–35.

Benedictus Polonus. "Relatio". In *Sinica* 1:133–43.

Berczik, A. "Vermutliche ungarische Spuren im Nibelungenlied." In *Akten des V. Internazionales Germanisten-Kongresses*. Jahrbuch für internazionale Germanistik, Reihe A II. Bern and Frankfurt, 1976, 383–88.

Bezzola, Gian Andri. *Die Mongolen in abendländischen Sicht (1220–1270)*. Bern and Munich: Francke, 1974.

Binder, Pál. "A Siebenbürgen fogalom jelentésváltozatairól" (Changes in meaning of the name Siebenbürgen). *Századok* 126 (1992): 355–80.

Bleyer, Jakab. "Die germanischen Elemente der ungarischen Hunnensage." *Beiträge zur Geschichte der deutschen Sprache und Literatur* 31 (1907): 429–599.

———. "A magyar hun-monda germán elemei" (German elements of the legend of the Huns in Hungary). *Századok* 39 (1905): 602–29, 712–53, 811–49, 902–40.

Bogyay, Thomas von. *Stephanus rex*. Vienna and Munich: Herold, 1976.

Bolla, Ilona. *A jogilag egységes jobbágyosztály kialakulása Magyarországon* (The development of a legally uniform tenant class in Hungary). Budapest: Akadémiai, 1983. Reprint, Budapest: Nap Kiadó, 1998.

Bollók, János, trans. "Kézai Simon, A magyarok viselt dolgai" (Simon of Kéza, The Deeds of the Hungarians).

In *A magyar középkor irodalma*. Edited by Sándor V. Kovács, 115–63. Budapest: Szépirodalmi, 1984.

———. "Ladislaus." In *Scripta manent. Festschrift József Gerics*. Edited by István Draskóczy, 63–74. Budapest: ELTE, 1994.

Bóna, István. *Das Hunnenreich*. Budapest: Corvina, n.d.

Borzsák, István. *A Nagy Sándor-hagyomány Magyarországon* (Alexander the Great's tradition in Hungary). Budapest: Akadémiai, 1984.

The Cambridge History of Poland from the Origins to Sobieski. Edited by W. F. Reddaway, J. H. Penson, et al. Cambridge: Cambridge University Press, 1950.

Cateura Bennasser, Pablo. "Sobre la aportacion aragonesa a la conquista de Mallorca, 1229–1232." In *Jaime I. y su epoca. X. Congreso de historia de la Corona de Aragon*. Zaragosa, n.d., vol. 1, 17–40.

Chronicon Hungaro-Polonicum. Edited by Joseph Deér. *SRH* vol. 2, 289–320. New edition edited by Béla Karácsonyi. Szeged: József Attila Tudományegyetem, 1969 (*Acta Historica Universitatis Szegediensis*, 26).

Cigada, Sergio. "La leggenda medievale del Cervo Biano e le origini della matière de Bretagne." *Atti della Accademia Nazionale dei Lincei, Scienze morali*, ser. 8., vol. 12/1. Rome, 1965.

Cobban, Alan B. *The Medieval University: Their Development and Organisation*. London: Methuen, 1975.

Constantine Porphyrogenitus. *De administrando imperio.* Edited by Gyula Moravcsik, trans. R. J. H. Jenkins. Budapest: Pázmány Péter Tudományegyetem, 1949. Rev. 2nd ed. Dumbarton Oaks Texts 1. Washington: Dumbarton Oaks Center, 1967.

Cordt, Ernst. *Attila - flagellum Dei. Etul, Atli. Zur Darstellung des Hunnenkönigs in Sage und Chronistik,* Quaderni dell'Istituto di Filologia Germanica. Trieste: Facoltà di lettere dell'Università di Trieste, 1984.

Corpus iuris canonici. Edited by Aemilius Friedberg. 2 vols. Leipzig: Tauchnitz, 1879. Reprint, Graz: Akademische Druckanstalt, 1995.

Cortese, Ennio. *La norma giuridica: Spunti teorici nel diritto comune classico* (Ius nostrum. Studi e testi dell'Univ. di Roma, vol. 6/1–2). Milan, 1962.

Cuozzo, Errico. *"Quei maledetti Normanni." Cavalieri e organizzazione militare nel mezzogiorno normano.* Naples, 1989.

Csóka, Lajos J. *A latin nyelvű történeti irodalom kialakulása Magyarországon a XI-XIV. században* (The formation of Latin historical literature in Hungary between the 11th and 14th centuries). Budapest: Akadémiai, 1967.

Deér, Josef. "Aachen und die Herrschersitze der Arpaden." *Mitteilungen des Instituts für Österreichische Geschichtsforschung* 79 (1971) 1–56. Reprinted as *Byzanz und das abendländische Herrschertum.* Sigmaringen: Thorbecke, 1977, 372–423.

————. "Entstehung des ungarischen Nationalbewusst-seins." *East Central Europe / l'Europe du Centre-Est* 20–23 (1993–96) Pt. 2, 11–54.

————. "Szkitia leírása a Gesta Ungarorumban" (Descrip-tion of Scythia in the Gesta Hungarorum). *Magyar Könyvszemle* 37 (1930): 243–63.

Déri, Balázs. "Marmorinus, Rex Agarenorum: Eine Be-merkung zu einem mittelalterlichen liturgischen Drama über den Heiligen Nikolaus." *Studia Musicologia Aca-demiae Scientiarum Hungaricae* 30 (1988): 303–7.

Dienst, H. *Die Schlacht an der Leitha 1246.* Vienna: Öster-reichische Bundesverlag, 1971.

Diplomata Hungariae antiquissima. Edited by György Györffy. Vol. 1. Budapest: Akadémiai, 1992.

Domanovszky, Sándor. "Attilától Árpádig" (From Attila to Árpád). In *Melich János emlékkönyv* (Memorial vol-ume for János Melich), 55–65. Budapest: Magyar Nyelv-tudományi Társaság, 1942.

————. "Die Chronik Simon von Kéza." *Ungarische Rundschau* 1 (1912): 137–54.

————. "Kézai és a húnkrónika" (Simon of Kéza and the chronicle of the Huns). In *Károlyi Árpád emlékkönyv* (Memorial volume for Árpád Károlyi), 110–32. Buda-pest: Sárkány, 1933.

————. "Kézai kódexéről." In *Békefi Remig emlékkönyv* (Memorial volume for Remig Békefi), 81–91. Buda-pest: Stepha- neum, 1912.

————. *Kézai Simon mester és krónikája* (Master Simon of Kéza and his chronicle). Budapest: MTA, 1906.

Dopsch, Heinz. "Die Hengistburg, Wildon und die Herkunft der Grafen von Güssing." In *Die Güssinger: Beiträge zur Geschichte der Herren von Güns/Güssing und ihrer Zeit (13./14. Jahrhundert)*. Edited by Heide Dienst and Irmtraut Lindeck-Pozza, 185–96. Eisenstadt: Burgenländisches Landesmuseum, 1989.

Dörrie, Heinrich. "Drei Texte zur Geschichte der Ungarn und Mongolen." *Nachrichten der Akademie der Wissenschaften in Göttingen, phil.-hist. Kl.* (1956): 125–202.

Dümmler, Ernst. "Über den furor Theutonicus." *Sitzungsberichte der Akademie der Wissenschaften, Berlin, phil.-hist. Cl.* 9 (1897): 112–26.

Eckhardt, Sándor. "Egy ismeretlen olasz hún krónika" (An unknown chronicle of the Huns from Italy). *Egyetemes Philologiai Közlöny* 60 (1936): 57–62.

————. "Micolt." *Magyar Nyelv* 26 (1930): 167–70.

————. "A pannóniai hún-történet keletkezése" (The origins of the Pannonian Hun history). *Századok* 61–62 (1927–28): 480–91.

————. "Sicambria." *Revue des Etudes Hongroises* (1928): 166–97.

Én, Anonymus (I, Anonymous). Budapest: Argumentum, 1998.

Engel, Pál. *The Realm of Saint Sephen. A History of Medieval Hungary.* London: Tauris, 1999.

Exordia Scythica. MGH SS AA 11/2. *Chronica minora saec. iv, v, vi, vii.* Edited by Theodor Mommsen, 308–22. Reprint, Berlin: Weidmann, 1956.

Fasoli, Gina. *Le incursioni ungare in Europa nel secolo X.* Florence: Samsoni, 1945.

————. "Points de vue sur les incursions hongroises en Europe au Xᵉ siècle." *Cahiers de civilisation médiévale* 2 (1957): 17–35.

Fehér, Géza. "Beiträge zur Erklärung der auf Skythien bezüglichen geographischen Angaben der ungarischen Chroniken." *Kőrösi Csoma-Archivum* 1 (1921): 52–76.

Fehértói, Katalin. *Árpád-kori kis személynévtár* (Handbook of first names from the age of the Árpáds). Budapest: Akadémiai, 1983.

Fine, John V. A., Jr. *The Early Medieval Balkans.* Ann Arbor: University of Michigan Press, 1983.

Fóti, József Lajos. "A római Attila-legenda" (The Roman legend of Attila). *Akadémiai Értesítő* 21 (1910): 52–64.

Freedman, Paul. "Catalan Lawyers and the Origins of Serfdom." *Mediaeval Studies* 48 (1986): 288–314.

————. "Cowardice, Heroism and the Legendary Origins of Catalonia." *Past and Present* no. 121 (November 1988): 3–29.

Friezberg, Helmut. "Die Burgen Wildon und Neuwildon." *Zeitschrift des historischen Vereins für Steiermark* 84 (1993): 41–50.

Fügedi, Erik. *Kings, Bishops, Nobles and Burghers in Medieval Hungary*. Edited by János M. Bak. London: Variorum Reprints, 1986.

──────. "Das mittelalterliche Ungarn als Gastland." In *Kings, Bishops*, ch. 8.; also in *Deutsche Ostsiedlung des Mittelalters als Problem der europäischen Geschichte*, 471–507. Sigmaringen: Thorbecke, 1975.

────── and János M. Bak. "Fremde Ritter im mittelalterlichen Ungarn." *Quaestiones medii aevi novae* 3 (1998): 3–18.

Gerard of Csanad. *Deliberatio supra hymnum trium puerorum*. Edited by Gabriel Silagi. Turnholt: Brepols, 1978 (*CCCM* 49).

Gerberding, Richard A. *The Rise of the Carolingians and the Liber historiae Francorum*. Oxford: Clarendon Press, 1987.

Gerics, József. "Adalékok a Kézai-krónika problémáinak megoldásához" (A contribution to the solution of the problems in Simon of Kéza's chronicle). *Annales Universitatis Scientiarum Budapestinensis, Sectio Historica* 1 (1957): 106–34.

──────. "Auslegung der Nacherzählung mittelalterlicher Quellen in unserer Zeit (Bischof Sankt Gerhard von Tschanad über König Aba)." *Acta Historica Academiae Scientiarum Hungaricae* 32 (1986): 335–48.

──────. "Domanovszky Sándor, az Árpád-kori krónikakutatás úttörője" (Sándor Domanovszky, founder of chronicle research for the Árpád period). *Századok* 112 (1978): 235–48.

————. "Das frühe Ständewesen in Ungarn und sein europäischer Hintergrund." In *Études historiques hongroises*. Budapest: Akadémiai, 1985, 285–302.

————. "Die Kirchenpolitik des Königs Peter und deren Folgen." *Acta Universitatis Budapestiensis, Sectio Historica* 24 (1985): 269–75.

————. *A korai rendiség Európában és Magyarországon* (The early system of estates in Europe and in Hungary). Budapest: Akadémiai, 1987.

————. "Krónikáink és a III. András-kori rendi intézmények friauli-aquileiai kapcsolatairól" (On the relation of the system of estates under King Andrew III and Friuli-Aquileia in Hungarian chronicles). *Filológiai Közlöny* 21 (1975): 309–26.

————. *Legkorábbi Gesta-szerkesztéseink keletkezésrendjének problémái* (Chronological problems of the earliest Hungarian Gesta redactions). Budapest: Akadémiai, 1961.

————. "Quedam puella de genere Tatun." *Annales Universitatis Budapestiensis, Sectio Historica* 9 (1967): 3–30.

————. "Zu den Quellen der gesellschaftlichen Ideologie in Ungarn nach dem Tod des Heiligen Stephan." *Acta Antiqua Academiae Scientiarum Hungaricae* 32 (1989): 431–63.

Gieysztor, Alexander. "La chrétienté et le pouvoir princier en Europe du Centre-Est des origines jusqu'à la fin du XIIe siècle." In *La christianità dei secoli XI e XII in occidente: coscienza e strutture di una società*, 123–45. Milan: Vita e pensiero, 1983.

Göckenjan, Hansgerd. *Hilfsvölker und Grenzwächter in mittelalterlichen Ungarn*. Wiesbaden: Steiner, 1972.

———. "Zur Stammesstruktur und Heeresorganisation altaischer Völker. Das Dezimalsystem." In *Europa Slavica – Europa Orientalis: Festschrift Herbert Ludat*. Edited by Klaus-D. Grothusen and Kl. Zernack, 51–86. Berlin: Duncker and Humblot, 1980.

———. "Der Westfeldzug (1236–42) aus mongolischer Sicht in Wahlstatt 1241." In *Beiträge zur Mongolenschlacht bei Liegnitz und zu ihren Nachwirkungen*. Edited by Ulrich Schmilewski, 35–76. Würzburg: Bergstadtverlag W. G. Korn, 1991.

Goldstein, Ivo. "Dinastija Arpadovića i ranosrednjovjekovna Hrvatska" (The Árpád dynasty and early medieval Croatia). In *Zvonimir, kralj Hrvatski: Zbornik radova*. Edited by I. Goldstein, 261–72. Zagreb: Hrvatska akademija, 1997.

Grzesik, Ryszard. "European Motifs in the Polish Medieval Chronicles." *Medium aevum quotidianum* 33 (1995): 41–53.

Guido. "Geographica." In *Ravennatis Anonymi Cosmographia et Guidonis Geographica*. Edited by M. Pinder and G. Parthey. Berlin, 1860.

Györffy, György. "Die Erinnerung an das Grossmährische in der mittelalterlichen Ungarns." *Acta Archeologica Academiae Scientarum Hungaricae* 17 (1965): 41–45.

———. *King Saint Stephen of Hungary*. Boulder, Col.: Social Science Monographs, 1994.

———. *Krónikáink és a magyar őstörténet* (Hungarian chronicles and Magyar prehistory). Rev. 2nd ed. Budapest: Balassi, 1993.

———. "Landnahme, Ansiedlung und Streifzüge der Ungarn." *Acta Historica Academiae Scientiarum Hungaricae* 31 (1985): 231–70.

———. "Die Landnahme der Ungarn aus historischer Sicht." In *Ausgewählte Probleme europäischer Landnahmen des Früh- und Hochmittelalters*. Edited by Michael Müller-Wille and Reinhard Schneider, vol. 2, 23–66. Sigmaringen: Thorbecke, 1994.

———. *Tanulmányok a magyar állam eredetéről* (On the origin of the Hungarian state). Budapest: Akadémiai, 1959.

———. "Ursprung der Szekler und ihre Siedlungsgeschichte." In *Siebenbürgen und seine Völker*. Edited by Elemér Mályusz, 76–131. Budapest, Leipzig, and Milan: Danubia, 1943.

———. *Wirtschaft und Gesellschaft der Ungarn um die Jahrtausendwende*. Vienna, Cologne, and Graz: Böhlau, 1983.

Györffy, György and János Harmatta. "Rovásírásunk az eurázsiai írásfejlődés tükrében" (Runic script in Hungary and the Eurasian development of script). In *Die heiligen Könige*. Edited by Thomas von Bogyay, Gabriel Silagi, and János M. Bak. Graz: Styria, 1976.

Honfoglalás és nyelvészet (Hungarian conquest and linguistics). Edited by László Kovács and László Veszprémy, 145–62. Budapest: Balassi, 1997.

Hadrovics, László. "A délszláv Nagy Sándor-regény és középkori irodalmunk" (The southern Slavic Alexander-romance and medieval Hungarian literature). *A Magyar Tudományos Akadémia nyelv- és irodalomtudományi osztályának közleményei* 16 (1960): 235–93.

Handwörterbuch zur deutschen Rechtsgeschichte. Edited by Adalbert Erler and Ekkehard Kaufmann. Berlin: Schmidt, 1971-.

Harmatta, János. "Érudition, tradition orale et réalité géographique: Le recit sur l'exode des Hongrois chez Anonyme." *Acta Antiqua Academiae Scientiarum Hungaricae* 27 (1979): 285–303.

Haug, Walter. "Die historische Dietrichsage. Zum Problem der Literarisierung geschichtlicher Fakten." *Zeitschrift für deutsches Altertum und deutsche Literatur* 100 (1971): 43–62.

Heinemann, Lothar von. "Zur Kritik ungarischer Geschichtsquellen im Zeitalter der Arpaden." *Neues Archiv der Gesellschaft für ältere Geschichtskunde* 13 (1888): 73–112.

Hesbert, René Jean. *Corpus antiphonarium officii*, vol. 3. *Invitatoria et antiphonae.* Rome: Herder, 1968.

Historia Alexandri Magni (Historia de preliis). Rezension J2. Edited by Alfred Hilka. Meisenheim am Glan: Anton Hain, 1976–77.

History of Transylvania. Edited by Béla Köpeczi. Budapest: Akadémiai, 1990.

Hoensch, Jörg K. *Přemysl Otakar II von Böhmen.* Graz, Vienna, and Cologne: Böhlau, 1989.

Hoffman, Richard C. "Outsiders by Birth and Blood. Racist Ideologies and Realities Around the Periphery of Medieval European Culture." *Studies in Medieval and Renaissance History* 6 (1983): 1–35.

Hóman, Bálint. *Geschichte des ungarischen Mittelalters.* 2 vols. Berlin, Gruyter, 1940–43.

———. *Geschichtliches im Nibelunglied.* Berlin and Leipzig, 1924.

———. *Magyar pénztörténet* 1000–1325 (Hungarian monetary history 1000–1325). Budapest: MTA, 1916.

———. *A Szent László kori Gesta Ungarorum és XII-XIII. századi leszármazói* (The *Gesta Ungarorum* of the time of St. Ladislas and its 12th- and 13th-century derivatives). Budapest: MTA, 1925.

Horváth, János. *Árpád-kori latin nyelvű irodalmunk stílusproblémái* (Stylistic problems in the Latin literature of the Árpád age). Budapest: Akadémiai, 1954.

———. "A hun-történet és szerzője" (The history of the Huns and its author). *Irodalomtörténeti Közlemények* 67 (1963): 446–76.

The Hungarian Illuminated Chronicle / Chronica de Gestis Hungarorum. Edited by Dezső Dercsényi, trans. Alick West. Budapest: Corvina, 1969. (with facsimile edition)

Isidore/Isidorus Hispalensis. *Chronica. MGH SS AA* 11/2, 391–488.

———. *Etymologiarum sive originum libri XX.* Edited by W. M. Lindsay. 2 vols. Oxford: Oxford University Press, 1911. Reprint, Oxford: Oxford University Press, 1962.

———. *Historia Gothorum.* Edited by Theodor Mommsen. *MGH SS AA* 11/2, 268–95.; also edited by C. Rodriguez Alonso. León, 1975.

Istványi, Géza. "A generalis congregatio" (The general congregation). *Levéltári Közlemények* 17 (1939): 50–83, 18–19 (1940–41): 179–207.

Jerome/Hieronymus. *Commentariorum in Esaiam libri I-XI.* Edited by M. Adriaen. Turnholt: Brepols, 1963 (*CCSL* 73).

Jordanes. *Romana et Getica. MGH SS AA* 5,1 Berlin: Weidmann, 1882, reprint, Munich: MGH, 1982.

Juhász, József. "Baracskai kő" (The stone of Baracska). *Székesfehérvári Szemle* 4 (1934): 75–80.

Kaindl, Raimund Friedrich. "Studien zu den ungarischen Geschichtsquellen, VII." *Archiv für österreichische Geschichte* 85 (1898): 431–507.

Kapitánffy, István. "Römisch-rechtliche und kanonistische Terminologie in der ungarischen Historiographie des 12.–14. Jh." *Acta Antiqua Academiae Scientiarum Hungaricae* 23(1975): 356–62.

Karácsonyi, János. *A magyar nemzetségek a 14. század közepéig* (Hungarian kindreds till the the middle of the 14th century). 3 vols. Budapest: MTA, 1900–1901. Reprint, Budapest: Nap Kiadó, 1995.

Keller, Hagen. "Die Aufhebung der Hörigkeit und die Idee menschlicher Freiheit in italienischen Kommunen des 13. Jhs." In *Die abendländische Freiheit vom 10. zum 14. Jh.* Edited by Johannes Fried. Sigmaringen: Thorbecke, 1991, 389–407.

Kiss, Lajos. *Földrajzi nevek etimológiai szótára* (Etymological dictionary of geographical names). 2 vols. 4th ed. Budapest: Akadémiai, 1988.

Klaniczay, Gábor. "I modelli della santità femminile tra i secoli XIII e XIV in Europa centrale e in Italia." In *Spiritualità e lettere nella cultura italiana e ungherese del basso medioevo.* Edited by Sante Graciotti and Cesare Vasoli, 75–110. Florence: Olschki, 1995.

Kódexek a középkori Magyarországon (Codices in medieval Hungary). Budapest: OSzK, 1985.

Kovács, Annamária. "Customs and Symbols: The Pictorial Representations of the Legend of King Ladislas of Hungary." *Medium Aevum Quotidianum* 39 (1998): 112–37.

Kovács, László. *A kora Árpád-kori pénzverésről* (Monetary history of the early Árpád age, 1000–1141). Budapest: MTA Régészeti Intézet, 1997.

Kristó, Gyula. *Hungarian History in the Ninth Century.* Szeged: Szegedi Középkorász Műhely, 1996.

———. "Kézai Simon és a XIII. század végi köznemesi ideológia néhány vonása" (Simon of Kéza and some features of the ideology of the gentry of the late 13th century). *Irodalomtörténeti Közlemények* 76 (1972): 1–22.

———. "Néhány megjegyzés a magyar nemzetségekről" (Some remarks about the Hungarian kindreds). *Századok* 109 (1975): 953–67.

———. "Volt-e a magyaroknak ősi hun-hagyományuk?" (Did the Hungarians have an ancient Hun tradition?). In ———. *Tanulmányok az Árpád-korról* (Papers on the Árpád age), 313–29. Budapest: Magvető, 1983.

Kulcsár, Péter. "La fondation de Venise dans l'historiographie humaniste en Hongrie." In *Venezia e Ungheria nel Rinascimento.* Edited by Vittore Branca, 353–67. Florence: Olschki, 1973.

———. "A magyar ősmonda Anonymus előtt" (Ancient Hungarian legends before Anonymus' time). *Irodalomtörténeti Közlemények* 91–92 (1987–88): 523—84.

Kunstmann, Heinrich. "Wer war der Heide Craco der Regensburger Dollingersage? Über einen allegorischen Epilog zur Lechfeldschlacht." *Verhandlungen des historischen Vereins für Oberpfalz und Regensburg* 132 (1992): 93–107.

Kusternig, Andreas. *Erzählende Quellen des Mittelalters: Die Problematik mittelalterlicher Historiographie am Beispiel der Schlacht bei Dürnkrut und Jedenspeigen 1278.* Vienna, Graz, and Cologne: Böhlau, 1982.

———. "Probleme um die Kämpfe zwischen Rudolf und Ottokar und die Schlacht bei Dürnkrut und Jedenspeigen am 26. August 1278." *Jahrbuch für Landeskunde von Niederösterreich* n.s. 44–45 (1978–79): 226–311.

Legendy a kroniky Koruny Uherské (Legends and chronicles of the Hungarian kingdom). Edited by Richard Pražák. Prague: Vyšehrad, 1988.

Lemaître, H. "Le refus de service d'ost et l'origine du servage." *Bibliothèque de l'Ecole des chartes* 75 (1914): 231–38.

Leyser, Karl J. "The Battle at the Lech, 955: A Study in Tenth Century Warfare." *History* 50 (1965): 1–25. (Reprint in ———, *Medieval Germany and Its Neighbours 900–1250*, 43–69. London: Humbledon Press, 1982)

"Liber Attilae." In *Attila: Poema franco-italiano di Nicola da Casola*. Edited by Gulio Bertoni, 111–19. Frieburg, 1907.

Löfstedt, Leena. "Attila, the Saintmaker in Medieval French Vernacular." In *Attila: The Man and his Image*. Edited by Franz H. Bäuml and Marianna D. Birnbaum, 65–74. Budapest: Corvina, 1993.

Losonczi, Ludovicus. *De Simonis de Keza chronicarum latinitate*. Kežmarok: Typis Pauli Sauteri, 1892.

Macartney, Carlile Aylmer. *The Magyars in the Ninth Century*. Cambridge: Cambridge University Press, 1930.

———. *The Medieval Hungarian Historians: A Critical and Analitical Guide*. Cambridge: Cambridge University Press, 1953.

————. *Studies on the Early Hungarian Historical Sources*, VI-VII. Oxford: Basil Blackwell, 1951.

————. *Studies on Early Hungarian and Pontic History*. Edited by Lóránt Czigány and László Péter. Aldershot: Ashgate, 1998.

Madzsar, Imre. "A hún krónika szerzője" (The author of the Hun chronicle). *Történelmi Szemle* 11 (1922): 75–103.

————. "Missitalius és missitalia. Kézai latinságáról" (Missitalius and missitalia. On the latinity of Simon of Kéza). *Egyetemes Philologiai Közlöny* 64 (1940): 222–23.

Maenchen-Helfen, Otto. "The Legend of the Origin of the Huns." *Byzantion* 17 (1944–45): 244–51.

————. *The World of the Huns: Studies in Their History and Culture*. Berkeley, Los Angeles, and London: University of California Press, 1973.

A magyar nyelv történeti-etimológiai szótára (Etymological dictionary of the Hungarian language). Edited by Loránd Benkő. 3 vols. Budapest: Akadémiai, 1967.

Magyarország története: Előzmények és magyar történet 1242-ig (History of Hungary. Antecendents and Hungarian history till 1242). Edited by György Székely. Budapest: Akadémiai, 1984.

Makk, Ferenc. *The Árpáds and the Comneni: Political Relations between Hungary and Byzantium in the 12th Century*. Budapest: Akadémiai, 1989.

Mályusz, Elemér. *Az V. István-kori Gesta* (The gesta of the time of Stephen V). Budapest: Akadémiai, 1971.

———— and Gyula Kristó. *Johannes de Thurocz, Chronica Hungarorum*, vol. II/1–2. *Commentarii*. Budapest: Akadémiai, 1988.

Marosi, Ernő. "Der Heilige Ladislaus als ungarischer Nationalheiliger. Bemerkungen zu seiner Ikonographie im 14.–15. Jahrhundert." *Acta Historiae Artium* 33 (1987–88): 211–55.

Melich, János. "Veznemut." *Magyar Nyelv* 28 (1932): 295–300.

Monneret de Villard, Ugo. *Le leggende orientali sui magi evangelici*. Vatican City: Bibl. Apost. Vaticana, 1952.

Nägler, Thomas. "Der Name Siebenbürgen." *Forschungen zur Volks- und Landeskunde* (Hermannstadt, Sibiu) 12 (1969): 63–71.

Novotny, V. "Beiträge zur Geschichte Premysl Otakars II." *Mitteilungen des Instituts für Österreichische Geschichtsforschung* 31 (1910): 291–301.

Österreich im Hochmittelalter, 907 bis 1246. Edited by Anna M. Drabek. Vienna: Österreichische Akademie der Wissenschaften, 1991.

Orosius, Paulus. *Historia contra paganos libri VII*. Edited by C. Zangemeister, Leipzig, 1899 (*CSEL* 5); also edited by M.-P. Arnaud-Lindet, Paris, 1990–91.

The Oxford Dictionary of Byzantium. Edited by Alexander P. Kazdhan. 3 vols. New York and Oxford: Oxford University Press, 1991.

Ozeoze Collodo, Silvana. "Attila e le origini de Venezia nella cultura tardomedioevale." *Atti dell'Istituto Veneto di Science* 131 (1972–73): 531–67.

Pálóczi Horváth, András. *Pechenegs, Cumans, Iasians: Steppe Peoples in Medieval Hungary*. Budapest: Corvina, 1989.

Pannonia régészeti kézikönyve (Archeological handbook of Pannonia). Edited by András Mócsy and Jenő Fitz. Budapest: Akadémiai, 1990.

Pauler, Gyula. *A magyar nemzet története az Árpád házi királyok alatt* (History of the Hungarian nation during the Árpád dynasty). 2 vols, 2nd ed. Budapest: Athenaeum, 1899. Reprint, Budapest: Állami Könyvterjesztő Vállalat, 1984)

Paul the Deacon/Paulus Diaconus. *Historia Romana*. Edited by H. Droysen. Berlin: Weidmann, 1879. Reprint, Munich: MGH, 1978 (*MGH SS AA* 2; *MGH SSrG* 49).

Petz, Gedeon. "A magyar krónikák német szavainak hangtani és helyesírási sajátságairól" (On the phonetical and orthographical characteristics of German words in Hungarian chronicles). In *Philologiai dolgozatok a magyar-német érintkezésekről*. Edited by Robert Gragger, 8–16. Budapest, 1912.

Płezia, Marian. "Ungarische Beziehungen des ältesten polnischen Chronisten." *Acta Antiqua Academiae Scientiarum Hungaricae* 9 (1959): 285–95.

Ploss, Emil. "Zeizenmure und die Helchenburg." *Forschungen und Fortschritte* 31 (1957): 208–15.

Posch, Fritz. "Die Herrschaft Riegersburg und Graf Poto (auch Boto) und seine Erben." *Zeitschrift des historischen Vereins für Steiermark* 83 (1992): 127–63.

Pryor, John H. *Geography, Technology and War: Studies in Maritime History, 649–1571.* Cambridge: Cambridge University Press, 1988.

Ransanus, Petrus. *Epithoma rerum Hungaricarum, id est Annalium omnium temporum liber primus et sexagesimus.* Edited by Péter Kulcsár. Budapest: Akadémiai, 1977.

Redlich, Oswald. "Die Anfänge König Rudolfs I." *Mitteilungen des österreichischen Instituts für Geschichtsforschung* 10 (1889): 341–418.

Regino of Prüm. *Chronicon cum continuatione Treverensi.* Edited by Fridericus Kurze. Hannover: Hahn, 1890. Reprint, 1978 as *MGH SSrG* 50; also edited by Reinhold Rau as *FvS* 7, 179–320. Darmstadt: Wissenschaftliche Buchgesellschaft, 1969.

Riesenberg, Peter. "Citizenship and Equality in Late Medieval Italy." *Studia Gratiana* 15 (1972): 424–39.

Rodericus Ximenius de Rada. *Historia de rebus Hispanie sive Historia Gothica.* Edited by Juán Fernández Valverde. Turnholt: Brepols, 1987 (*CCCM* 72).

Rokay, Péter. *Salamon és Póla* (Solomon and Pula). Új-vidék (Novi Sad): Forum, 1990.

Róna-Tas, András. *A honfoglaló magyar nép* (Hungarian people of the conquest period). Budapest: Balassi, 1996.

———. *Hungarians and Europe in the Early Middle Ages. An Introduction to Early Hungarian History.* Budapest: Central European University Press, 1999 (forthcoming).

———. "Ugor, gour or ugur." In *Mikola Tibor emlékkönyv* (Memorial volume for Tibor Mikola), 265–69. Szeged, 1996.

Runciman, Steven. *A History of the Crusades.* 3 vols. Cambridge: Cambridge University Press, 1951.

Russell, Frederick R. *The Just War in the Middle Ages.* Cambridge: Cambridge University Press, 1979

Schünemann, Konrad. *Die Deutschen in Ungarn bis zum 12. Jahrhundert.* Berlin and Leipzig: Gruyter, 1923.

Silagi, Gabriel. "Die Ungarnstürme in der ungarischen Geschichtsschreibung: Anonymus und Simon von Ké-za." In *Popoli delle steppe: Unni, Avari, Ungari,* vol. 1, 245–72. Spoleto, 1988.

Simon, V. Péter. "A Nibelung-ének magyar vonatkozásai" (Hungarian references in the Nibelungenlied). *Századok* 112 (1978): 271–325.

Sinor, Denis. "The Historical Attila." In *Attila: The Man and His Image.* Edited by Franz H. Bäuml and Marianna D. Birmbaum, 3–15. Budapest: Corvina, 1993.

Solymossi, Sándor. "Lél vezér kürtmondája" (The legend of chieftain Lél's horn). *Ethnographia* 40 (1929): 17–39.

Sós, Ágnes Cs. *Die slawische Bevölkerung Westungarns im 9. Jahrhundert*. Münchener Beiträge zur Vor- und Frühgeschichte, vol. 22. München, 1973.

Spiegel, Gabrielle M. *Romancing the Past: The Rise of Vernecular Prose Historiography in Thirteenth Century France*. Berkeley, Los Angeles, and Oxford: University of California Press, 1995.

Stanescu, Eugen. "La crise du Bas-Danube byzantin au cours de la seconde moitié du XIe siècle." *Zbornik radova. Recueil des travaux de l'Institut d'Études byzantines* 9 (1966) 49–73.

Sulpicius Severus. *Vita Sancti Martini*. Edited by Jan W. Smit. n. p.: Fondazione Lorenzo Valla / Mondadori, 1975.

Die Summa des Stephanus Tornacensis über das Decretum Gratiani. Edited by Johann Friedrich von Schulte. Giessen: Emil Roth, 1891.

Sweeney, James Ross. "Hungary in the Crusades, 1169–1218." *The International History Review* 3 (1981): 467–481

Szentpétery, Imre. *Magyar oklevéltan* (Hungarian diplomatics). Budapest: Magyar Történelmi Társaság, 1930.

Szűcs, Jenő. "Kézai-problémák." In *Középkori kútfőink kritikus kérdései* (Problems of Hungarian medieval sources). Edited by János Horváth and György Székely, 187–202. Budapest: Akadémiai, 1974.

————. "Társadalomelmélet, politikai teória és történet-szemlélet Kézai Simon Gesta Hungarorumjában" (Social thought, political theory and the idea of history in Simon of Kéza's *Gesta Hungarorum*). *Századok* 107 (1973): 569–643, 823–78.

————. "Theoretische Elemente in Meister Simon von Kézas Gesta Hungarorum 1282–1285." In *Nation und Geschichte: Studien*, 263–328. Cologne, Vienna, and Graz: Böhlau / Budapest: Corvina, 1981.

————. *Theoretical Elements in Master Simon of Kéza's Gesta Hungarorum*. (Studia Historica, vol. 96) Budapest: Akadémiai, 1975. A revised version appears as an introductory study in this volume.

————. *Az utolsó Árpádok* (The last Árpádians). Budapest: História, 1993.

Theiner, Augustinus. *Vetera monumenta historica Hungariam sacram illustrantia*. 2 vols. Rome: Typis Vaticanis, 1859–60. Reprint, Osnabrück: Zeller, 1968.

Thietmar of Merseburg. *Chronicon libri VIII*. Edited by Werner Trillmich, Darmstadt: Wissenschaftliche Buchgesellschaft (*FvS* 9).

Thomas Archidiaconus, *Historia Salonitana*. Edited by Fr. Rački. Zagreb: Academia scientiarum, 1894; also edited by Nada Klaič, Belgrade, 1967.

Tóth, Endre. "Hoholt-Hahót." In *Kubinyi András emlékkönyv* (Memorial volume for András Kubinyi). Budapest, 1998 (forthcoming)

————. "Ókor a középkorban" (Ancient history in the middle ages). In *Szombathely város története 1526-ig* (History of the city of Szombathely till 1526). Edited by Gábor Kiss, Endre Tóth, and Balázs Zágorhidy Czigány. Szombathely, 1999 (forthcoming).

Tóth, Melinda. "La Cathedral de Pécs au XIIᵉ siècle." *Acta Historiae Artium* 24 (1978): 43–59.

Tóth, Zoltán. *Attila's Schwert. Studie über die Herkunft des sogenannten Säbels Karls des Grossen in Wien.* Budapest: MTA, 1930.

————. "A Botond monda eredete s az anonymusi Botond-hagyomány" (Origins of Botond's legend and its tradition in Anonymus' work). *Hadtörténelmi Közlemények* 35 (1988): 466–83.

————. *A hun krónika kialakulásának kérdéséhez* (On the origins of the chronicle of the Huns). Unpublished paper, Department of Manuscripts and Rare Books of the Library of the Hungarian Academy of Sciences, Ms 5034/1).

Váczy, Péter. "The Byzantine Emperor Constantine VI Porphyrogenitos and the Saga of the Hungarian Conquest." *Hungarian Studies* 4 (1988): 129–35.

————. "A népfelség elvének magyar hirdetője a 13. században: Kézai Simon mester" (A Hungarian propagandist of the principle of the people's sovereignty in the 13th century: Master Simon of Kéza). In *Károlyi Árpád emlékkönyv* (Memorial volume for Árpád Károlyi), 546–63. Budapest: Sárkány, 1933.

———. "A Vazul-hagyomány középkori kútfőinkben" (Vazul's tradition in Hungarian medieval sources). *Levéltári Közlemények* 18–19 (1940–41): 312–13.

Vajay, Szabolcs de. "Dominae reginae milites. Árpádházi Jolánta magyarjai Valencia visszavétele idején" (Hungarians of Queen Violante at the time of Valencia's recapture). In *Mályusz Elemér emlékkönyv* (Festschrift for Elemér Mályusz). Edited by Éva H. Balázs, Erik Fügedi, and Ferenc Maksay, 395–414. Budapest: Akadémiai, 1984.

———. *Der Eintritt des ungarischen Stämmebundes in die europäische Geschichte (862–933)*. Mainz: Hase and Koehler, 1968.

———. "Grossfürst Geysa von Ungarn." *Südost-Forschungen* 21 (1962): 45–101.

Vásáry, István. "Medieval Theories Concerning the Primordial Homeland of the Hungarians." In *Popoli delle steppe: Unni, Avari, Ungari*, vol 1, 213–42. Spoleto, 1988.

Verbruggen, J. F. *The Art of Warfare in Western Europe during the Middle Ages, from the Eight Century to 1340*. Amsterdam and New York: North Holland Publishing Company, 1977.

Veszprémy, László. "Der Hl. Adalbert im wissenschaftlichen Geschpräch ungarischer Historiker." *Bohemia* (1999) (forthcoming).

———. "Kézai Simon a 'fajtiszta' Magyarországról" (Simon of Kéza on a "thoroughbred" Hungary). *Magyar Könyvszemle* 4 (1993): 430–33.

———. "A kővetőgép egy elfelejtett említése a magyar krónikákban" (An unnoticed mention of a mangonel in Hungarian chronicles). *Hadtörténelmi Közlemények* 35 (1988): 139–41.

———. "Martin von Troppau in der ungarischen Historiographie des Mittealters." In *Die Anfänge des Schrifttums in Oberschleisen bis zum Frühhumanismus*. Edited by Gerhard Kosellek, 225–36. Frankfurt: Peter Lang, 1997.

———. "Az 1167-es magyar zászlóskocsitól (carroccio) a székesfehérvári zászlóbontásig. A magyar hadi zászlóhasználat kezdetei" (From the Hungarian flag-car (carroccio) of the year 1167 to the flag-unfurling at Székesfehérvár). *Történelmi Szemle* 37 (1995): 209–16.

———. "Szent Isván felövezéséről" (On the girding of St. Stephen). *Hadtörténelmi Közlemények* 102 (1989): 3–13.

———. "La tradizione unno-magiara nella Cronaca universale di Fra Paolino da Venezia." In *Spiritualità e lettere nella cultura italiana e ungherese del basso medioevo*. Edited by Sante Graciotti and Cesare Vasoli, 355–75. Florence: Olschki, 1995.

Wenczel, Gusztáv. *Magyar diplomacziai emlékek az Anjoukorból* (Hungarian diplomatic sources from the Angevin period). Budapest: MTA, 1874.

William of Rubruck. "Itinerarium." In *Sinica* 1: 147–332.

Williams, Jennifer. *Etzel der rîche*. Europäische Hochschulschriften R.1. vol. 364. Franfurt: Peter Lang, 1981.

Wisniewski, Roswitha. *"Pestis patriae*: Die Ungarneinfälle in der *Kaiserchronik*." In *Deutsche Literatur und Sprache von 1050–1200. Festschrift Ursula Hennig*. Edited by Annagret Fiebig Hans-Jochen Schwiewer, 347–57. Berlin: Akademie Verlag, 1995.

Wolfram, Herwig. *Die Geburt Mitteleuropas: Geschichte Östereichs vor seiner Entstehung 378–907*. Vienna: Kremayr and Scheriau, 1987.

Zsoldos, Attila. *Az Árpádok és alattvalóik: Magyarország története 1301-ig* (The Árpádians and their subjects: A history of Hungary till 1301). Debrecen: Csokonai, 1997.

———. "Téténytől a Hód-tóig. Az 1279 és 1282 közötti évek politikatörténetének vázlata" (From Tétény to Lake Hód. Hungarian political history in the years 1279–1282). *Történelmi Szemle* 39 (1997): 69–98.

GAZETTEER OF GEOGRAPHICAL NAMES

Abbreviations for Languages

Cr: Croatian

Ge: German

Hu: Hungarian

It: Italian

Ro: Romanian

Sl: Slovakian

Slo: Slovenian

T: Turkish

Uk: Ukrainian

FORM USED IN THE TRANSLATION	FORM USED IN THE LATIN	OTHER VARIANTS
Adrianopolis	Idropolis	Edirne[T]
Altenburg[Gc]	Altumburg	Magyaróvár[Hu, today Mosonmagyaróvár]
Bratislava[Sl]	Posonium	Pozsony[Hu] Pressburg[Ge]
Csanád[Hu]	Chenad	Cenad[Ro]
Chiraleş[Ro]	Kyrioleis	Kerlés[Hu] Kirieleis[Ge]
Güssing[Ge]	Kyscen	Németújvár[Hu]
Hlohovec[Sl]	Golgocha	Galgóc[Hu] Freistadtl[Ge]
Hron[Sl]	Goron	Garam[Hu]
Koper[Cr]	Campistyria	Capodistria, Capo d'Istria[It]
Ljubljana[Slo]	Leopah	Laibach[Ge]
Martinsdorf[Ge, today Mattersburg]	Martinsdorf	Nagymarton[Hu]
Morava[Sl]	Morowa	March[Ge]
Moson [Hu, today Moson-magyaróvár]	Musun	Wieselburg[Ge]
Nin[Cr]	Nona	Nona[It]
Nitra[Sl]	Nitria	Nyitra[Hu] Neutra [Ge]

FORM USED IN THE TRANSLATION	FORM USED IN THE LATIN	OTHER VARIANTS
Oradea[Ro]	Warod	Nagyvárad[Hu] Grosswardein[Ge]
Poreč[Cr]	Parentia	Parenzo[It]
Pula [Cr]	Pola	Pola [It]
Sabaria	Sabaria	Szombathely[Hu] Steinamanger[Ge]
Senj[Cr]	Sena	Segna[It] Zengg[Ge, Hu]
Šibenik[Cr]	Sebenicum	Sebenico[It]
Skradin[Cr]	Scardona	Scardona[It]
Solin[Cr]	Salona	Salona[It]
Sopron[Hu]	Supronium	Ödenburg[Ge]
Split[Cr]	Spaletum	Spalato[It]
Székesfehérvár[Hu]	Alba, Albensis	Stuhlweissenburg[Ge]
Trieste[It]	Triestina	Triest[Ge] Trieszt[Hu]
Trogir[Cr]	Tragura	Trau[It]
Ung[Hu]	Hung, Ung	Už[Uk] Uh[Sl]
Zadar [Cr]	Iadra	Zára [Hu] Zara[It]
Zemun[Yu, today in Beograd]	Zemin	Zimony[Hu] Semlin[Ge]

INDEX OF PROPER NAMES

Persons and places appearing in Simon's work are
indexed under the form that appears in the translation

Demetrius, son of Michael, of the clan Rosd   159
Dietrich of Bern   35, 37, 39, 45, 67, 69
Dula, prince of the Alans   17

Eberhard, duke   87
Ed, Csaba's son   73
Edemen, Csaba's son   73
Egyptians   65
Előd, mythical ancestor of the Árpád   81
Emeric, St., Hungarian duke   103, 105, 151
Emeric, Hungarian king   145, 169, 171, 173
Eneth   15
Érd, Hungarian clan   27
Ernest, known as Pot, of Lébény   165

Filimer, Aldaric's son   5
Frederick, II, the Quarrelsome, Austrian duke   147
Frisians   51

Gauls   51
Geoffrey, margrave of Austria   113
Geoffrey, of Meissen   173, 175
Geoffrey, duke of Merania   87
Georgians   19
Gerard, St., Hungarian bishop   117, 125
Germans   35, 39, 53, 71, 73, 85, 91, 95, 107, 109, 111, 115, 119, 123, 127, 135
Géza, I, Hungarian king   131, 133, 139, 179
Géza, II, Hungarian king   143
Géza, Hungarian duke   29, 43, 101, 159, 161, 163, 175, 179
Gisela, Hungarian queen   105, 107, 169
Godfrey, of Viterbo, historian   9
Goths   5, 49
Greeks   73, 99, 175
Gregory (with Becse), ancestor of a Hungarian kindred   143
Gregory, Keled's son   173
Gut and Keled, Hungarian kindred   165
Gyula, Hungarian leader   83
Gyula, King Stephen's uncle   103

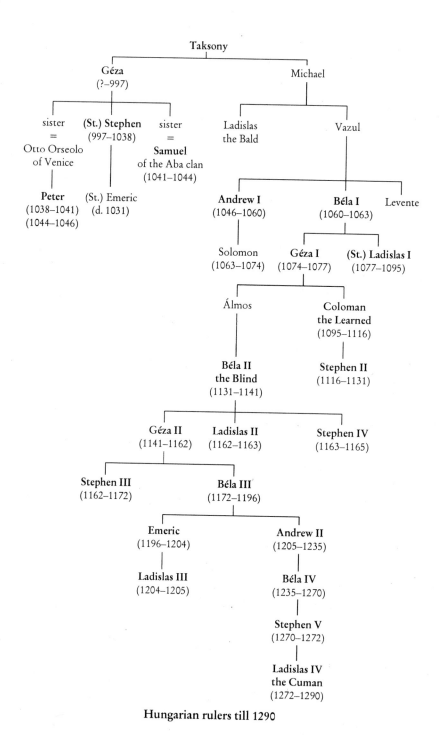

Taksony

- **Géza** (?–997)
  - sister = Otto Orseolo of Venice
    - **Peter** (1038–1041) (1044–1046)
  - **(St.) Stephen** (997–1038)
    - **(St.) Emeric** (d. 1031)
  - sister = **Samuel** of the Aba clan (1041–1044)
- Michael
  - Ladislas the Bald
  - Vazul
    - **Andrew I** (1046–1060)
      - Solomon (1063–1074)
    - **Béla I** (1060–1063)
      - **Géza I** (1074–1077)
        - Álmos
          - **Béla II the Blind** (1131–1141)
            - **Géza II** (1141–1162)
            - Ladislas II (1162–1163)
            - Stephen IV (1163–1165)
      - **(St.) Ladislas I** (1077–1095)
        - **Coloman the Learned** (1095–1116)
          - **Stephen II** (1116–1131)
    - Levente

- **Stephen III** (1162–1172)
- **Béla III** (1172–1196)
  - **Emeric** (1196–1204)
    - **Ladislas III** (1204–1205)
  - **Andrew II** (1205–1235)
    - **Béla IV** (1235–1270)
      - **Stephen V** (1270–1272)
        - **Ladislas IV the Cuman** (1272–1290)

Hungarian rulers till 1290

INDEX OF GEOGRAPHICAL NAMES

Ethiopia   19
Etul, river   19, 21
Etzelburg, *also* Óbuda, Sicambria   53
Europe   19

Fanberg (Schaumburg ?)   161
Ferrara   61
Flanders   51
France   3, 51, 77, 89, 95, 97, 127
Frankfurt am Main   149
Friedburg   165
Friuli   61, 89
Fulda   95

Germany   3, 45, 53, 67, 77, 97, 127, 137, 153, 159, 173
Greece   69, 73, 77, 99, 101
Güssing, Mt.   165
Gvozd, Mts.   141

Havilah, biblical   13
Hersfeld   173
Hlohovec   85
Holy Land   145
Hron, river   163
Hyrcania   21

India Minor   19
Island of the Blessed Virgin (Margitsziget, Budapest)   149
Italian Alps   97
Italy   3, 61, 65, 77, 89

Keveaszó   37
Kiev   79
Knin   141
Koper   55

Langres   47
Lébény   165

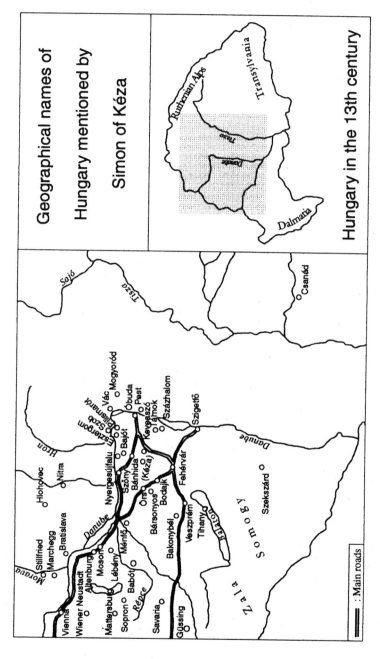

Geographical names of

Hungary mentioned by

Simon of Kéza

Hungary in the 13th century

Map 3